FRENCH POLICY AND THE AMERICAN ALLIANCE
OF 1778

EDWARD S. CORWIN, Ph.D.

PROFESSOR OF POLITICS, PRINCETON UNIVERSITY;
AUTHOR OF "NATIONAL SUPREMACY," "THE
DOCTRINE OF JUDICIAL REVIEW," ETC.

*"La Diplomatie . . . ne peut, elle ne doit
avoir qu'un but, la force et la grandeur
du pays qu'elle représente."—Capefigue.*

GLOUCESTER, MASS.

PETER SMITH

1969

TO
MY SISTERS
"BELOVED ALLIES"
THIS BOOK IS AFFECTIONATELY
INSCRIBED

PREFACE

The materials for the following study were assembled more than ten years ago as a part of work done for the doctorate, at the Universities of Michigan and Pennsylvania. About two years ago I had prepared for publication the portion of the present volume comprising, essentially, chapters I, V, and VIII-XV, when Mr. P. C. Phillips' *The West in the Diplomacy of the American Revolution* appeared, covering much of the ground of several of these chapters. I then decided to enlarge the scope of the volume to that of a general history of the one entangling alliance to which the United States has been party.

I have been particularly interested in these pages in emphasizing the idea that France's intervention in the American Revolution was motivated primarily by her desire to recover her lost preëminence on the Continent of Europe. Writers have sometimes made verbal recognition of this fact, but in the case of American writers at least, they have generally failed to appreciate its really controlling importance for the subject, and in the end have usually contrived—thanks,

no doubt, to Professor Seeley's famous dictum—
to present French intervention as an episode
in the British-French struggle for colonial dominion in the Western Hemisphere rather than
for what it really was, an episode in the European policy of the *Ancien Régime*. A second
phase of the general subject to which I have
given prominence is the embarrassment which
resulted to France from the conflict of interest
between her new ally, America, and her hereditary ally, Spain, a conflict which greatly enhanced the difficulty of getting Spain into the
war in the first place; which subsequently forced
France to make a very restrictive interpretation
of certain of her engagements with the United
States; and which finally eventuated in the
breach of their instructions by the American
commissioners at the negotiations of 1782. Lastly, I have felt that it would be a service to
American students to make the materials in
Doniol's monumental work more available.
These materials, supplemented by the other
sources that I have used, will be found, I think,
to furnish adequate basis for judgment with reference to most, if not all, of the more important
questions likely to suggest themselves to an
American student of the Alliance of 1778.

In gathering my materials I have incurred obligations to several libraries, which I gladly take
this opportunity to acknowledge: to the Penn-

sylvania Historical Society, the American Philosophical Society, and the Ridgeway Branch Libraries of Philadelphia, for the use of numerous eighteenth century publications, both French and English; to the University of Pennsylvania Library, for the use of its extensive collection of materials on the Mercantile System; to the Harvard University Library, for the use of the Jared Sparks Manuscripts; to the American Antiquarian Society Library at Worcester, for the use of newspapers of the Revolutionary period; to the Library of Congress for numerous services. I should also note a more special obligation to the staffs of the University of Michigan and the University of Pennsylvania Libraries and of the Princeton University Library, for many courtesies.

My other indebtednesses are not extensive, but they are deep. I wish especially to record my grateful recognition of the aid which I received from my teachers, Professors A. C. McLaughlin and W. E. Lingelbach, in the early stages of my labors.

E. S. C.

May 25, 1916.

CONTENTS

CHAPTER   PAGE

I—The Question of Motive 1

II—The Classical System and British Sea-Power 23

III—Vergennes Discovers the American Revolt 54

IV—The Portuguese and Corsair Questions... 80

V—Florida Blanca Defines Spain's Position.. 105

VI—Vergennes, Alarmist and Propagandist... 121

VII—The Treaty of Alliance and Outbreak of War 149

VIII—Spanish Mediation and the Convention of Aranjuez 173

IX—The Two Alliances Compared.......... 195

X—The Mississippi and Western Land Question 217

XI—Sieur Gérard and the Continental Congress 243

XII—The Mission of La Luzerne............ 263

XIII—The Crisis of the Revolution.......... 284

XIV—Jay's Mission to Spain............... 318

XV—Jay and the Negotiations of 1782....... 329

XVI—Profit and Loss..................... 361

Bibliographical Note 379

Appendices 385

Index 415

ix

CONTENTS

CHAPTER

CHAPTER I

THE QUESTION OF MOTIVE

The great majority of students today would, I suppose, concede that but for our alliance with France, the War of Independence would have ended without independence, and that but for the aid which France lent us secretly in the months preceding Burgoyne's surrender at Saratoga, we should hardly have become allies of His most Christian Majesty, at least on anything like terms of equality. To emphasize the efficacy and indispensability of French aid in the Revolution is, however, only to throw into higher light its aspects of paradox: the oldest and most despotic monarchy of Europe making common cause with rebels against a sister monarchy; a government on the verge of bankruptcy deliberately provoking a war that, to all appearances certainly, it might have easily avoided. Ignorance of the dangers it invited might conceivably afford a partial explanation of the course taken by the French government in the years between 1776 and 1783, but in fact the explanation is available in only slight measure. The risk to a monarch in

1

promoting rebellion, albeit in another's dominions, was clearly present to Louis' mind, while the unfitness of the royal exchequer for the burdens of war was pressed upon him by Turgot with all possible insistence.

Bancroft explains France's championship of American independence thus: "Many causes combined to produce the alliance of France and the American republic, but the forces which brought all influences harmoniously together, over-ruling the timorous levity of Maurepas and the dull reluctance of Louis XVI was the movement of intellectual freedom."[1]

The important element of truth in this theory is unquestionable. The direction and momentum of French popular sentiment established, to some extent certainly, the possibilities and limitations of French official action, and this sentiment was in turn to no inconsiderable extent the product of the liberalism of the age. Nevertheless, the idea that France ought to intervene, if chance offered, between England and her North American colonies in behalf of the latter, came in the first instance, not from the *salon* but the Foreign Office. And it is not less clear that the precise policy pursued by the French government toward the United States from 1776 on was shaped, not by philosophers but by professional diplomatists.

[1] *History of the United States* (Author's last revision), V. 256. See also *ib.*, 264 ff.

Confining then our attention from the outset to the question of what were the *official* motives of French intervention, we have naturally to consider in the first instance the Count de Vergennes' argument in behalf of his program, which eventually became that of the French government, that however the American situation eventuated, it carried with it the substantial risk for France of having to come finally to the defense of her Caribbean possessions against an English attack; since if England subjugated America she would be tempted to turn the large forces she would have on hand to some profitable employment, whereas if she did not, she would make allies of those whom she had lost as subjects in an endeavor to compensate herself at the expense of France.[2]

It was a theory calculated to appeal strongly to the French mind of that day and generation. The Seven Years War had been begun by the British government in the midst of negotiations without a word of warning. It had been conducted by Chatham in a spirit of ferocious antipathy toward France and her ruling House.[3] It had been concluded by a peace which had been

[2] Henri Doniol, *Histoire de la Participation de la France à l'Établissement des États-Unis d'Amerique* (Paris, 1886-99), I. 273-5; II. 460, 462-3. Cited hereafter as "Doniol."

[3] Expressions of Vergennes' distrust of Chatham will be found in Doniol I. 61-2, 67-72. At the same time he admits in effect the unlikelihood of George III's calling him to power, *ib.*, 62.

roundly denounced by an influential section of
the English public for restoring to France English conquests in the Caribbean. Moreover, the
violence of English party contests was notorious;
and to men to whom it had not yet become evident
in what a powerful leash George III held Parliament it was natural to suppose that, rather than
incur the penalty of a too long delayed triumph
in America, the North ministry would be ready,
if worse came to worst, to resort to the most
desperate expedients.

And not only did the argument in question
strike hands with the popular French estimate of
British policy; it also countered admirably the
strongest argument against French intervention
in America, namely, that it meant war with England. Yet these very considerations should
perhaps put us on our guard against too spon-
taneously crediting Vergennes with complete
sincerity in this matter; or if we decide to accord him that, we should at least remember his
own warning, that "it is human nature to
believe readily that which one desires most
ardently."[4]

The evidence presented by Vergennes to support a plea of self-defense in behalf of France's
action in America we shall pass upon later.
Here we need only weigh some more general considerations militating against that plea: To

[4] *Ib.,* II. 790.

begin with, the risks involved in attempting to aid the Colonies secretly were obvious from the first; yet it is on the increment of danger resulting from his own policy at this point that Vergennes based in part his argument for an open alliance with the Colonies.[5] Again, by his own argument, the danger that confronted France arose alike from the prospect of English victory and of English defeat in America; yet it will be found that he was quite ready to retreat from his program of alliance with America whenever English victory seemed seriously to impend.[6] In other words, it would seem that, while the danger menacing France from the prospect of an immediate English triumph in America was one to be awaited in calm—the calm of despair, forsooth—the danger which threatened from the opposite contingency was one that must be met half-way. Yet it was the latter contingency precisely which the policy of secret aid was designed to make sure![7] But, again, while a British attack upon her Caribbean possessions would, of course, have forced France to come to their defense, it may be seriously doubted whether French official opinion held these possessions after 1763 in sufficient esteem to have warranted a policy that materially increased the likelihood of a serious war of which

[5] *Ib.*, 724.
[6] *Ib.*, I. 567-75 and 613-21; also II. 526-9, 534-6, 539, and 551-5.
[7] *Ib.*, I. 247-8.

their security would be the main objective.[8] Indeed Vergennes himself declared more than once
that the French West Indies could offer but
slight temptation to English cupidity, that England already had enough of that sort of thing;[9]
and it is significant that during the negotiations
of 1782 he stood ready to surrender some of the
most valuable items of these possessions if he
could thereby procure Gibraltar for Spain.[10]
Finally, there is good reason for believing that
France could, at any time before 1778, have obtained from England a specific guaranty of her
American holdings—a guaranty which Spain
would have been glad to sanction, and which England would have been slow to violate, so long at
any rate as peace continued on the Continent.[11]

[8] See the remarks of M. Abeille, quoted *infra*. In the same
connection one should also recall the pacifist attitude of the
French government early in 1777 toward the question of defending
Santo Domingo, the obvious explanation of it being the fear of
arousing suspicion on the part of Great Britain that would prejudice the policy of secret aid: Doniol, II. 234-41, 253, 264-5, 272-5.

[9] *Ib.*, II. 643-4; III. 50-1. See also *Life of Arthur Lee,* I. 361.

[10] *Ib.*, V. 220. It should also be noted that throughout the war
France definitely subordinated obvious opportunities to enlarge
her holdings in the West Indies to other objectives. "Au vrai,"
says Lavisse, "les intérêts coloniaux paraissaient à Vergennes,
comme à presque tous les hommes d'Etat français, de médiocre
importance," *Histoire,* IX.[1] 117.

[11] Both at the end of 1776 and in the spring of 1777, the
British Government suggested a common disarmament on the
part of England, France, and Spain, Doniol, II. 145-54, 232.
An earnest advocate of such a plan, which was to be accompanied

The principal reason for Vergennes' constant employment of the line of argument under discussion undoubtedly lies in its propagandist use. Before, of course, any diplomatic program could be entered upon it had to receive the assent of the king. Had the idea of an aggressive program been unbiased by other considerations it would probably have had Louis' assent from the start, for ignorant as he was of domestic affairs, he was well versed in dynastic politics and jealous for the honor of his House. But unfortunately for such a program, Louis had ascended the throne promising reforms that forbade ambitious schemes abroad; and besides, an endeavor to

by a joint guaranty by the parties to it—France, Spain, England, and Portugal—of their possessions in America and the two Indies, was Beaumarchais' friend Lord Rochford, a member of the ministry, Wharton, III. 727-8. Vergennes however had from the first been averse to seeking any sort of understanding with England, Doniol, I. 51-2; P. C. Phillips, *The West in the Diplomacy of the American Revolution* (Univ. of Ill., 1913), 38 fn. 25 and 54 fn. 74; B. F. Stevens, *Facsimiles of Manuscripts in European Archives Relating to America, 1773-1783* (London, 1889-98, 25, vols., cited hereafter as SMSS.), Nos. 1533, 1544, and 1549. In Aug., 1777, we find Vergennes arguing against France's accepting a British guaranty of French and Spanish possessions, Doniol, II. 528-9. At the very end of the year, that is after Saratoga, if we are to credit a statement attributed by the Spanish ambassador Aranda to Vergennes, the English government was offering France the Island of Cape Bréton and Nova Scotia, together with extensive rights in the Newfoundland fisheries, if France in return would close her ports to the rebels. Aranda to Florida Blanca, Jan. 31, 1778, Sparks MSS. (Harvard Univ. Library), CII. See also SMSS., No. 1838.

strike at England through America involved the naturally unwelcome idea of assisting rebels."[11a] Nor could Vergennes' calculations stop short with his own sovereign. For the logic of the Family Compact clearly exacted that the Spanish court too should be consulted about measures that might involve it in war. How, then, could the Foreign Office better meet the twofold necessity before it than by giving its program as much as possible of the appearance of a program of defense? With Louis the device succeeded, and probably no other would have. At Madrid, on the contrary, though the argument was plumed especially for the favorite anxieties of that court, it failed utterly; with the result however that the argument of defense had to be pressed upon Louis with fresh insistence, in order to induce him to take a line different from that of his uncle and ally.

In short, while the argument that England designed to attack her Caribbean possessions assisted materially in bringing France into the Revolution, especially by tending to minimize

[11a] One of the few literary remains of any importance from the hand of Louis XVI is a note scribbled on the margin of a Projet of the "Exposé des Motifs de la Conduite de la France," etc., of 1779, to protest against Vergennes' assertion that France had only recognized a people already free. "Cette observation," runs the royal gloss, "pourrait autoriser . . . l'Angleterre à aider ouvertement les mécontents si souvent agités en Bretagne, nos protestants, et tous les Français discordants d'avec l'autorité royale." Capefigue, *Louis XVI* (Paris, 1856), 107-9. See also Appendix IV.

with the king the weightiest consideration against such a project, it does not follow that the defense of these possessions furnished the principal purpose of French intervention. The central core of Vergennes' program from the first was *aid* to the Americans in the achievement of their *independence*; and the prospect of American independence necessarily brought into view objectives which far overshadowed the security of the French West Indies, either momentary or permanent. French intervention in the Revolution was, in other words, determined by motives of "aggression" rather than of "defense"; which is to say that its real purpose was the upsetting of the *status quo* in certain particulars rather than its preservation in certain others. But in what particulars? Was France's objective territory, or commerce, or was it something less tangible than either of these?

The possibility that it was territory is raised by the contention of Professor Turner that France hoped in the Revolution to replace England in Canada and Spain in Louisiana. In support of this thesis Professor Turner adduces first, the testimony of Godoy, "the Prince of Peace," that after the war was over, Vergennes, counting upon the close union between France and Spain, sought to induce the latter, "already so rich in possessions beyond the sea, to give to

France her ancient colony"; secondly, the fact
that during the war Vergennes appeared anxious
"to protect the interests of Spain in the country
between the Alleghenies and the Mississippi";
and thirdly, a document published in Paris in
1802 under the caption *Mémoire historique et
politique sur la Louisiane par M. de Vergennes.*[12]

Upon closer scrutiny each item of this evidence
must for one reason or other be disallowed. The
reliability of the testimony of Godoy, who did
not come into power until six years after Vergennes' death, is in itself questionable, but even
if it be accepted at face value it says nothing of
Vergennes' intentions *before* and *during* the
Revolution. Vergennes' attitude *during* that
period toward Spain's claims to the territory between the Alleghenies and the Mississippi is
sufficiently accounted for by his feeling that it
was necessary to harmonize the conflicting interests of the United States and Spain, each of
whom was in alliance with France against England. The document published in 1802, though
it may *possibly* date from the Revolution, was not
the work of Vergennes nor yet of any one who
spoke for him. Not only does the program that
it proposes directly traverse, in its reference to
Canada, the pledge of His Most Christian Majesty in article VI of the Treaty of Alliance, renouncing "forever the possession . . . of any

[12] *American Historical Review*, X. 249 ff.

part of the continent" that had lately belonged
to Great Britain, but it materially conflicts with
the policy which Professor Turner himself acknowledges that Vergennes pursued, of supporting Spain's claims in the region between the
Alleghenies and the Mississippi. This policy
was clearly designed to allay Spain's alarm at
the prospects of American independence. The
program urged in the *Mémoire* of 1802 proposed,
on the contrary, the deliberate aggravation of
this alarm as the easiest means of inducing Spain
to relinquish Louisiana to the stronger hands of
France.[13]

[13] See the *Mémoire,* pp. 25-30. Other considerations that forbid
the attribution of this document to Vergennes or official associates of his are the following: It is to be noted that while the
anonymous editor of the *Mémoire* assumes to vouch for "the style,
the thoughts" of the document as being those of the French secretary, he says nothing of a signature, nor does any appear in the
published form. The *Mémoire* is also devoid of certain distinctive
marks of a French official document addressed to royalty. The
most obvious consisting in the failure of the writer (or compiler)
ever to refer to France and Spain by the titles of their Bourbon
rulers. If we are to rely upon the silence of the *Inventaire Som-
maire,* no memoir on Louisiana exists in the French archives of the
date to which the *Mémoire* published in 1802 is assigned by its
editor, though several are to be found there of an earlier date
from which this one might have been fabricated, and to one of
these the editor makes specific reference in a footnote. Furthermore, the fact that the *Mémoire* of 1802 was, if at this point we
are to follow the editor, found among Vergennes' own papers of
itself casts doubt on its ever having been presented to the king.
In connection with his statement that "both French and American bibliographers have accepted" the "genuineness" of the

But if France's objective was not territory, perhaps it was commerce? Unquestionably there was a widespread belief in France early in the Revolution, which was appealed to not only by

Mémoire, Professor Turner cites only the *Voyage à la Louisiane* of Baudry des Lozieres. Yet Baudry, while praising the *Mémoire* for "plusieurs des ses vues qui sont très sages," directly challenges the assertion that it was the work of Vergennes. "If," says he, "M. de Vergennes has any part in these memoirs, it is only a very small part." But perhaps the most remarkable feature of the document under consideration is (assuming it to date from before 1783) the ignorance it discloses on the part of its author that by the Treaty of 1763 Florida belonged to Great Britain (see pp. 26 and 30). The Duke of Newcastle is reported to have once addressed a despatch to "the Governor of the Island of Massachusetts." But Vergennes was neither a British peer nor a spoilsman in office, but a man noted among his contemporaries for the range and accuracy of his information in the field of diplomacy. It may be safely assumed, therefore, that he was fully aware that France's closest ally had lost an extensive province by the Peace of Paris and had been compensated by France herself with a still more extensive one. Besides, as is shown below, the *Mémoire* of 1802, considered as an entity, must by any assumption date from a period later than early January, 1778. Before this however, Holker, in instructions dated Nov. 25, 1777, was informed by the French Foreign Office that his government wished to see England left in possession of Florida, Nova Scotia and Canada, Doniol, II. 616. Upon careful examination of it I am convinced that the *Mémoire* of 1802 comprises two earlier documents loosely joined together by the author of the short address "Au Roi," chapter I, and certain paragraphs of chapter X of the published document. The first of these two earlier documents comprises most of chapters II-X of the *Mémoire* of 1802 and was written before the outbreak of the Seven Years War to refute Great Britain's claim to the region then in dispute between France and Great Britain. It closed with a plan of compromise in the form of a proposed treaty between the two nations, which plan is

the American envoys but by Vergennes himself on occasion, that if France assisted the United States to their independence, American trade

touched up at points by the compiler of the 1802 document. The second of the earlier documents was written after the events described in pages 162 to 169 of the published volume—*i.e.* about 1769—to protest against the then recent cession of Louisiana to Spain. The entire separateness of the two documents is attested by the words with which the second one opens ("Ce mémoire a pour but," etc., p. 115), by the vastly different styles of the two documents, and by their diverse spelling of certain proper names. (In the latter connection compare pp. 57 and 150-1; also pp. 61 and 172.) When, then, was this compilation made? Dismissing the editor's assertion that the document was the work of Vergennes, but taking the document itself at face value, it was brought together after the outbreak of the War of Independence (Chapters I and X), but before the Treaty of Alliance recognizing American independence was known (the United States are always referred to as "colonies" and "provinces" and on p. 180, the compiler speaks of "strengthening the peace "between France and Great Britain"); also during a warlike situation on the Continent (pp. 27 and 103, by the compiler). But this last condition can be satisfied, for the period between 1775 and 1781, only by supposing the references just cited to have been to the events leading up to the so-called War of the Bavarian Succession. If, then, the *Mémoire* of 1802 is to be assigned as a whole to the period of the American Revolution, it must be placed between late January and the middle of March, 1778. We know that, in the months preceding France's intervention, numerous memoirs were transmitted to the Foreign Office, and the *Mémoire* of 1802 may therefore represent one from a sheaf of similar later productions. Doniol I. 242 footnote. Mr. Paul C. Phillips, on the other hand, conjectures plausibly that the document published in 1802 owes its existence to an effort to bolster up Napoleon's then recent acquisition of Louisiana, *The West in the Diplomacy of the American Revolution* p. 30 fn. 2.

would turn forthwith to French ports.[14] Yet
squarely confronted with the theory that this
belief had been material in determining his program, Vergennes unqualifiedly rejected the notion. "They perhaps think at Madrid," he wrote
after the alliance had been determined upon,
"that the interest of acquiring a new trade had
principally decided us."   But he repelled the
suggestion thus: "This motive, assessed at its
true worth, can be only a very feeble accessory.
*American trade, viewed in its entirety and sub-
ject to the monopoly of the mother-country, was
undoubtedly a great object of interest to the
latter and an important source of the growth of
her industry and power.*   But American trade,
thrown open as it is to be henceforth to the avid-
ity of all nations, will be for France a very petty
consideration."[15]

These words of Vergennes have, however, no
merely negative value; they bring us in fact to the
very threshold of the object of our quest.   Official thinking about trade was moulded in the

[14] Wharton, *Diplomatic Correspondence of the American Revolution* (Washington, 1889), II. 79; *Deane Papers* (N. Y. Hist'l Soc.
Cols., 1886), I. 181, 184 ff., 207; Doniol, I. 244.   Deane later
changed his views on this as well as certain other subjects.   In
his letter of June 10, 1781, to Robert Morris, he says: "America
left at liberty will, I am persuaded, take at least three-fourths
of the European articles she wants from Great Britain," *Deane
Papers*, IV. 406.

[15] Doniol III. 140.   Madrid received its impression from Aranda,
Aranda to Florida Blanca, Jan. 31, 1778, Sparks MSS., CII.

eighteenth century in vast part by the categories
of what is called "the Mercantile System," and
it is the significance of the words just quoted
that they show Vergennes to have been of this
school. The salient features of Mercantilism
mark it at once a system of *statecraft* rather
than of *economics,* at least in any modern sense of
these terms. Thus wealth was identified with
that form of it in which, in a period when the
machinery of public credit was rudimentary and
the usual cement of international alliances was
provided by cash subsidies, it was most available
for political purposes. Again, the welfare of the
subject was assessed for its contribution to the
power of the state. Finally, the power of the
state was evaluated in the terms furnished by the
doctrine of the Balance of Power. But granting
these premises and it followed, first, that the principal advantage to be sought from trade was a
balance payable in coin or bullion, and secondly,
that the most desirable branch of trade was that
which was most susceptible of manipulation to
produce such a balance, in other words, *colonial
trade.* For subject as it was, within the laws of
nature, to the unlimited control of the mother-
country, the colony could be compelled to obtain
all its manufactures from the mother-country
and to return therefor raw materials and a cash
balance. At least, by furnishing the mother-
country raw materials which she would otherwise

have to purchase from her political rivals, the colony would contribute directly to the maintenance of a favorable *balance of trade* and, *pro tanto,* to that of a favorable *balance of power,* against those rivals.[16]

[16] A good general account of the rise of Mercantilism and of its principles is to be found in C. F. Bastable's *Commerce of Nations* (1899), ch. IV. For an admirable statement of the connection which mercantilist theory and policy established between colonies and commerce, see Prof. C. M. Andrews, *American Historical Review,* XX. 43 ff. "During the greater part of our colonial period commerce and colonies were correlative terms, unthinkable each without the other," *ib.* 43. See also the same writer's article, *ib.,* XX. 589 ff., entitled "Anglo-French Commercial Rivalry, 1700-1750." "France and England were fairly matched rivals, in that their policies were the same, to acquire colonies in the interest of trade, shipping, and manufactures, to exclude the foreigner from the colonial market, and to make the welfare and wealth of the mother state the first and chief object of the efforts of all, colonies and mother-country alike," *ib.,* 546. It will be noted that Professor Andrews makes welfare the objective of the mercantile policy, but *power* would perhaps be the better word even for English mercantilism. Note the following passage quoted by Professor Andrews from Otis Little's *The State of the Trade of the Northern Colonies Considered* (1748), pp. 8-9: "As every state in Europe seems desirous of increasing its trade, and the acquisition of wealth enlarges *the means of power,* it is necessary, in order to preserve an equality with them, that this kingdom extend its commerce in proportion; but to acquire a superiority due encouragement ought to be given to such of its branches as will most effectually enrich its inhabitants. As trade enables the subject to support the administration of government, the lessening or destroying that of a rival has the same effect as if this kingdom had enlarged the sources of its own wealth. But as an ascendancy is to be gained by checking the growth of theirs, as well as by the increase of our own, whenever one of these happens to be the consequence of the other to this nation, *its figure and*

Applying these considerations to the case of
French intervention in the American Revolution,
we note at once that by the Treaty of Amity and
Commerce all privileges of trade were to be "mutual" and none given France but what the United

reputation will rise to a greater height than ever." *Ib.*, 543 footnote. In other words, the mercantilist looked beyond the *welfare*
of the subject to the *power* and *reputation* of the State, and these
he measured by the standard set by the doctrine of the Balance
of Power. The same point is also brought out by a passage from
Postlethwayt's *Britain's Commercial Interest Explained and Im-
proved* (1757): "I next enter upon the general principles whereon
the balance of trade is founded—the consideration of which is
earnestly recommended to the public regard, in order to throw
the balance of trade so effectually into the hands of Great Britain
as to put the constant balance of power in Europe into her hands,"
ib., II. 551. See also *Gentleman's Magazine*, XII. 589 (Nov..
1742): "Now, that Money is the Sinews of War, is become a
proverbial Expression; and, with Respect to Great Britain, it is
notorious we can do nothing without it. Almost all we did in
the last Struggle with the Grand Monarch, was by the Dint of
Money. If we had Numbers of Allies, we were obliged to pay them
all; and whereas every other Power in the Confederacy run into
Arrears with their Engagements, we not only made good our
Proportions, but often exceeded them. . . . But, to suppose what
is impossible, that we still roll in Riches, who is to join with us in
this mighty Enterprise, of wrestling the *Balance of Europe* out
of the strong Hand that hath lately held it?" See further the
index of this same periodical under titles, "Balance of Power"
and "France," for other instructive passages along the same
lines, especially in the volumes covering the years from 1737 to
1742. Naturally in France, where the dynastic principle was the
exclusive basis of the state, the political aspect of Mercantilism
was predominant. Recall Colbert's assertion: "I believe that
most people would be agreed that the quantity of gold in a state
alone determines the degree of its greatness and power," *Lettres,*
etc. (P. Clement, ed.) II. pt. 2, ccvii. See also *infra*.

States were left at liberty to grant to any other nation, while by the Treaty of Alliance, its "essential and direct end" was stated to be the achievement of American *independence* not only in *matters of government* but *of commerce* also.[17] In other words, we discover that the *real* commercial motive underlying the alliance was not the hope of *building up French trade*—which it was supposed could hardly be done effectively or advantageously without the machinery of monopoly—but that of *breaking down British trade at the point at which, by mercantilist premises, it most immediately supported British power.* The commercial motive merges itself with a larger political motive: *the enfeeblement of England.*[18]

The lesson that Englishmen themselves drew from their magnificent triumph in the Seven Years War is to be found in the famous lament of Chatham on the news of Saratoga: America "was

[17] Treaty of Amity and Commerce, preamble; Treaty of Alliance, art. II.

[18] Congress' original intention was to throw open its commerce to all friendly nations on terms of equality, and the argument was made with France that if she gave America aid the gratitude of the American people would secure her a preëmption of American trade. Wharton, II. 79 and 235. Later, December 30, 1776, the instructions of Congress enlarged the discretion of the commissioners as to the terms they might offer France and Spain very greatly, *ib.*, 240-1. Eventually, the commissioners offered France certain exclusive privileges in connection with American trade, but these Vergennes declined, in order to remove every temptation from the way of the Americans that might lead them to a reconciliation with England, Doniol, II. 837.

indeed the fountain of our wealth, the nerve of
our strength, the nursery and basis of our naval
power."[19] But what should be especially noted
of these words is that they refer to the part of
America then in revolt, that is, to *continental*
America.   Anterior to 1760 this could hardly
have been the case.   For then the emphasis was
still on colonies as sources of supply, with the result that when British opinion appraised the two
parts of British America, it gave the preference
to the island and tropical portion.   The Treaty
of Paris, however, signalizes a new point of view.
Not only had continental America made direct
contributions to the military forces of the mother-
country in the course of the war just closed, but
its increasing importation of British manufactures in exchange for raw materials now netted a
favorable balance that quite eclipsed the calculable benefits from the West Indian trade.   Furthermore, inasmuch as the colonial trade had
always been regarded as the essential matrix of
British naval strength, popular esteem naturally
turned increasingly to that branch of this trade
which promised a progressive extension.   The
upshot of these developments is to be seen in the
decision of the British government, registered in

[19] Speech of Nov. 18, 1777, *Parliamentary History*, XIX. col.
365, footnote. See to the same effect Burke's speech of Nov. 27,
1781, *ib.*, cols. 721-2. See also the opening paragraph of Deane's
memoir on the "Commerce of America and its Importance to
Europe," cited above, *Deane Papers*, I. 184.

the Treaty of Paris, to retain Canada instead of Guadaloupe and Martinique from its French conquests. No doubt the decision was in part motivated by a desire to meet the demands of New England; but the discussion that attended it proves that it is also to be regarded as a deliberate reappraisement by England of the relative value of the two sections of her western empire.[20]

The reaction of France, on the other hand, to the lesson of the Treaty of Paris was conditioned in the first instance by the plain impossibility of further competition with Great Britain in the field of colonization, at least so long as British naval strength remained predominant. However, the doctrine of the Balance of Power which, as I have already pointed out, was the political obverse of Mercantilism, emphasized the notion that the grand desideratum for a state was not so much a certain absolute quantum of power as a certain rank of power in relation to other rival states, that, in short, *power was relative*. But this premise assumed, the opportunity presented France by the American revolt was a deduction at once inevitable and irresistible. England was France's ancient and hereditary enemy. The essential basis of English power was English commerce and English naval strength. The most important source of these, in turn, was England's colo-

[20] For the matter of this paragraph, see George Louis Beer, *British Colonial Policy, 1754-1765* (N. Y. 1907), ch. IV.

nial empire, and especially her holdings in North America. The striking down once and for all time of the connection between England and her rebellious provinces would deprive her of the greatest single source of power and, by the same token, elevate the power of the House of Bourbon against its most dangerous and unscrupulous rival. To achieve that would be worth a war otherwise "somewhat disadvantageous."[21]

Nor was the enfeeblement of England the only benefit, though the most important one, to be anticipated from American independence. For one thing, from being an ever available base of operations against the French West Indies, the new nation would be converted into their joint protector "forever."[22] Again, from being a beneficiary and so a prop to those rules of naval warfare by which Great Britain bore so hard upon the commercial interests in wartime both of her enemies and of neutrals, the new nation would be pledged to a more liberal system.[23] Again, by leaving England her non-rebellious provinces in

[21] See especially the following passages: the "Réflexions" of Dec. 1775, Doniol, I. 243-4; the "Considérations" of Nov. 5, 1776, ib., 686-7; the unofficial "Reflexions" of Jan. 7, 1777, given in Appendix II; the despatch of Mar. 11, 1777, ib., II. 239; the despatch of May 23, 1777, ib., 295; "Mémoire" of July 23, 1777, ib., 461; the despatch of Dec. 13, 1777, ib., 643-4; Broglie's "Mémoire" of Jan., 1778, ib., 674 ff.; the despatch of June 20, 1778, ib., III. 140.

[22] Treaty of Alliance, art. XI.

[23] Treaty of Amity and Commerce, arts. XV. ffg.

North America, a certain portion of England's strength and attention would be permanently diverted from the European balance to the maintenance of a minor balance in the Western Hemisphere.[24] Yet it is obvious that these considerations too connect themselves, and for the most part rather directly, with the logic of the doctrine of the Balance of Power. Thus the real question raised by our search for the main objective of French intervention in the Revolution becomes the question of *the main objective in the thinking of French statesmen of a balance of power favorable to France.* The answer to that question reveals the third dimension of French diplomacy of the Old Régime—a certain dynastic tradition.

[24] Doniol, III. 156-58, 557; IV. 74.

CHAPTER II

THE CLASSICAL SYSTEM AND BRITISH SEA POWER

"The diplomatic object of this crown has been and will always be to enjoy in Europe that rôle of leadership which accords with its antiquity, its worth, and its greatness; to abase every power which shall attempt to become superior to it, whether by endeavoring to usurp its possessions, or by arrogating to itself an unwarranted pre-eminence, or finally by seeking to diminish its influence and credit in the affairs of the world at large."[1]

In these words of the French Foreign Office, penned in 1756 to justify the Diplomatic Revolution, is sketched the picture that dominated French diplomacy throughout the declining years of the Old Régime. In "the fair days of Louis XIV" the picture had been a reality,

[1] *Recueil des Instructions données aux Ambassadeurs et Ministres de la France depuis les Traités de Westphalie jusqu'à la Révolution Française* (Ed. Sorel, Paris, 1884), I. (Autriche), 356; see also p. 383. See also the significant definitions of the function of Diplomacy, in Capefigue, *Louis XVI, ses Relations diplomatiques*, 84; and in P. L., Comte de Ségur, ainé, *Politique de tous les Cabinets* (2nd ed., 1801, 3 vols.), III. 370. Both Capefigue and Ségur were of the Old Régime and wrote from its point of view.

which, alack, that monarch's later aggressions had gone far to shatter. Then Cardinal Fleury had come forward with his *Système de Conservation* by which France pledged Europe that in return for *influence* she would forego extension of *dominion* and that she would devote the influence vouchsafed her on these terms to the cause of Europe's peace.[2]

The success of the System for France's diplomatic position was astonishing. On the eve of the War of the Austrian Succession the elder branch of the House of Bourbon, the protector of Christian interests in the East, of Poland, Sweden, Turkey, Saxony, Sardinia, the German princes, of Don Carlos of Naples, of the emperor himself, and the ally of the maritime powers and of Spain, was the nodal point of every combination of powers in Europe. At the same time His Most Christian Majesty's services as mediator were sought, now by Austria and Spain, now by Rus-

[2] M. de Flassan, *Histoire générale et raisonnée de la Diplomatie française depuis la Fondation de la Monarchie jusqu'à la Fin du Règne de Louis XVI* (2nd. ed., Paris 1811, 7 vols.), V. 167 ff. On the general principles and outlook of French diplomacy following the death of Louis XIV and the orientation of Vergennes' policy in these, see Albert Sorel, *L'Europe et la Révolution française*, Pt. I. (*Les Meours politiques et les Traditions*) (3rd ed., Paris, 1893), 331-6, 299-304. For some excellent eighteenth century expressions of the "Tradition of Grandeur," dating from Louis XIV, see Abbé Raynal's *Philosophical and Political History of the Settlements, etc.* (Trans. by Justament, London, 1777), IV. 560 ff.; V. 457 ff.; also Anquetil's *Motifs des Guerres et des Traités de Paix de la France* (Paris, 1797), 187 ff.

sia and Turkey, now by Austria and Russia, now
by Spain and Portugal, now by England and
Spain.[3] "Thanks to Cardinal Fleury," exclaimed the advocate Barbier, "the king is the
master and arbiter of Europe."[4] The aged
Fleury himself complacently compared the position of France to what it had been "at the most
brilliant epoch of Louis XIV's reign."[5] Frederick II, just ascending the throne of Prussia,
found "the courts of Vienna, Madrid, and Stockholm in a sort of tutelage" to Versailles.[6] The
Sultan's ambassador at the coronation of Charles
VII apostrophized Louis XV as "Grand Mon-
arque," "King of Christian Kings," "Emperor
of the Franks."[7] The enemies of Walpole, who
in return for commercial favors to England had
willingly connived in the extension of French influence, declared that England had been made a
cat's-paw of, that the House of Bourbon was at

[3] For these data, see Lavisse et Rambaud, *Historie Générale,*
VII. 119-60.

[4] *Ib.,* 158.

[5] *Recueil des Instructions,* I. 246. A pamphlet of the period
contains a squib entitled "Jeu de Piquet entre les Puissances de
l'Europe en 1730." "La France" heads the list, with the motto:
"C'est à moi à jouer, j'ai la main." Far down the list is "L'Angleterre," who says: "Ce n'est pas à mon tour de jouer." Capefigue, *Diplomatie de la France et de l'Espagne"* (Paris, 1846), 108.

[6] *Posthumous works of Frederick II* (Trans. by Holcroft, London, 1789), I. 16.

[7] *Gentleman's Magazine,* XII. 54 (1742).

the summit of power, that the balance of power was at an end.[8]

Nor did the war of the Austrian Succession, rising like a drama to its climax in the stage-triumph of Fontenoy,[9] though obviously a defeat for salient principles of Fleury's System,[10] signify any lessening of France's influence on the Continent in the estimate of those who then guided her destinies. Foremost of these was the Marquis d'Argenson, who became in 1744 the king's secretary of state for Foreign Affairs on a platform, so to speak, interpreting the rôle of France among the nations in the light of the rising philosophy of the age. The period of conquests, Argenson declared—though unhappily not of war—was at an end, and France especially had reason to be content with her greatness. Those therefore who spoke of perfecting the boundaries of France or forming leagues for her

[8] See the "Debate in the Lords on Carteret's Motion for the Removal of Sir Robert Walpole," especially Carteret's own speeches, *Parliamentary History*, XI. col. 1047 ff.

[9] See Voltaire's description in his "Précis du Siècle de Louis XV," *Oeuvres Complètes* (Paris, 1792), XXI. 129-48. Note especially his words on p. 148: "Ce qui est aussi remarquable que cette victoire, c'est que le premier soin du roi de France fût de faire écrire le jour même à l'abbé de la Ville . . . , qui'l ne demandait pour prix de ses conquêtes que la pacification de l'Europe."

[10] For the policy of a friendly understanding with the maritime powers and Austria. In his instructions of Dec. 11, 1737, to the Marquis de Mirepoix, Fleury suggests definitely a rapprochement between the Houses of Bourbon and Hapsburg, *Recueil des Instructions*, I. 245-6.

defense were ill-advised. "Our neighbors have
everything to fear from us—we nothing from
them." The only alliances which France should
form should be "for the purpose of repressing the
ambitious," and should be made only with lesser
states, "such as Portugal, Sweden, Denmark,
Holland, Venice, Modena, Switzerland, Bavaria,
Prussia, Saxony, etc." In brief, France was in
the position to give the law to Europe, so it be a
just law. Let her, then, "sustain the feeble and
oppressed" and in her part as "paternal protector," "arrest disorders for many centuries."[11]   In
1748 France, by the Treaty of Aix-la-Chapelle,
restored her conquests of the war just closed.
Sinful Paris pronounced it "a beastly peace."
The royal ministers, on the other hand, contrast-
ing His Most Christian Majesty with those rulers
who were forced by necessity to seek only their
own aggrandizement and were ever masking selfish designs with a pretended solicitude for the
balance of power, defended the treaty as marking
precisely France's station and magnanimity.[12]

[11] *Journal et Mémoires du Marquis d'Argenson* (ed. Ratheray,
Pairs, 1859), I. 325-6; 371-2; IV. 131 ff. See also Saint-Beuve,
"Argenson," *Causeries du Lundi*. The idealistic, not to say sentimental, character of Argenson's point of view is illustrated by his
"maxim," "le roi aime mieux être trompé que de tromper."

[12] For the Parisian estimate of the Peace, see Lavisse et Rambaud, *op. cit.*, VII. 204. Argenson testifies to the popular criticism
evoked by the Peace, thus: "Le Français aime la gloire et l'hon-
neur, de sorte qu'après les premiers moments de joie de la paix
conclue, tout le public est tombé dans la consternation de la

And thus much for the successful aspect of Fleury's System: it gave France for the time being the preponderance in Europe and it accustomed her statesmen to claim for her in relation to the minor states of the Continent in general the rôle which the Treaty of Westphalia had conferred upon her in terms, in relation to the lesser members of the Germanic Body.[13] Unfortunately the System had its Achilles' heel, its indifference to the decline of French sea-power and to the rise of English sea-power. The earliest protest against an attitude so obviously defiant of the tenets of Mercantilism came from Fleury's own associate, the young Count de Maurapas, who between 1730 and 1740 headed the Department of the Marine. Now in an official report on the state of the marine, now in a letter purporting to emanate from the shade of Louis XIV, now in a memoir on the condition of French commerce abroad, Maurepas reiterated again and again the favorite premises of his school and their obvious deductions for France: Commerce that kept gold at home and drew it from abroad was a source of public greatness. Foreign trade was the essential root of naval strength. Against

médiocrité des conditions." For the ministerial viewpoint, see *Recueil des Instructions*, I. 286 ff., 319 ff. On the preëminence of Louis' position in Europe after Aix-la-Chapelle, see Wraxall, *Historical Memoirs* (Phila., 1845), 55.

[13] On France's guaranteeship of the Treaty of Westphalia, see *Recueil des Instructions*, I. 208.

no two states in the world could France so profit-
ably turn her arms as against Holland and England. The latter moreover was an active menace
to Bourbon interests in all parts of the world. It
behooved His Most Christian Majesty "to put to
flight this usurping race" and to curtail the commerce which already rendered "these ancient
enemies of his crown almost the masters of the
fate of Europe."[14] It is not impertinent to recall
that at the outbreak of the American Revolution
the author of these words was His Most Christian
Majesty's chief-minister.

The warning thus sounded was soon reëchoed
by others. In a council of ministers shortly before France's entrance into the War of the Austrian Succession, the Duke de Noailles opposed
this step with vigor and insight. England's system, said he, is obvious. "It is to arrive at supreme power by superiority of wealth, and
America alone can make smooth the road for
her." It could be predicted at the outset that His
Britannic Majesty would not waste his substance
in Germany, but would seize the opportunity afforded by a war on the Continent to wage war
for his own purposes in America. France's real
concern should be for her colonies, and only motives of vainglory could distract her attention to
the Empire.[15] Two years later Deslandes' *Essai*

[14] Maurepas, *Mémoires* (ed. Soulavie, Paris, 1792), III. 93 ff.,
161 ff., 194 ff., especially 205-6 and 241.

[15] Anquetil, *Motifs des Guerres*, p. 376.

sur la Marine et le Commerce appeared, addressed to "those at the Helm." In these pages one will find proclaimed the theory to be made familiar to us a hundred and fifty years later through Admiral Mahan's famous work, that from the beginning of history the marine has been a decisive factor in the rise and fall of states. And particularly, Deslandes went on to argue, had the greatness of France always rested on a strong navy. The restoration of the marine was therefore the first duty of French statesmen. Its neglect could lead only to calamity.[16]

The mercantilist propaganda, aptly confirmed as it was by the events of the War of the Austrian Succession, began in time to show promise of fruition. Even Argenson, despite his general complacency, yet gave warning that English ambition, fraud, and aggressiveness in the way of trade, and the prosperity of the English colonies, menaced Europe with the prospect of British dominion "of the seas and of all the commerce in the world."[17] Saint-Contest, who became secretary of state for Foreign Affairs in 1751, was of like opinion, holding that, on account of her naval strength, England even then exerted a greater influence in European concerns than France. At

[16] *Op. cit., passim.* See also the same writer, *Essai sur la Marine des Anciens et particulièrement sur leurs Vaisseaux de Guerre* (Paris, 1748). Curiously enough Admiral Mahan does not seem to be aware of Deslandes' works.

[17] *Journal et Mémoires,* I. 372.

the same time, he contended that naval strength
was a highly vulnerable sort of strength, and that
with prudent measures, it would be easy for
France to reduce Great Britain to her proper
rank.[18] Meantime, in 1749, Rouillé had become
minister of the Marine. Under his administration and that of his successor Machault the navy
was brought to comparative efficiency, as was attested by the capture of Minorca in June, 1756.

Unfortunately the Seven Years War, thus
auspiciously begun for France, was not long to
remain predominantly a war with England, to
be waged on the sea for commerce and colonies.
The simple fact is that with the *haute noblesse*
the army was popular and the navy, for all the
zeal of the mercantilists, was not. The prejudices of the nobles moreover fell in with the pique
of the king at what he considered the ingratitude
and faithlessness of his protégé, the king of Prussia, in making a defensive alliance with England.
In vain was it urged upon Louis that the Treaty
of Westminster, far from implying hostility on
Frederick's part toward His Most Christian Majesty, was really a matter for thanksgiving, in
that it guaranteed peace on the Continent and,
by the same sign, a free hand for France in India
and America. By the first Treaty of Versailles,
of May 1st, 1756, the famous Diplomatic Revolu-

[18] Flassan, *op. cit.*, VI. 14-16; *Recueil des Instructions* XII.'
(Espagne, pt. II), 298 ff.

tion was effected by a defensive alliance between France and Austria. Even so, the general opinion at first was that this arrangement also was calculated to conserve the peace of Europe. On August 29th, 1756, however, Frederick invaded Saxony and the war thus precipitated speedily became general. By the second Treaty of Versailles, May 1st, 1757, the resources of France were placed at the disposal of the House of Austria.[19]

The fortunes of the ensuing war it is, of course, unnecessary for us to follow further than to note that for France they were *misfortunes*. These were the days when Mme. du Deffand rechristened France "Madam Job." Cardinal Bernis, minister of Foreign Affairs and so official sponsor for the Austrian alliance, was soon in the depths. "Everything is going to pieces," he wrote. "No sooner does one succeed in propping the building at one corner than it crumbles at another." France "touches the very last period of decay." She "has neither generals nor ministers." "Ah that God would send us a directing will or some one who had one! I would be his valet if he wished it, and gladly!"[20]

[19] Lavisse et Rambaud, *op. cit.*, VII. 217-20; Richard Waddington, *Louis XV et le Renversement des Alliances* (Paris, 1896), 249-62, 358-517.

[20] Lavisse et Rambaud, *op. cii.*, VII. 244-5; Richard Waddington, *La Guerre de Sept Ans*, II. 432-3; Sainte-Beuve, "Bernis," *Causeries du Lundi*.

In Choiseul, who succeeded Bernis in November, 1758, the directing will was found and the mercantilist point of view again assured utterance in the royal council. It is true that Choiseul's first official act was to renew with the empress the onerous engagements of his predecessor, but to this he was fairly committed by the circumstances in which he had taken office.[21] Presently we find him declaring to the Austrian court with entire candor that the war with England involved French power and honor more directly than did the struggle on the Continent. Indeed, he proceeded, the interest of Austria herself demanded the preservation of France's seapower. For "this it is," said he, "which enables His Majesty to sustain numerous armies for the defence of his allies, as it is the maritime power of England which today arms so many enemies against them and against France."[22] And the same point of view again found expression in his despatch of March 21st, 1759, to Havrincourt, the king's ambassador at Stockholm:

We must not deceive ourselves. *The true balance of power really resides in commerce and in America.* The war in Germany, even though it should be waged with better success than at present, will not prevent the evils that are to be feared from the great superiority of the English on the sea. The king will take up arms in vain.

[21] Waddington, *op. cit.,* II. ch. VIII. and III. 452-4.
[22] "Instructions to the Count de Choiseul," June 1759, *Recueil des Instructions,* I. 386.

For if he does not have a care, he will see his allies forced to become, not the paid auxilliaries of England, but her tributaries, and France will need many a Richelieu and Colbert to recover, in the face of her enemies, the equality which she is in peril of losing.[23]

In October came the news of the fall of Quebec. "The balance of power," wrote Choiseul to Ossun, the king's ambassador at Madrid, "is destroyed in America, and we shall presently possess there only Santo Domingo. France, in the actual posture of affairs, cannot be regarded as a commercial power, which is to say that she cannot be regarded as a power of the first order."[24]

Choiseul now set himself the task, failing a peace with England on reasonable terms, of restoring to the war its original character of a contest with that power for commerce, colonies, and naval supremacy. Auspiciously for his purpose, Don Carlos, a much better Bourbon than Ferdinand VI had ever been, was now Charles III of Spain. In the negotiations during the summer of 1761 between France and England Choiseul seized the opportunity of championing certain claims of Spain against His Britannic Majesty, which however were rejected by Pitt in terms that aroused not only Charles' indignation but positive apprehensions for his own colonial empire.[25]

[23] Flassan, *op. cit.,* VI. 160.

[24] *Ib.,* 279.

[25] Waddington, *op. cit.,* III. 427-42, and IV, 428-37, 555-72. See

The result was that on August 15th, 1761, the second Family Compact, making France and Spain practically one power for all warlike purposes, was signed at Paris.

The intention [runs the preamble of this document] of His Most Christian Majesty and of His Catholic Majesty, in contracting the engagements which they assume by this treaty, is to perpetuate in their descendants the sentiments of Louis XIV of glorious memory, their common august ancestor, and to establish forever a solemn monument of reciprocal interest which should be the basis of the desires of their courts and of the prosperity of their royal families.

The treaty itself announced its basic principle to be that, "whoever attacked one crown, attacked the other." Thus, when at war against the same enemy, both crowns were to act in concert. When either was at war, offensively or defensively, it was to call upon the other for certain forces— Spain upon France for 18,000 infantry, 6,000 cavalry, 20 ships of the line, and 6 frigates; France upon Spain, for the same naval forces, 10,000 infantry, and 2,000 cavalry. The Bourbon holdings in Italy were guaranteed absolutely.

also *Recueil des Instructions*, XII.² 338. Of further interest is Alfred Bourget's "Le Duc de Choiseul et l'Angleterre: la Mission de M. de Bussy," *Revue historique*, LXXI. 1-32. In a letter dated Aug. 25, 1761, Bussy, who was then acting as Choiseul's special envoy to England, wrote: "M. Pitt paraît n'avoir d'autre ambition que celle d'elever sa nation au plus haut point de la gloire et d'abaisser la France au plus bas degré de l'humiliation," *ib.* 12.

On the other hand, Spain was excused from assisting France in the guaranty of the Peace of Westphalia unless a maritime power should take arms against the latter. Each power extended to the subjects of the other the commercial privileges of its own subjects in its European dominions.[26]

The renewal of the Family Compact was Choiseul's greatest achievement and is to be regarded as the starting point of the restoration of France's position in Europe; notwithstanding which, at the outset, it brought only fresh calamities and new losses. In October Pitt fell from power for urging a declaration of war upon Spain. None the less, the declaration followed in January. The English and provincial forces now turned from the capture of France's West Indian islands to that of Havana, which fell in July. But Choiseul, his eyes fixed on remoter developments, was determined that Spain should not suffer for her devotion to the Bourbon cause. On November 3rd, 1762, France agreed to give Spain New Orleans and all of Louisiana west of the Mississippi, an arrangement which permitted the latter to exchange the Floridas for Havana. The ensuing February 10th the Peace of Paris was signed. By it France ceded England

[26] G. F. de Martens, *Recueil de Traités . . . des Puissances et Etats de l'Europe depuis 1761 jusqu' à présent* (Gottingen, 1871), I. 16-28.

the vast part territorially of what was still left of her colonies. Of the great empire that had once comprised half of North America and the richest of the American islands, and that had given fair promise to include eventually India and the West African coast, she retained Gorée on the African coast; Santo Domingo, which thanks to the English diversion against Havana, her forces still held; Guiana, Martinique, Guadeloupe, Santa Lucia, and their dependencies; the small fishing islands St. Pierre and Miquelon, off Newfoundland; and a few factories in India, together with the islands of France and Bourbon, which she must not fortify, as also she must not the fishing stations.[27]

Nevertheless, we must be on our guard against exaggerating the merely material aspect of the losses wrought France by the Seven Years War. On the map, no doubt, Canada and Louisiana comprised an impressive domain, but regarded from the point of view of commerce and trade-balances they were essentially worthless, Louisiana being practically uninhabited and Canada hardly returning the cost of administration. On the other hand Guadeloupe and Martinique, in place of which England had finally and somewhat reluctantly consented to take Canada, were commercially of great value.[28] France's real loss, apart from the enormous outlay of the war, was

[27] *Ib.*, 104-20; Lavisse et Rambaud, *op. cit.*, VII. 256-7.
[28] On these points, see Flassan, *op. cit.*, VI. 480 ff.

in prestige. Her armies had been defeated, her
fleets annihilated, her allies disappointed and dis-
gruntled. The Treaty of Peace itself signalized
her humiliation most graphically by renewing
the defunct provisions of the Treaty of Utrecht
against the fortification of Dunkirk, to which was
later added provision for an English commissioner at that port, "without whose consent not a
pier could be erected, not a stone turned." And
not less ominous was the sort of demand that now
began being made by His Britannic Majesty's
diplomatic representatives at various courts,
that in view of the outcome of the war they were
entitled to the precedence over His Most Christian Majesty's representatives. French pride
could not possibly have been flouted more
shrewdly.[29]

How, then, was France to recover her prestige
and the influence that this assured her upon Continental affairs? This was the question that addressed itself, and in terms ever more poignant,
to the guardians of her diplomacy in the period
between the Treaty of Paris and the death of
Louis XV. And the answer returned to this
question by all schools of opinion on questions
diplomatic carried with them the implication at
least that, before France could hope to regain her
station in Europe, English power must be diminished. The story however is one that should be

[29] *Ib.*, VI. 183-7; VII. 26-7.

told in more detail, and in connection with it I desire to draw particular attention to two highly important documents: Choiseul's *Mémoire* of February, 1765, which comprises a general defense of his policy,[30] and Broglie's *Conjectures Raisonnées* of 1773, which voices the views at that date of an adherent of the more narrowly Continental viewpoint.[31]

Choiseul begins his exposition of the fundamentals of French diplomacy by tracing the calamities of the late war to one cause: the fact that the Austrian alliance was allowed to convert "the war on seas and in America, which was the true war," to a purely land war. Also it is admitted that the Austrian connection was always bound to be a precarious one. Nevertheless, it is insisted, it was of value as tending to conserve the peace on the Continent, for which reason it should be continued so long as it exacted no further material sacrifices by France. And the historical connections with the princes of the Empire should be viewed in the same light. The old policy of paying subsidies in advance should be discontinued. The English system was to pay for services rendered and this

[30] Soulange-Bodin, *La Diplomatie de Louis XV et le Pacte de Famille* (Paris, 1894), 236-53.

[31] "Conjectures Raisonnées sur la Situation actuelle de la France dans le Système politique," etc.: "Oeuvre dirigé par de Broglie et exécuté par M. Favier": dated Apr. 16, 1773, and comprising vol. I. p. 211 to the end, all of vol. II, and vol. III. to p. 104 of Ségur's *Politique de tous les Cabinets,* (1801). Cited hereafter as "Ségur."

had proved much more effectual. But the one indispensable alliance of His Most Christian Majesty was with His Catholic Majesty. The foremost precept of His Majesty's policy henceforth must be, accordingly, "to manage with the most scrupulous attention his system of alliance with Spain, to regard the Spanish power as a power necessary to France." Nor would this be difficult, for the king of Spain was "just, firm, and one upon whom you can count even beyond the point at which France herself would fail you." The *Mémoire* concludes thus:

It remains for me to speak to Your Majesty of the maritime powers. England is the declared enemy of your power and of your state, and she will be so always. Many ages must elapse before a durable peace can be established with this state, which looks forward to the supremacy in the four quarters of the globe. *Only the revolution which will occur some day in America, though we shall probably not see it, will put England back to that state of weakness in which Europe will have no more to fear of her.*

Thus the *Mémoire* closed on something like a note of despair. Despair, however, was not Choiseul's normal attitude. Even a year before this he had sent an agent named Pontleroy to British North America to report upon its resources and the strength of the lines connecting it with the mother-country,[32] and now in 1766,

[32] C. De Witt, *Thomas Jefferson, Etude historique sur la Dé*

with the news of the American outbreak against
the Stamp Act at hand, the results of Pontleroy's
investigation and their significance for France became the subject of active correspondence between Choiseul and His Most Christian Majesty's representatives at the Court of St. James.

Judging from the small number of arrangements
with reference to colonial possessions in America [Du-
rand wrote Choiseul in August, 1767] Europe has only
lately begun to sense their importance. England herself
has discovered with surprise that they are the sources
of the power which she enjoys and that these great
objects of power and ambition draw in their wake the
balance of power in Europe. In brief, money has become so necessary to the sustenance of a government
that without commerce no state has the wherewithal to
uphold its dignity and independence; and commerce
would dry up if it were not sustained by that branch of
it which traffics in the products of America. It is there
that England finds the outlet for her manufactures, and
to what dimensions would these be reduced if they supplied only the market of Europe at a time when every
nation is endeavoring to make its own resources suffice
and to prevent the departure of specie from its
territory?[33]

This, of course, is all in the best strain of the
most rigorous Mercantilism. Nevertheless, pro-

mocratie américaine (3rd ed., Paris, 1861), 407. Most of the
citations to this work are to the documents in the Appendices,
pp. 393-559. See also F. Kapp, *Life of Kalb* (N. Y., 1870), 43-4.

[33] De Witt, *op. cit.*, I. 420-1. See also to same effect pp. 427-8.
Choiseul's viewpoint was precisely the same: *ib.*, 47-51.

fessing to fear the American colonies more than
England herself, Durand advised against foment-
ing revolution among them, since to do so "might
have the result of handing over the other colonies
of Europe to those who by their excessive energy
and strength had detached themselves from the
parent stem."[34] Durand's successor Chatelêt, on
the other hand, was strongly of the opinion that
France ought to seize the first opportunity of
intervening in America.

In the case of a rupture [he inquired of Choiseul early
in December, 1767] even were it an open and premature
one, between the colonies and Great Britain, could
France and Spain remain idle spectators of an opportunity which in probability would never occur again?
. . . Before six months have elapsed America will be
on fire at every point. The question then is whether
the colonists have the means of feeding it without the
aid of a foreign war, and whether France and Spain
should run the risk of taking an active part in foment-
ing the conflict and making it inextinguishable, or
whether it would be more their policy to leave it to
itself at the risk of its going out for want of fuel and the
means of spreading.[35]

As a matter of fact Choiseul had already taken
a definite step toward interesting his government
in the American situation. On April 22nd, 1767,

[34] *Ib.*, 52. See also, to some effect, pp. 432-3.

[35] *Ib.*, 56-7 footnote. Choiseul regarded these views as "profound": *ib.* For further correspondence to the same effect, see
ib., 433-55.

he had despatched Kalb, who was later to distinguish himself as a major-general in Washington's army, to Amsterdam, there to inquire into "the rumors in circulation about the English colonies" and, should these be well founded, to "make preparations for a journey to America." In conformity with these and further instructions, Kalb finally sailed for America from Gravesend, on October 4th, and arrived in Philadelphia January 2nd.[36] In essence, the conclusions he drew from his inquiries into the American situation were, that the moment had not yet arrived for France to embroil herself with her neighbors; that while the remoteness of the American population from their central government made them "free and enterprising," at bottom they were "but little inclined to shake off the English supremacy with the aid of foreign powers"; that "such an alliance would appear to them to be fraught with danger to their liberties"; that "a war with us would only hasten their reconciliation," so that "on the footing of restored privileges, the English court could even direct all the troops, resources, and ships of this part of the world against our islands and the Spanish Main."[37]

There can be little doubt that these observations, in the general assessment they made of American sentiment, squared with the facts, but

[36] F. Kapp, *Life of Kalb,* cited above, 45-51.
[37] *Ib.,* 53-7 *passim.*

that was small consolation to Choiseul, who in his disappointment petulantly charged Kalb with superficiality and pronounced his labors useless.[38] The result however was that now, abandoning any idea of actually interfering in America, the French minister began to formulate a plan whereby France and Spain should indirectly foster discontent in the English colonies by throwing open the ports of their own colonies to the products of North America.[39] This was on the basis of the theory, that while the English colonies augmented the strength of England, those of France weakened her. "The thing to be aimed at," therefore, in the words of M. Abeille, Choiseul's secretary-general of Commerce, was "to diminish the artificial strength of England and to relieve France of the burdens that obstruct the development of her native strength."[40] Indeed M. Abeille was for granting the French colonies their independence. But these views naturally encountered some opposition at Madrid; and in 1770 Choiseul fell from power.

[38] *Ib.*, 71. At this very time Franklin was writing, with reference to Choiseul's policy: "That intriguing nation would like very well to blow up the coals between Britain and her colonies, but I hope we shall give them no opportunity," Bancroft, III. 261. As late as Apr. 6, 1773, Franklin predicted that a war with France and Spain on the part of England would heal the breach with the colonies, *Complete Works* (Ed. Bigelow), V. 126.

[39] De Witt, *op. cit.*, 60-3.

[40] *Ib.*, 61-2.

Two years later occurred the first partition of Poland, all things considered, the most humiliating episode from the French point of view in the history of French diplomacy. Poland had been for centuries, with a fair degree of constancy, the ally and protégé of France. Since 1745, moreover, Louis himself had been endeavoring, through the subterranean channels of the *Secret du Roi,* which indeed he had created for the purpose, to secure the succession of the House of Conti to the Polish throne.[41] The project of the royal brigands, however, was never known to His Most Christian Majesty's agents till it was *fait accompli,* and thus the most important transfer of territory since the Peace of Westphalia, involving ultimately the extinction of the greatest state territorially in western Europe, was effected not only without the consent but without the knowledge of France. But worst of all, France's own ally Austria was *particeps criminis* to the act, even though a reluctant one at first. "She wept but she took," was the adequate account that Frederick gave of the empress' part in the transaction. Her course published to the world at large in a way that tears more copious and more sincere than hers could not obliterate, that the desires of France no longer greatly counted in Europe.[42]

[41] Lavisse et Rambaud, *op. cit.,* VII. 212-14.
[42] *Ib.,* 503-11.

"The Tragedy of the North" it was that incited
Broglie, the principal agent of the *Secret du Roi,*
to the composition, in collaboration with the ver-
satile Favier, of his elaborate *Conjectures Raisonnées,* referred to above. "One would wish in
vain," this document begins, "to conceal the rapid
degradation of the credit of France in the courts
of Europe, not only in consideration but even in
dignity. From the primacy among great powers
she has been forced to descend to a passive rôle
or that of an inferior."[43] Putting then the question as to the cause of this unhappy transfor-
mation, Broglie first assailed "the change of system produced by the Treaty of Versailles."[44] The
preponderance in Europe was the rightful pat-
rimony of the French crown: this was a dogma
consecrated by a thousand years.[45] But the
Treaty of Versailles had accustomed Europe "to
regard France as . . . subject to orders from
Austria." To the same cause was it due that
France had abandoned her ancient allies Sweden,
Poland, Turkey, and the German princes; and
worse still, that she had made to fill the rôle of
dupe in the recent developments in Poland and
Turkey, the result of which was her own reduction to the fourth grade of powers.[46] The Family

[43] Ségur, I. 212.
[44] *Ib.,* 212-13.
[45] *Ib.,* 229.
[46] *Ib.,* 213, 258-64, 303-4; II. 33-4, 64, 88-92.

Compact of 1762, too, had had the worst possible
effect upon European opinion, since by it Spain
was admitted to virtual equality with France.
"France for the first time admitted the equality
of another power."[47]

Thus far spoke the critic and rival of Choiseul.
The longest section of the *Conjectures* however
deals with England and the tone here is signifi-
cantly harmonious with that of Choiseul's *Mémoire*. The attitude of England toward France
was that of ancient Rome toward Carthage.
England of course did not expect to wipe out the
French monarchy; her inferiority on land forbade
the idea. But she had adopted the principle of
keeping the French marine reduced, "of watching
our ports, of surveying our dockyards and arsenals, of spoiling our projects, our preparations, our
least movements." Her policy in this respect was
to be explained in part by that spirit of rapine
native to the English people, but also in part by
the knowledge of the English ministers that the
edifice of English power was still supported by
factitious resources and forced means and that
its natural tendency, in face of the approaching
danger of a schism between the mother-country
and her colonies, would be to crumble and dis-
solve. In short, it was *fear* that determined England's policy toward France, though a fear that
knew how to choose its weapons. In view of this

[47] *Ib.*, I. 229-30.

fact, France should know her real strength,
should know that her industry, resources, patriot-
ism, and intelligence were sufficient to overturn
"the colossus of English power," could she once
restore her marine. She should know too that
the feeble line of conduct taken with England in
the immediate past had but nourished English
pride and disdain and that what was needed was
a firm line of conduct. France's military system
and her diplomatic policy must alike sustain the
dignity and preëminence of the crown of France
on sea as well as on land.[48]

The influence of the *Conjectures Raisonnées*
upon those who were interested in France's diplomatic position is beyond all question, and the
same is true of Abbé Raynal's contemporaneous
Histoire des Indes.[49] "The marine," declared
this writer, "is a new kind of power which has
given, in some sort, the universe to Europe. This
part of the globe, which is so limited, as acquired, by means of its fleet, an unlimited empire
over the rest, so extended." Yet the benefit of
this control had passed, in effect, to one nation
alone, England, and with it had passed the balance of power. Such had not always been the
case. In the days of Louis XIV France had

[48] *Ib.*, II. 165-97.
[49] Sorel, *op. cit.*, I. 304-10. "La doctrine de Favier se ramène à
une proposition essentielle: l'anéantissement de l'Angleterre," *ib.*,
306.

given the law to Europe, and the basis of her greatness had been in her marine. Unfortunately, the excesses of that monarch, while cementing the alliance of the maritime states against France, had also turned the martial energies of the latter from the fleet to the army; and so French power had been doubly undermined.[50] The connection between England's greatness as a colonial power and her influence among the states of the world and the memory of France's greatness under Louis XIV are constantly reiterated thoughts in Raynal's pages, and the course to which they incited French sentiment, both official and unofficial, is plain. "Favier," writes Sorel, "made disciples and Raynal proselytes."[51]

France's intervention in the American Revolution is often described as an act of Revenge. The description is less erroneous than incomplete, for while it calls to mind the fact that France had humiliations to be redressed, it fails to indicate the even more important fact that she had also a rôle to be retrieved. Furthermore, it leaves entirely out of account the logic by which, in an Age of Reason, the purpose of either revenge or restoration was brought into relation with a concrete situation. This logic comprised the follow-

[50] *Histoire des Indes* (Paris edition of 1781), V. 203; VII. 208 ff.; IX. 88 ff., 219 ff.; and especially, X. 136 ff.

[51] Sorel, *op. cit.*, I. 309.

ing ideas: That France was entitled by her wealth, power, and history, to the preponderating influence in Continental affairs; that she had lost this position of influence largely on account of Great Britain's intermeddling; that Great Britain had been enabled to mingle in Continental concerns by virtue of her great naval strength, her commercial prosperity, and her preparedness to maintain Continental subsidiaries; that these in turn were due in great part to her American colonial empire and especially to the policies controlling her trade therewith; that America, become independent, would be an almost total loss from the point of view of British interests; that this loss would mean a corresponding diminution of British power; that since the two were rivals, whatever abased the power of Great Britain would elevate the power of France. By calling into existence the New World, France would "redress the balance of the Old."

But while these ideas define the principal advantage which France hoped to obtain from the course she took, there were also supporting ideas that should not be lost to view. For one thing, it was by no means impossible that whether she intervened or not in behalf of the American rebels, France would find herself, sooner or later, at war with Great Britain in defense of the French West Indies. Again, it had for centuries been France's rôle to back the smaller fry against

her greater rivals. Again, it was generally felt
that, formidable as it was at the moment, British
power was in reality more or less spurious. Furthermore, recent diplomatic developments had
most miraculously paved the way for French intervention in North America. The withdrawal of
France from Canada had left America no reason
to fear her; the Family Compact convenanted the
assistance of the Spanish marine; the Austrian
alliance constituted a reasonable guaranty of
peace on the Continent. Finally, it was felt to
be not only allowable but right for France to seize
so favorable an opportunity to tear down a
power that had been used so outrageously as England had used her power on the sea. In the end,
the project did not lack some of the aspects of a
crusade.

The primary requisite, however, to an understanding of Louis XVI's espousal of the cause
of American independence is that due weight be
given the fact that Europe was still organized on
the dynastic principle, and to the further fact,
especially noteworthy in the case of the elder
branch of the House of Bourbon, that position
and influence were the essential objectives of diplomacy, even in the age of "Benevolent Monarchy."[52] To-day with the voice of the common

---

[52] Indeed among a people so fond of glory as the French the very
security of the crown demanded that the dishonor it had suffered
abroad in the detested latter years of Louis XV should be wiped

man dominant in the direction of society, historical investigators are apt to give too slighting
attention to all but bread-and-butter interests as
interpretative of the conduct of states.   But this
is plain anachronism.   The doctrine of the equal-

away as speedily as possible. "Or la France, passionnée comme
elle était pour la gloire, et qui aurait excusé bien les fautes du
gouvernement intérieur, ne pardonna pas au Roi . . . son humiliation." Lavisse, *Histoire de France,* VIII.² 411. It is interesting to
note that as early as November, 1775, Burke had predicted French
intervention. "He observed, that from being the first, she was,
with regard to effective military power, only the fifth state in
Europe. That she was fallen below her former rank solely from
the advantages we had obtained over her; and that if she could
humble us, she would certainly recover her situation." *Parl. Hist.,*
XVIII. 967. Eighteen months before this Col. Barré in the debate
in Commons on the "Bill for Regulating the Government of
Massachusett's Bay," had declared that "during these troubles
with our colonies, France would not lie quiet," *ib.,* XVII. 1307.
A hint of foreign interference is conveyed in Franklin's "Rules
by Which a Great Empire May Be Reduced to a Small One,"
Works (Ed. Sparks), IV. 396. In a sermon delivered June 6,
1774, in the Second Church of Boston, the Rev. John Lathrop
declared, "France and Spain will take satisfaction for their
losses in the late War," *Pennsylvania Packet,* No. 147. In his
"Farmer Refuted," which was published in Feb., 1775, Hamilton
put the question whether "the ancient rivals and enemies of Great
Britain would be idle," in the event of an open breach between
Great Britain and her colonies; and answered, that ere this could
come about, "the French, from being a jealous, politic, and
enterprising people, must be grown negligent, stupid, and inat-
tentive to their own interest. They could never have a fairer
opportunity or a greater temptation to aggrandize themselves
and triumph over Great Britain than would here be presented."
Works (Constitutional Ed.), I. 164-5. A year later John Adams
raised the same question on the floor of Congress (Mar. 1, 1776).
"Is it," he inquired, "the interest of France to stand neuter, to

ity of man was indeed a tenet of the schools in 1776, but it had made little headway among the professional diplomatists, who still assessed the general welfare in terms furnished by the competition for station of rival reigning houses.[53]

join with Britain, or to join with the colonies? Is it not her interest to dismember the British empire? Will her dominions be safe if Britain and America remain connected? Can she preserve her possessions in the West Indies? . . . In case a reconciliation should take place between Britain and America, and a war should break out between Britain and France would not all her islands be taken from her in six months?" *Life and Works,* II. 487-8. There was, of course, a strong possibility, even probability, of such a reconciliation at this date. For this and other reasons the danger to France cited by Adams was much more real than after Saratoga. See *infra.* Adams, at this date, wished only a "commercial" connection with France, and declared flatly against a "political' or "military" connection. "Receive no troops from her," he advised, *ib.* For some further items on American expectation of French aid because of the rivalry between France and England, see the *Continental Journal and Weekly Advertiser* of Boston, issues of July 11, 18, and 25, and Oct. 17, 1776.

[53] See further the document given in Appendix II.

CHAPTER III

Louis XVI ascended the throne in May, 1774, and was at once confronted with the task of choosing a ministry. The queen, anxious to see the policy of friendship with Austria continued, urged that Choiseul be again called to power. The dull and priggish Louis, however, abhorred both the aggressive talents and tawdry morals of the former minister, and his scruples carried the day. When the new cabinet was formed in the course of June and July the post of chief-minister was assigned to the old and decrepit Count de Maurepas, while that of secretary of state for Foreign Affairs was bestowed upon the Count de Vergennes.[1]

Charles Gravier, later the Count de Vergennes, was born at Dijon, in 1717, of one of those families of the lesser *noblesse* whose function it was, under the Old Régime, to replenish the ranks of French officialdom. He began his diplomatic career in 1740 by accompanying his uncle Chavigny to the latter's post as ambassador at Libson.

[1] Lavisse, *Histoire de France*, IX.[1] 5, 6.

Six years later he won the praise of Argenson by
the clarity of his views on questions then at issue
between Portugal and Spain. In 1750 he became
minister plenipotentiary at Trèves, and a little
later His Most Christian Majesty's representative at the Congress of Hanover, where he is said
to have shown great dexterity in foiling the designs of George II's representative, the Duke of
Newcastle. This and other successes brought him
four years later the great post of ambassador to
Constantinople, where for fourteen years he represented both the official diplomacy and the *Secret
du Roi.* Then followed a short term of retirement on account of an altercation with Choiseul.
But in 1771, at the instance of Aiguillon, he became the king's ambassador at Stockholm; and
here the year following he successfully engi-
neered a *coup d'état,* which by transferring the
governing power in Sweden from the antiquated
and corrupt estates to the king, saved that country from the fate which had just overtaken
Poland and was even then overshadowing
Turkey.[2]

[2] *La Grande Encyclopédie,* title "Vergennes"; *Magazine of Amer-
ican History,* XIII. 31 ff.; Flassan, *op. cit.,* VI. 12-13, 234-58;
Arthur Hassall, *The Balance of Power* (N. Y., 1898), *passim;*
Le Bonneville de Marsangy, *Le Chevalier de Vergennes, son Am-
bassade à Constantinople* (2 Vols.; Paris, 1894); H. Doniol, "Le
Ministère des Affaires étrangères de France sous le Comte de
Vergennes," *Revue d'Histoire diplomatique,* VII. 528-60 (1893).
This reference is chiefly valuable for the extracts it contains from
the "Souvenirs" of Vergennes' friend Hennin, written at the time

Compared with the brilliant Choiseul, the new secretary is a somewhat prosaic figure, an impression which Carlyle has recorded in the dictum that "M. de Vergennes was a clerk, a mere clerk with his feet under the table." The fact is that, to a taste for methodical employment, and to the minute knowledge of the diplomatic systems of Europe that stirred the admiration of Ségur, Vergennes added an ambition for patriotic achievement that was none the less real because it was controlled by the prudence of a man who had risen to station by his own efforts. Nor is the traditional Vergennes less remote from fact, the Vergennes who is pictured to us as "a difficult and dangerous man with whom to have dealings," a washed-out version of the legendary Machiavelli. It is certain that Vergennes was no sentimentalist, for which, however, he is hardly to be blamed, since the happy thought of blending sentimentalism and diplomacy had not yet occurred to men. On the other hand, the Machiavellian principle that self-interest is the only feasible basis of a public policy was applied by him with certain very essential qualifications and limitations. England, it is true, he treated from the outset to a policy of duplicity and falsehood, but that nation, he held, had put herself beyond the

of the minister's death. See also a eulogy of Vergennes' Continental policy by Sorel in the *Revue historique*, XV. 273 ff., and a criticism of the same by Tratchevsky, *ib.*, XVI. 327 ff.

pale. On the Continent itself he sought unremittingly to bulwark the *status quo* behind
the maxims of the *Système de Conservation*.
"Force," he wrote, "can never vest a title, nor
convenience bestow a right"; and the partition of
Poland he denounced as "political brigandage."
Moreover, he regarded the honor of the king as
setting very definite limits beyond which political advantage was not to be sought. Capable
himself of playing the Jesuit with most admired
skill when occasion required, yet once the word of
His Majesty was distinctly pledged, he deemed
it inviolable.

In a word, expert that he was in the use of the
conventional weapons of eighteenth century
French diplomacy, Vergennes had no thought of
casting these aside or of greatly changing them.
And the same is true of his attitude toward the
accepted axioms of his profession. He believed
in the doctrine of the Balance of Power, and till
he was disillusioned by the results of the American Revolution, in the tenets of Mercantilism.
He adopted without reservation the fundamental
postulate of the Classical System, that France
by virtue of geographical position, wealth, intelligence, and military resources, was entitled to
the preponderance in Europe. "France," he
wrote in 1778, "placed in the center of Europe
has the right to influence all great affairs. Her
king, comparable to a supreme judge, is entitled

to regard his throne as a tribunal set up by Providence to make respected the rights and properties of sovereigns."[3] Alas! in 1774, the age-long prerogative of France was in eclipse, her prestige dimmed. "Among all nations," he afterward declared of this period,

the opinion prevailed that France no longer had either will or resources. The envy which till then had governed the policy of other courts toward France became contempt. The cabinet of Versailles had neither influence nor credit in any quarter. Instead of being, as formerly, the center of all great affairs, it became their idle spectator. Everywhere men treated its approval and its disapproval as alike negligible.[4]

It was a situation that touched him hardly less acutely than if it had been his own personal misfortune.

How, then, was France to recover her influence and what use would she make of it, once it was recovered? Like Argenson, Vergennes linked the reputation of the House of Bourbon with the cause of Continental peace.

[3] Mémoire of Apr. 18, 1778, Flassan VI. 140 ffg. See also *Recueil des Instructions*, I. (Autriche), 488. See SMSS., No. 861, where Vergennes compares the wealth of France and Great Britain favorably to France. At the same time he envied the British government the facility with which it commanded the resources of the realm. "Nous avons assurement," he wrote, "des resources plus reelles que l'Angleterre, mais il s'en faut bien que le jeu en soit aussi facile. Cela tient à une opinion qui ne peut pas s'établir dans une monarchie absolue comme dans une monarchie mixte." Doniol, II. 18.

[4] *Ib.*, I. 3-4. See also Sorel, *op. cit.*, I. 309.

Like Broglie, he censured the overestimation of
the Austrian connection that had eventuated in
neglect of France's guardianship of the Peace of
Westphalia, "one of the most beautiful jewels"
of the Gallic crown. On the other hand, following Choiseul, he admitted that the Austrian alliance, kept within due bounds, might yet prove
useful to France in that its tendency was to prevent England and Austria from striking hands
once more. It thus guaranteed, he argued, the
peace of the Continent, where France could desire only peace, and, by the same sign, it left
France at liberty "to direct her efforts to counter-
balancing the power of England, whose naval
superiority most necessarily enlisted her foresight." Finally, from the same point of view,
he acclaimed the Family Compact as the very
"cornerstone of France's whole system." This
connection, it was true, required France always
to stand ready to come to the defense of Spain's
vast possessions beyond the sea, but it was, for
all that, more valuable to France than to Spain.
England was loath to break with Spain on account of her profitable commerce there, from
which she drew riches and employment, while
with France no such motive held her back. "If
there is anything capable of giving England
pause, it is the thought of France and Spain
united; it is the certainty that the first cannon-

shot directed at the one or the other will be answered by both."[5]

None the less, it would seem that at the moment of taking office Vergennes' policy looked toward an effort at amity with England; and it is certain that he first assessed the American revolt as guaranteeing England's continued peaceableness rather than as furnishing a fulcrum for an actively anti-English policy.[6] For this there were three reasons: In the first place, the American business itself was still much "in the vague." Again, Vergennes was aware that Louis had taken the throne pledged to a program of economy and internal reform and to this program, he naturally assumed, diplomatic programs would have to be subordinated.[7] Finally, in July, 1774, by the Treaty of Kutchuk-Kainardji Russia had established herself on the shores of the Black Sea in territory wrested from Turkey. Alarmed at the prospect of a repetition of what had just occurred in Poland, as well as for France's monopoly of the Levantine trade, Vergennes felt that his first attention must be given to the South-

[5] "Instructions to the Baron de Breteuil," Dec. 28, 1774, *Recueil des Instructions*, I. 478 ffg.; "Exposé succinct" of Dec. 8, 1774, Doniol I. 14 ff.

[6] *Ib.*, I. 13, 40.

[7] See *Recueil des Instructions*, I. 488: "La grandeur de la puissance du Roi, la position de ses États et ses soins que sa Majesté est résolvé de donner à leur administration intérieure, le mettront en effet . . . en état de choisir entre tous les systèmes politiques celui qui conviendra le mieux à ses vues et à ses interêts."

eastern situation. Indeed, he seems at one moment to have considered the possibility of persuading England herself to join in an effort to curb Russia's assaults upon the established equilibrium.[8]

But this attitude was, after all, weakly rooted in a thin soil. Moreover, Turkey's cession of the Chersonese was soon seen to be *fait accompli*. Vergennes' real disposition toward England found expression in connection with the dispute which began brewing in July, 1774, between Spain and Portugal over some aggressions of the latter in South America. The possibility of war between Portugal and Spain raised the possibility of war between Spain and England and that, in turn, the possibility of war between England and France. Commenting on the report that England desired an amicable settlement of the affair, Vergennes remarked: "We share the wish, rather from necessity than inclination."[9] And equally illuminative is an episode which occurred early in 1775 in connection with the destruction which the king had just then ordered of the correspondence of the *Secret du Roi*. Among the papers about to be consigned to the flames was a plan that had been drawn up by Broglie in 1766 for the invasion of England. Vergennes

[8] See Hassall, *The Balance of Power*, 320; *Recueil des Instructions*, IX. (Russe), 318-20; and Doniol, I. 15.

[9] Vergennes to Ossun, Oct. 31, 1774, Doniol, I. 33.

and his associate, the Count du Muy, at once petitioned Louis to be allowed to save this document, a request which was promptly granted.[10]

But all other sources of instruction as to the new secretary's attitude toward England yield place to a document I have already cited more than once, his *Exposé Succinct,* which was prepared early in December, 1774. This was, in brief, a plea for military preparation based on a survey of the whole diplomatic situation with which France was then confronted. "People," its author wrote, "respect a nation which they see prepared to make a vigorous resistance and which, without abusing the superiority of its forces, desires only that which is just and useful for the whole world, to wit, peace and general tranquillity." Unfortunately, however, while this was the objective of diplomacy, diplomacy itself was unable "to fix conclusively the choice of route thereto." It was a truth albeit a trite one,

that the longer a peace has endured the less likely is it to continue. The fact that the present peace has lasted twelve years furnishes a strong prejudgment against its further stability. It is then not to transgress the limits of allowable prevision to insist upon the necessity of being ready for any event; and besides, one is never better assured of peace than when one is in position not to fear war. Opinion, 'tis said, is queen of the world.[11]

[10] Ségur, I. 104-6; Doniol, I. 23-4.
[11] Ségur, I. 169-70; Doniol, I. 20.

Nor did Vergennes leave those whom he addressed in doubt as to the practical bearing in the main of these generalizations:

If [he wrote] having surveyed the Continent we turn our eyes coastward, do we find there greater pledges of security? We see lying alongside us a nation greedy, restless, more jealous of the prosperity of its neighbors than awake to its own happiness, powerfully armed and ready to strike on the instant. Let us not deceive ourselves; whatever parade the English ministers may make of their pacific intentions, we cannot count upon this disposition longer than their domestic difficulties continue. These however may come to an end, or indeed they may increase to such a point as to cause the government to direct the general uneasiness against objects abroad. It is not without precedent that the cry of a war against France has become the rallying point of all parties in England. . . . Having nothing to gain with France by the prosecution of a legitimate commerce, England looks with envy upon the vast extent of our plantations in America and our industry in Europe.[12]

Rarely has a minister of state drawn a more sinister picture of the purposes and policies of an ostensibly friendly government; and to the picture so delineated, rumor soon added the touch of imminent menace. Within a few days of the preparation of the *Exposé,* Vergennes received

[12] *Ib.,* 18-9. Note the point of view revealed by the assertion that England has nothing to gain from "a legitimate commerce with France."

from Garnier the report then circulating about
London that Chatham had a plan by which peace
could be reëstablished in America without offense
to the dignity of England. This plan, he at once
inferred, could only be at the expense of France.
True, he wrote Garnier, England was burdened
with debts and was the object of universal enmity.
True too, George III has little love for Chatham.
But the very extremity of the situation in America might compel his Britannic Majesty to conquer his prejudices and call this "enemy of peace"
to power once more. His doing so would signal a
situation for which desperate remedies had been
determined upon and France would have need
to beware.[13]   Six weeks later Garnier wrote still
more alarmingly.   Speaking on his own responsibility, he asserted very confidently that if the
measures of the existing ministry "do not meet
with complete success, the end of the administration will follow immediately and the king will be
forced to yield to circumstances and place my lord
Chatham at the head of affairs.   He will come in
clothed with absolute power."[14]

There now ensued a considerable pause; and it
was the end of July, 1775, when the Count de
Guines wrote that Lord Rochford, a member of
the British ministry, had confided to him the belief of men in both parties, that the only way

[13] Vergennes to Garnier, Dec. 26, 1774, *ib.*, 60-2.
[14] *Ib.*, 69.

to end the war in America was to declare war upon France, the argument being that, if confronted with the necessity of choosing between England and France, the Americans in fear of seeing the latter once more in Canada would certainly cast in their lot with the former, even at the expense of liberty.[15] A little later advices reached Vergennes by way of Madrid that, even though Chathan did not come again to power—which was improbable—the existing ministers seemed to wish to imitate his way of thinking, from which it resulted that war was not unlikely to break out at the least expected moment.[16] Finally in the middle of September Vergennes sent Beaumarchais, the famous author of *Figaro,* to pump from Rochford, who was an old acquaintance of his, further information as to British intentions. Beaumarchais, in a letter which was handed the king September 21st, summarized his conclusions thus: "In short, America is lost to the British in spite of their efforts. The war is waged more ferociously in London than in Boston. The crisis will end with war against France if the opposition comes in, whether it is Chatham or Rockingham who replaces Lord North."[17]

[15] *Ib.* 116-17.

[16] *Ib.,* 117-19. See also the letter of Aug. 7 from Louis to Charles III, indicating the former's persuasion of the possibility of war with England, *ib.,* 131-2.

[17] John Durand (Ed.), *Documents on the American Revolution* (N. Y., 1889), 53-4

Already, however, the secretary's interest in the American situation had ceased to be exclusively one of alarmed concern. Thus, late in August the ambassador had forwarded from London the text of the royal proclamation pronouncing the Americans "rebels," and Vergennes had concluded thence that, so long as the existing ministry remained in office, there was little danger of an alliance between America reconciled and the mother-country, which would turn its combined forces against France and Spain.[18]   Furthermore, the little likelihood there had been at any time that the arch-enemy of France would come again to power was for the time being at an end. This great man, "the world forgetting, by the world forgot," was now in a mysterious seclusion from which he did not emerge till the beginning of 1777.   For many months the name of Chatham, its magic in abeyance, drops out of the despatches altogether.[18a]

A clue to the new point of view of the Foreign Office is afforded by its response to Guines' despatch of September 8th, reporting a statement by Rochford that the American Lee, now in London, had sworn "on his honor" that the colonists had assurance of aid from France and Spain, and his own positive denial that this

[18] Doniol, I. 172-4.

[18a] *The Correspondence of King George the Third with Lord North,* from 1768 to 1783.   (Ed. W. B. Donne, London, 1867, 2 vols.), II. 10.

statement had basis in fact. Replying ten days later Vergennes had commended the ambassador's method of parrying his English interlocutor but at the same time had cautioned him against putting anything in writing. "The king," said he, "wishes neither to augment the difficulties of the British government nor to encourage the resistance of the Americans, but neither does it suit his interest to serve as a means of putting the latter down."[19]

Late in October Vergennes received the British ambassador Stormont and engaged him in an extended conversation on the American situation with the aim, at once, of reassuring the English government as to French intentions and of discovering how seriously that government regarded its trans-Atlantic affairs. That which was now happening in America, the French secretary declared, he had himself foreseen when as ambassador at Constantinople he had learned of the cession of Canada to England. He then proceeded to suggest that what the Americans were plainly aiming at was independence and to conjecture the consequences should they attain their object:

In that case they would immediately set about forming a great marine, and as they have every possible advantage for ship-building, [it] would not be long before they had such fleets as would be an overmatch for the

[19] Doniol, I. 150-1.

68   FRENCH POLICY AND

whole naval power of Europe, could it be united against
them. . . . In the end they would not leave a foot of
that hemisphere in the possession of any European
power.

To these speculations the Englishman assented
eagerly.[20]   It is evident that against the background furnished by the siege of Boston, the news
of which was already producing an immense stir
in Paris, Choiseul's observation that "the balance
of power lay in America" revealed a new
significance.

In the closing days of 1775 the French Foreign
Office proceeded, under Vergennes' direction, to
formulate the problem with which the American
revolt confronted France.   It had before it
memoirs and letters from a variety of quarters,
some even from the French West Indies, but
what is much more to the point, it had before
it the plans and projects of Choiseul, wherein
was clearly set forth the connection that existed
between the American insurrection and the restoration of French power and prestige, and
wherein the large general problem was reduced to
the more precise question whether the Americans
would really proclaim their independence, or if
they once proclaimed it, be of a mind to make a
persistent effort for it.[21]

[20] SMSS., No. 1306.
[21] Doniol, I. 240-2. Vergennes had, upon taking office, reorgan-
ized the archives of the Foreign Office, and had had his secretaries

The answer that the Foreign Office returned to this question and the consequences that it deduced from its answer are set forth in the *Réflexions,* which was penned by Vergennes' secretary, Gérard de Rayneval, probably early in November, 1775.[22] "There is reason to believe," this most important document begins, "that the colonies are not in quest simply of a redress of grievances, but that they are resolved to throw off the yoke of the mother-country altogether." Yet, it continues, "if the colonies are left to themselves, it is probable that Great Britain will succeed in subjugating them." What then is the course that France should pursue at this juncture? "If England subjugates the colonies she will at least retain the commercial benefits that she has always drawn thence and which will accordingly continue to sustain both her manufactures and her marine. She will, moreover, prevent the colonies from becoming what they would be if independent, a considerable weight in the balance of power in favor of some other state." France's interest was therefore plain. "England is the natural enemy of France, and a greedy, ambitious, unjust, and

prepare elaborate summaries of French foreign policy in all directions from the time of the Peace of Westphalia, *Revue d'Histoire diplomatique,* VII. 540.

[22] *Ib.,* 243-9; SMSS., No. 1310. The conjecture as to date is based on M. Doniol's very probable theory that Beaumarchais' activities in behalf of the idea of secret aid came after the secretary had formulated his program in the "Réflexions": see Doniol I. 251.

treacherous enemy, the constant and cherished object of whose system is, if not the destruction of France, at least her abasement, humiliation, and ruin." But now at this moment, England's "colonies are in open war against her, their purpose is to cast off her yoke, they ask us to furnish them aid and supplies." Suppose then we meet their desires and our assistance proves effective, what advantages will result to us?

1. The power of England will shrink and ours will expand correspondingly; 2. Her commerce will suffer an irreparable loss while ours will increase; 3. It is very probable that in the course of events we may be able to recover some of the possessions that the English ridded us of in America, as for instance, the Newfoundland fisheries, those of the gulf of St. Lawrence, the Isle Royal, etc. I do not speak of Canada.[23]

But if these were the premises upon which France should base her course, what precisely should that course be? Of men capable and willing to bear arms the colonies had a great sufficiency, but they lacked: "first, provisions of war; secondly, currency; thirdly, a good navy." To obtain the first it would only be necessary for them to send their vessels to French ports laden with produce which they should there exchange for arms and munitions. This commerce could easily proceed without the government having any visible hand in it: "it would only be necessary

[23] Ib., 243-4.

to have at each of the ports to which the American vessels resorted an intelligent merchant whose loyalty and discretion could be relied upon." The demand for money was somewhat more difficult, but given legitimate dimensions, it could be met in the same way as the demand for munitions. Most difficult of all would it be to furnish the insurgents vessels of war without declaring openly for them and so "precipitating war with Great Britain." Still it would perhaps be feasible to send some merchant vessels adapted to the uses of war to Santo Domingo, where they could pass to the Americans by a simulated purchase. But the essential thing was that France should lose no time in reinforcing the courage of the Americans, and by doing it secretly she would avoid compromising herself either with the insurgents or the court of London, while at the same time "she would be putting herself in shape to strike decisive blows" when the time was ripe.[24]

Thus, it was admitted, that secret aid looked forward to possible war. But then, it was argued, a policy of inaction would be no guaranty of peace either, whether England triumphed or the insurgents. For in the one case as in the other the court of London would believe itself warranted in attacking France's colonies. Prudence therefore dictated that the means of waging war with success should be prepared beforehand,

[24] *Ib.*, 246-8.

and one of the most essential of such means was "to make sure" of the Americans.[25]

With the appearance of the *Réflexions* began in good earnest the contest for the support of the king, earlier alluded to, between those who wished to see a brilliant diplomatic program adopted and those who, headed by Turgot, urged domestic reform and economy.[26] At the outset the royal conscience was in the possession of the reformers. Happily for the program of the Foreign Office, in the lively and inventive Beaumarchais, a veritable Cagliostro in the blend he presents of interested calculation and generous enthusiasm, Vergennes had a zealous missionary of his cause and one who, moreover, stood high in the favor of the royal family. On December 7th Beaumarchais handed Vergennes a letter addressed "to the king alone, very important" and headed with the motto *summum jus summa injuria*. In this extraordinary document the author of *Figaro* proceeded to attack with vigor the conscientious scruples which he thought stood in the way of the king's adopting the plan of secret aid: "The national policy which preserves

[25] *Ib.*, 249.

[26] See Lavisse, *op. cit.*, 46-51.

[27] On Beaumarchais' part in the American Revolution see Wharton, I. §§ 56-75; John Durand, *op. cit.*, 38-159; Louis de Lomenie, *Beaumarchais and his Times* (Trans. by H. S. Edwards, N. Y., 1857), Chs. XVII-XX; Blanche E. Hazard, *Beaumarchais and the American Revolution* (Boston, 1910).

states," he argued, "differs in every respect almost entirely from the civil morality which governs individuals." *"Salus populi suprema lex."* But even if this were not the case good faith would not be due England, "that natural enemy, that jealous rival of your success, that people always systematically unjust to you."

Indeed not even a treaty would have justly restrained you on this occasion. For when have the usurpations and outrages of this people ever had any limit but that of its strength? Has it not always waged war against you without declaring it? Did it not begin the last one, in a time of peace, by the sudden capture of five hundred of your vessels? Did it not humble you by forcing you to destroy your finest seaport? Has it not recently subjected your merchant vessels to inspection on the northern seas?—a humiliation which would have made Louis XIV rather eat his hands than not atone for it?

Finally, Beaumarchais again invoked general principles. Tranquillity is most safely based on the division of one's enemies, the way to conquer iniquity is to arm it against itself. And if, he concluded, there is anyone who does not agree with me, "beginning with M. de Vergennes," "I close my mouth, I cast into the fire Scaliger, Grotius, Puffendorf, Gravina, Montesquieu, every writer on public rights, and admit that the study of a lifetime has been only a waste of effort."[28]

Meantime, in August, 1775, the Count de

<hr>

[28] Durand, *op. cit.*, 59-73.

Guines, acting under instructions from Vergennes, had despatched a certain Bonvouloir to
America to travel in a private capacity, to gather
impressions, and to insinuate to such influential
Americans as he met the admiration felt in
France for their noble efforts after liberty, the
entire disinterestedness of the French government so far as Canada was concerned, and the
welcome which American merchantmen would
receive in French harbors.   Early in March, 1776,
Bonvouloir's first report, which was highly sanguine of American prospects, reached Paris.[29]
Thus confirmed in his idea of the military competence of the Colonies, Vergennes proceeded at
once to shape up his plan of secretly aiding them.
for discussion by his associates in office. At the
same time he still had before him the certainty
of Turgot's opposition, with the result that there
is a marked difference in tone between the *Mémoire de Considérations*[30] and the earlier *Réflexions*. Thus at the outset of the *Considérations,*
in an effort to supersede the language of
advocacy with that of scientific detachment, Vergennes concedes ostensibly that whether France
and Spain should desire the subjection or the
independence of the English colonies was "perhaps problematical," that either event perhaps

[29] Wharton, I. §§38-40. For the report itself, see Doniol, I. 287-
92, especially 287-8; and for a translation, Durand, 2-16.

[30] Doniol, I. 273-9; SMSS., No. 1316.

threatened "dangers that it was not within human foresight to provide against."[31]   Also the notion that "Providence had marked out this moment for the humiliation of England by striking her with the madness which is the sure precurser of destruction" is ostentatiously disavowed in the name of both the Bourbon kings.[32]   On the other hand, two propositions are offered as axiomatic: first, that the prolongation of the American war would be "highly advantageous to both France and Spain, inasmuch as it would be calculated to exhaust both the victors and the vanquished";[33] and secondly, that whatever the final result of the struggle between England and her Colonies, France could hardly hope for peace, since if England conciliated or subjected the Colonies she would be tempted by the large forces on hand to make an easy conquest of the West Indies, whereas if she lost them, she would be driven thus to indemnify herself.[34]   And from these supposed facts it is held to follow that it was for the interest of both France and Spain, while "dexterously reassuring" England as to their intentions, to "extend the insurgents secret aid both in money and military stores without seeking any return for so doing beyond the political objective

[31] Doniol, I. 273
[32] Ib., 275.
[33] Ib., 276.
[34] Ib., 274-5.

of the moment". This should be the program for at least the ensuing twelve months. Meantime "the idea of independence, which seems to germinate rather slowly among the Americans," would perhaps have come to maturity. At any rate the two crowns would have had opportunity to perfect their forces.[35]

Adroitly, however, as this argument was framed to anticipate the objections of the controller-general, it did not conceal the essential risk of the program it supported. It is significant, therefore, that the burden of Turgot's criticism of the *Considérations* is a protest against any program likely to precipitate an avoidable war, the expense of which must necessarily aggravate the already serious state of the royal finances. For the rest, striking to the very heart of the foreign secretary's argument, its mercantilist presuppositions, the controller-general predicted that the day of "colonies exclusively riveted to the mother-country" was over, and counselled that that nation would show itself wisest and most deserving of happiness which should first convert its colonists from subjects to allies. Spain, said he, "ought to expect to see herself abandoned by her colonies; it was necessary to make ready for the commercial revolution which the new régime would bring about: by the same sign, there was little need of uneasiness lest England pounce

[35] *Ib.*, 277-8.

upon France's colonies, since there was no advantage involved in longer possessing them."
"What difference did it make, then, whether
England subjugated her colonies or not? Subjugated, they would occupy her attention by their
desire to become free; freed, their whole commercial system would be altered and England would
have no further interest than to appropriate to
herself the benefits of the new system."[36] As to
the likelihood that England was planning to
attack France, Turgot was frankly sceptical, but,
he argued, if that were found to be the case, then
France ought to prepare for the danger nearer
at home, and especially by strengthening her
fleet. Meantime it would be proper to put the
Americans in the way of procuring the munitions
and even the money they needed by means of
trade, but there should be no departure by the
government itself from neutrality and no act of
direct aid.[37]

Turgot, however, was fighting what from the
first was foreordained a losing battle. In the
words of Soulavie, the cause of "Reform, Re-
trenchment, and Rights to be realized" could not
hold its own with a selfish and ambitious court
against a program of "Revenge, Glory, and Hu-

[36] Ib., 281.
[37] Ib., 282-3. Turgot also makes the point, later to be emphasized by the Spanish government, that "an attack on England
would be a signal for the reconciliation of England and America
and would precipitate the very danger" which the Foreign Office's
policy ostensibly sought to avoid.

miliation to be retrieved"; and even liberals like LaFayette found the idea of shedding blood for liberty abroad more to their taste than that of shedding feudal immunities at home. There had, indeed, been a period at the end of February and early in March when the Maurepas cabinet had seemed about to succumb to the joint attacks of the friends of Choiseul and Guines. But while the sentiments of the latter nobleman were so excessively pacific that he had just been superseded by the Duke de Noailles at Saint James',[38] Choiseul was loudly critical of the ministry's apparent failure to appreciate the possibilities of the American revolt;[39] and the total result of the episode had been to solidify the ministry, except for the Liberals Turgot and Malesherbes, in support of a more enterprising policy. In their comments on the *Considérations,* St. Germain, the minister of War, and Sartines, the minister of Marine, did little more than reëcho the arguments of Vergennes, while Maurepas took a line that was frankly belligerent.[40]

[38] See Doniol, I. 359-68.

[39] Stormont to Weymouth, Dec. 6, 1775; Jan. 10 and Feb. 14, 1776: SMSS., 1307, 1313, 1314. For the circumstances attending the recall of Guines from London, for which, curiously enough, Turgot was primarily responsible, and the intrigue that had for its purpose to bring Choiseul into power, see *Last Journal of Horace Walpole* (Ed. Doran, London, 1859, 2 vols.), II. 9-13.

[40] *Ib.,* 280, 284-6. The statement as to Maurepas' attitude is based on the assumption, sanctioned by M. Doniol, that the "Réflexions sur la Nécessité de secourir les Américains et de se préparer à la Guerre avec l'Angleterre" was his work. This document

The ministerial arguments, moreover, were
again supplemented by the ardent advocacy of
Beaumarchais, to whose effusion entitled *La
Paix ou la Guerre* is generally credited Louis'
final conversion to the plan of secret aid.[41]   On
May 2nd the king at last definitely authorized the
advance of a million livres to Beaumarchais for
the purchase of supplies to be transferred to the
Americans.   Six weeks later the Spanish court
made a similar advance, and the following August the famous house of *Hortalez et Cie* opened
its doors.   Within a twelvemonth it had despatched to America eight ship-loads of warlike
stores, valued at more than six million livres
and drawn in large part from the royal arsenals.[42]
Meantime, on May 12th, Turgot had been dis-
missed, leaving Vergennes the directing influence
in the ministry.

closes with the following illuminating observation: "Toutes ces considérations réunies pourroient donc porter à conclure même l'offensive comme le seul moyen de rétablir notre marine d'une part et de
l'autre d'affaiblir celle de l'Angleterre, et comme le seul moyen
d'assurer pour longtems la paix du Continent qui n'a jamais été
troublée que par leurs intrigues ou leur argent." "The ablest man
I knew," wrote Horace Walpole, "was the old Comte de Maurepas.
. . . Knowing his enmity to this country, I told him . . . that it
was fortunate for England that he had been so long divested of
power." Trevelyan, *The American Revolution*, Pt. III. 413 fn.

   [41] Durand, *op. cit.*, 74-85; Lomenie, *op. cit.*, 267-71.

   [42] See the references in note 27, *supra*, especially Wharton, I.
§§ 60 ff.; also C. J. Stillé, "Beaumarchais and the Lost Million,"
Pennsylvania Magazine of History and Biography, XI. 1-36.

CHAPTER IV

THE PORTUGUESE AND CORSAIR QUESTIONS

For many months secret aid was a mystery closely guarded from even its beneficiaries. The decision to render it, none the less, involved certain diplomatic consequences at once. Beaumarchais had not yet begun operations when England lodged a complaint against Americans being allowed to procure powder in the French West Indies and to fly the French flag from their mastheads.[1] Perceiving the bearing of the question, Vergennes promptly took up an aggressive position. He recalled England's traffic in arms with Corsica when France was subjugating that island. He asserted entire willingness to abide by the English doctrine that contraband must have a hostile destination, wherefore vessels plying between France and the French islands would not be subject to seizure on the charge of carrying it. He ridiculed the idea that England could pretend a grievance in the fact that the Americans were getting aid from France through the channels of trade: the French markets were open

[1] Garnier to Vergennes, May 6, 1776, Doniol, I. 463.

to all and those who paid best would have the preference. Thus, to use a more modern terminology, Vergennes gave notice of his government's intention to treat the Americans as possessed of "belligerent rights", including the right of an inviolable asylum in neutral ports for their peaceful traders.[2]

But the question of the trading rights of neutrals was from the outset but one ingredient of the diplomatic situation between England and France, and not the most important ingredient at that. Far more ominous was the stage which the dispute between Spain and Portugal, arising

[2] Vergennes to Garnier, June 15 and 21, *ib.*, 466-9. See also Vergennes to Noailles, March 21, 1777, *ib.*, II. 334: "Nous en [the question of prizes] usons avec les insurgens comme nous ferions avec toute nation amie qui seront en guerre avec l'Angleterre." Other interesting documents in the same connection are Dumas' letter to the Committee of Secret Correspondence, May 14, 1776, Wharton II. 90-2; the "Exposé des Motifs de la Conduite du Roi Très-Chrétien relativement à l'Angleterre," Doniol, III. 823-56; and *Observations on the Justificatory Memorial of the Court of London* (see Appendix IV), 102-12. That the modern distinction between "Belligerency" and "Independence" in the case of communities seeking admission to the Family of Nations found no place in the Public Law of the period is shown by the following passage from the pen of Horace Walpole: "An American privateer had carried three prizes into Bilboa. The governor had detained them. . . . He was ordered by Grimaldi's letter to restore them, the king of Spain professing an exact neutrality, which was in effect owning our colonies for an independent state," *Last Journals,* II. 87. It it an interesting speculation, to what extent the French alliance with the United States was made necessary by the absence of a distinction which would have enabled France to aid the Americans without violating England's rights.

from the latter's aggressions in South America, had now reached. Because of the alliances of these powers with France and England respectively, the outbreak of war between them meant almost inevitably war between England and France as well.[3] The Spanish ambassador at Paris, the Count d'Aranda, who was a bitter enemy of England, had from the first proclaimed this a welcome development in view of England's growing embarrassment in North America.[4] Vergennes, on the other hand, disliking the obvious ambition of Spain to annex Portugal, both because he regarded such a project as contrary to the precepts of the *Système de Conservation* and also because he feared for the smooth working of the Family Compact should Spain become the equal of France, had sought to compose the differences of the Iberian states. His efforts at pacification had, however, been followed by fresh aggressions on Portugal's part, instigated, Spain hinted, by the English;[5]

[3] "Si la guerre entre l'Espagne et le Portugal devient indispensable, ce que la situation présente des affaires entre les deux puissances ne donne que trop sujet d'appréhender, il est inévitable que la guerre avec l'Angleterre en sera la suite et que la France ne pourra pas se dispenser d'y prendre la part la plus directe." Such are the opening words of the memoir read by Vergennes to the council of ministers held at Marly, July 7, 1776, Doniol, I. 527.

[4] *Vd. ib.*, 352 ff. For an interesting characterization of this unique individual, see Ségur, *Mémoirs*, I. 390. *Cf.* Doniol, V. 30.

[5] On the whole matter, see Doniol, I. 75-6, 298-312, 330-7, 525, 532-3.

and by the beginning of July, Vergennes had come quite around to Aranda's viewpoint.

A warlike situation now developed rapidly.[6] To a council of ministers held at Marly on July 7th Vergennes presented the Spanish-Portuguese matter as offering France the opportunity "to break the power of the single enemy she had cause to fear," provided only French diplomacy was equal to the occasion. First and foremost, the war must be kept from spreading to the Continent, which could be readily guaranteed by Austria's standing by to prevent Russia from falling upon Sweden. Again, in Holland the ashes of the old Republican party must be fanned to flame once more and Dutch neutrality be secured by appeal to Dutch avarice. Finally, it was essential "to let the Americans know of the present state of affairs and the results which it presaged, and, without assuming engagements with them, yet to make them understand the full advantage which existing circumstances promised had they but the hardihood and patience to await their unfolding."[7]

[6] Vergennes' English correspondence at this period contains many sharp criticisms of the treatment French subjects were alleged to be receiving in Newfoundland and Hindoostan. Most of these supposed grievances were long-standing ones. Their revival at this moment is indication of the French government's belligerent intention. See generally the references in note 2, above.

[7] *Ib.*, 527-8. Compare Garnier's "Lettre particulière" of May 15, SMSS., No. 868.

Four days later Deane, the Continental Congress' first agent to France, who had just arrived at Paris, was admitted by Vergennes to a secret interview. The secretary would not express himself on the subject of American independence, especially as "the United Provinces" had not yet expressed themselves; but he gave assurance that no obstacles would be placed in the way of Americans trading in French ports, whether in munitions or other products. He proposed that Deane should keep the Foreign Office *en rapport* with all important happenings in America, and strongly advised him to steer clear of Englishmen.[8] Then on August 13th Garnier wrote from London that the Americans had at last declared their independence.[9] In a "committee" consisting of the king and cabinet, held on August 31st, Vergennes, casting equivocation aside, proclaimed that, as between the advantages and disadvantages of a war "against England in the present juncture, . . . the former outweigh the latter so unmistakably that no comparison can be made": The Americans had now declared their indepen-

[8] Deane to the Committee of Secret Correspondence, Wharton, *op. cit.*, II. 112-6. The British government protested against Deane's having been allowed to land in France, a protest at which Vergennes professed to take great umbrage: "Le Roy est le maître chez lui, . . . il n'a compte à rendre à qui que soit des étrangers qu'il juge à-propos d'admettre dans ses États," Doniol, I. 583.

[9] *Ib.*, 561.

dence. These same Americans it was, their sailors and soldiers, who had made "those vast conquests of which France has in times past so keenly felt the humiliation." They were now available allies; and, thanks to commerce, the connection now formed with them could not fail to be lasting.[10] Against these arguments no voice was raised, and a week later the memoir embodying them was despatched to Madrid for approval by that court.

Why, then, did not the war come? The answer is supplied by the fact that the very day that the response of the Spanish government arrived accepting its ally's program, though with a characteristic stipulation for further delay,[11] the news came from Garnier of the American defeat at Long Island.[12] Vergennes at once decided that the policy of secret aid still remained the better part of valor, but he was able to conceal his retreat under the pretext of disapproving of Spain's plan, which still included the conquest of Portugal.[13] "The king," he wrote, "will always regard the aggrandizement of the Spanish monarchy with satisfaction but His Majesty is unable to conceal from the king, his uncle, that the conquest of Portugal would be alarming to all states

[10] Ib., 567-77, especially 570-1; SMSS., No. 897.

[11] Grimaldi to Aranda, Oct. 8, 1776, Doniol, I. 603-13. The main points of the document are summarized on pages 612-13.

[12] Ib., 615-6.

[13] "Réflexions," ib., 681-8.

interested in maintaining the balance of power."
"If," he continued, "it is a universal maxim, as
contended by the Marquis de Grimaldi, that one
makes war only for the purpose of gain, yet this
maxim ought to be adopted by the two crowns in
the existing situation only with the idea in mind
that *everything* is to be gained by breaking down
the power of England." Could that be done,
then would

France and Spain have achieved an advantage more
precious than could be represented by the conquest of a
rich province. For once England is unable to keep
going the flame of discord among the great sovereigns
of Europe, then will the two monarchs no longer be ham-
pered in exercising their better inclinations, which look
only to securing to their own subjects and to all Europe
the sweet fruits of a sure and durable peace.[14]

A few weeks later we find Vergennes penning
the British ambassador the following *billet:*

Versailles, December 21st, 1776. Monsieur: I am
indeed touched at the attention shown me by Your Excellency in admitting me to share your joy at the satisfactory news of the success of British arms in Connecticut and New York. I beg Your Excellency to accept
my many thanks at this testimonial of your friendship,
and my sincere felicitations upon an event so calculated
to contribute to the reëstablishment of peace in that
part of the globe. I shall impart the communication
made me to the king and now take it upon myself to
assure you that His Majesty will always receive with

[14] *Ib.*, 685-7.

pleasure news of whatever may contribute to the satisfaction and glory of the king your master.[15]

Vergennes' policy during the late months of
1776 and the early months of 1777 may be characterized in the poignant phrase of today as one
of "watchful waiting." The secretary had abandoned none of his fundamental premises: "The
purpose of every offensive war is either to aggrandize one's self or to enfeeble the rival power,
whose superiority one fears. . . . As everything
is relative in the political order, they [the two
crowns] will necessarily increase by reason of the
enfeeblement of their rival. . . . By renouncing
every idea of supremacy the English would be
free to recognize the independence against which
they are armed": and more to like effect.[16] On

[15] *Ib.*, II. 107, fn. 2. A month earlier than this, Vergennes had
told Stormont that it was contrary to the king's intention that his
subjects should go to America, SMSS., No. 905. On Dec. 10, the
secretary ordered Lenoir to arrest all persons giving out that they
were intending to go to America, *ib.*, No. 1385. Vergennes' despatches to Noailles at this period display considerable uneasiness
as to British intentions, *ib.* Nos. 907, 913, and 917. The fact is
that Vergennes, relying on American and Spanish assistance, had
been planning an attack upon England for which the French
marine was not at all fit. See Doniol, II. 156-70. Hence, the extent
of his reaction after the American defeat at Long Island.

[16] Vergennes to Ossun, Mar. 11, 1777, *ib.*, 238-41. See also the
document given in Appendix II. Though the work of a "private
citizen" it was prepared, Doniol thinks, for the Council. *Vd. ib.*, 118.
Its speculations as to the effect of the success of the Revolution
on France's position in Europe take a wide range.

the other hand, it is quite apparent that his confidence in the military capacity of the Americans —indeed, in the vitality of their cause—had suffered a great shock from the disaster of Long Island. Of these facts he must again be persuaded before he would consent to risk the dignity of the French crown, and meantime, between American importunity and British suspicion, he must take his way charily.

The clue to the period is furnished by the comparison of two memoirs from the secretary's pen that are dated respectively April 12th and April 26th, 1777. The latter, a criticism upon certain propositions of the Spanish government, which still continued in a warlike frame of mind, contained the following homily in favor of peace:

"One knows well enough where war begins, but no one can know where or how it will end. If one could be sure that England would concentrate against us and not extend her efforts to the Continent, the present occasion would be very seductive and it would require a sublime exercise of virtue to repulse it. But the existence of England is a matter of concern from the point of view of the equilibrium of Europe; it is accordingly necessary to anticipate that she will not be left alone. . . . The uprising in America has remained up to the present a purely domestic matter so far as England is concerned; she sees in the insurgents only a people in revolt whom she has a right to recall to their obedience by whatever means lie within her reach and without other powers having any title to mix up in the affair. To offer to

intervene would be in some sort to recognize and support
the independence which the American provinces have
declared, since it is only between equal powers that
intervention ordinarily takes place.[17]

The earlier memoir struck a quite different note.
Composed in anticipation of a visit of the emperor to Paris, it urged the necessity of the
Austrian connection to France, because, by assuring the peace on the Continent, it paved the way
for "taking measures against England, the
natural and most inveterate enemy of France, her
glory and prosperity."[18]

[17] "Lettre . . . communiquée au Roi," etc., *ib.*, 271 ff., 272-4
See also passage to like effect in Vergennes to Ossun, Mar. 22,
1777, *ib.*, 248. Also, same to same, Apr. 12, where the following
words occur: "Si nous pouvions rétablir l'opinion du bon état de
nos finances, toutes nos possessions servient bien plus en sureté
sous cet abri que sous la protection d'escadres nombreuses qui
peuvent être primées ou surpassées," *ib.*, 261,—a sentiment altogether worthy of Turgot!

[18] *Ib.*, 428; Flassan, *Histoire générale et raisonnée,* etc., VII. 135.
See also Vergennes' note of February 12 to Aranda in response
to propositions emanating from the British government looking
to a general disarmament by France, Spain, and Great Britain:
"Si nous accordons à désarmer nous epargnons sans doute une
grande dépense mais l'oconomie sera plus grande pour l'Angleterre," etc. Doniol, II. 155, 208-9. It was also during this period
that the controversy occurred between the French and Spanish governments over the question of sending further reinforcements to
Hayti and Santo Domingo, in view of the continued possibility
of war over the Portuguese question. Vergennes argued against
the idea on the ground that the climate was fatal to Europeans
and on the ground that such a step would tend to alarm Great
Britain and make her less ready to accept France's friendly as-

Inevitably, it was a period of episodes. It was at this time that LaFayette, eluding the deceptive vigilance of the royal officers, made his way to America, though he would have preferred to lead a filibustering expedition against the English settlements in the East.[19] It was at this time that the minister of War, St. Germain, induced Steuben to come to America to assist in training the Continental Army. It was also at this time that the Count de Broglie launched his scheme, which had the approval of Deane, for making himself a sort of temporary stadtholder of the United States and commissioned Kalb, Choiseul's former emissary to America, to enlist the interest of Congress.

Writing Kalb from his country-seat at Ruffec, December 11th, Broglie set forth the outlines of his plan as follows:

A military and political leader is wanted, a man fitted to carry the weight of authority in the colonies, to unite its parties, to assign to each his place. The main point of the mission with which you have been entrusted will therefore consist in explaining the advantages, or rather, the absolute necessity of the choice of such a man. The rank accorded the candidate would have to be of the first eminence, such for instance, as that of the Prince of Nassau; but his functions would have to be

surances. As the troops were sent later on (in July: see Doniol, II. 453), we man conclude that the second was the important consideration. See references in Chapter I., *supra,* note 8.

[19] Doniol, II. ch. 2; SMSS., No. 756.

confined to the army, . . . with perhaps the single
exception of the political negotiations with foreign
powers; . . . the assurance of the man's return to
France at the end of three years will remove every apprehension in regard to the powers to be conferred and
will remove even the semblance of an ambitious design
to become governor of the new republic.   Of course
large pecuniary consideration would have to be claimed
for the preparation of the journey and for the journey
itself and a liberal salary for the return home.   You
can give the assurance that such a measure will bring
order and economy into the public expense, that it will
reimburse the cost a hundred-fold in a single campaign.
You will be equally mindful to dwell upon the effect
necessarily produced by such an appointment on its
mere announcement in Europe.[20]

I know of no documentary evidence connecting
Vergennes with this extraordinary scheme.   Yet
it seems to me hardly supposable that a great
noble like Broglie, who obviously had none of the
youthful enthusiasm of LaFayette and who was
already more or less at outs with the court on
account of his connection with the *Secret du Roi,*
would have risked the king's further displeasure

[20] Friedrich Kapp, *Life of Kalb,* pp. 94-5.   See also Kalb's
memoir of Dec. 17, addressed to Deane, which is to be found in the
French Archives des Affaires étrangeres.   Here the additional
argument is offered that the step proposed by Broglie would so
enlist the interest of the nobility that they would force the king
to make an alliance with the Americans.   Broglie's own expectations from the scheme are also set forth in greater detail.   SMSS.,
No. 604; *Deane Papers,* I. 426-31.

by lending himself to a project of incalculable possibilities without some sort of assurance as to the attitude of his government. Moreover, the plan lent itself rather nicely to the requirements of the American situation as these appeared to the French government at the moment: The American cause was on the verge of collapse for want of competent military leadership; it also lacked prestige in Europe; the king did not dare openly take up the cudgels for so feeble a client; French officers were departing daily for America on their own account; if Broglie failed, it would be as easy to disavow him as to disavow LaFayette, Coudray, or any other; if he succeeded, France would reap the fruits of his success; His Most Christian Majesty has proffered Poland a Conti, why not America a Broglie?[21]

But now a policy of marking time is one that from the nature of things ceases in time to be feasible, for either the event awaited is upon one or it has descended below the horizon of sensible probability. Even by January 1st, 1777, there was in train a series of events that by mid-summer of that year had forced Vergennes finally to choose his position. The rendition of secret aid to the Americans through the channels of commerce still continued, but subject to be inter-

[21] See generally C. J. Stillé, "The Comte de Broglie, Proposed Stadtholder of America," *Pennsylvania Magazine of History and Biography*, XI. 369-405; Doniol, II. Ch. 2; Wharton, I. 391-6.

rupted at any time by measures of the government meant to allay British suspicions. The result was discontent on both hands. The, perhaps designedly, bungling methods of the agents of secret aid were constantly furnishing Lord Stormont texts for remonstrance,[22] and meantime American gratitude took on a tinge of resentment.[23]

But of far more importance was the fact that Franklin was now in France. Almost from the outset had Franklin's assured front restored the American cause to the footing it had had in popular estimation before the news of Long Island. The prestige of his immense reputation—"more universal than that of Leibnitz or Newton, Frederick or Voltaire"[24]—had suggested, for the first

[22] SMSS., Nos. 1306, 1309, 1418, 1427, 1496, 1519, 1531, 1593, etc. In his despatch to Weymouth of Jan. 7, 1778, Stormont declares that "the very existence of the American army depends upon the arrival of these succors," ib., No. 1822.

[23] See, for instance, Franklin, Deane, and Lee to Vergennes, Jan. 5, 1777: "We are also instructed to solicit the court of France for an immediate supply of twenty or thirty thousand muskets. . . . This application has now become the more necessary, as the private purchase made by Mr. Deane of those articles is rendered ineffectual by an order forbidding their exportation": Wharton, II. 245. Also, to like effect, ib., 257. The inadequacy of secret aid to establish any hold on the Americans is recognized by Vergennes in his despatch to Ossun of Apr. 7, Doniol, II. 341. And see ib., generally, pp. 305-12.

[24] Life and Works of John Adams (Boston, 1856), I. 660. The passage is worthy more extended quotation: "His reputation was more universal than that of Leibnitz or Newton, Frederick or Voltaire, and his character more beloved and esteemed than any

time perhaps, that if America was to be made an
ally at all, it must be on terms of exact equality.
The charm of his unique personality, the interesting phases of which he exploited with faultless
facility and with just the touch of charlatanism
that the sentimentalism of the age demanded, had
served from the moment of his landing at Auray
to focus to a blaze of enthusiasm the diverse lines
of opinion making among all classes of Frenchmen for the king's espousal of the American
cause.[25]

or all of them. Newton had astonished perhaps forty or fifty
men in Europe. . . . But this fame was confined to men of letters.
The common people knew little and cared nothing about such a
recluse philosopher. Leibnitz's name was more confined still. . . .
Frederick was hated by more than half of Europe. . . . Voltaire,
whose name was more universal . . . was considered as a vain and
profligate wit, and not much esteemed or beloved by anybody,
though admired by all who knew his works. But Franklin's fame
was universal. His name was familiar to government and people,
to kings, courtiers, nobility, clergy and philosophers, as well as
plebeians, to such a degree that there was scarcely a peasant or a
citizen, a *valet de chambre,* coachman or footman, a lady's cham-
bermaid or a scullion in a kitchen, who was not familiar with it,
and who did not consider him a friend to human kind." Matthew
Arnold somewhere comments on the curious fact that America
contributed her only world-wide reputation, that of Franklin, while
she was still a province.

[25] See generally Edward Everett Hale and Edward Everett
Hale, Jr., *Franklin in France* (Boston, 1886-8, 2 vols.). "Tout
Paris visitait Franklin dans sa maison de Passy. Admiré par les
savants et les philosophes qui le comparaient à Socrate et à Newton, il charmait le populaire par sa bonhomie et par la simplicité
de ses habits bruns et de ses gros souliers." Lavisse, *op. cit.,* IX.[1]
104. See also an undated pamphlet by Hilliard d'Auberteuil on
Franklin (Penn. Hist'l Soc. Lib.).

Franklin arrived in Paris December 21st, and
two days later he and his associates, Deane and
Lee, requested an audience with the French secretary, which was accorded them the 28th.[26] The
suggestion of a formal audience having been
evaded by Vergennes, on January 5th, 1777, the
commissioners made explicit their expectations
of France in a note: "Eight ships of the line
completely manned," with which to clear the
American coast of British cruisers, and twenty
or thirty thousand stand of muskets and bayonets,
together with a "large quantity of ammunition
and brass field pieces, to be sent under convoy."
In return for these favors, Congress offered
France and Spain a treaty of amity and commerce and also "to guarantee in the firmest manner to those nations all their possessions in the
West Indies, as well as those they shall acquire
from the enemy in a war that may be consequen-
tial of such assistance as" it requested.[27] It is
hardly surprising that Vergennes found these
demands rather staggering. However, he argued his refusal of them with the utmost suavity
and good nature;[28] and, what is more, followed
it up with an advance of 250,000 *livres,* the first
instalment, as he announced, of a loan of two mil-

[26] Franklin, Deane, and Lee to Committee of Secret Correspondence, Jan. 17, 1777, Wharton, II. 248; SMSS., No. 606.

[27] Franklin, Deane, and Lee to Vergennes, Wharton, II. 245-6.

[28] Note approved by the king, Jan. 9, Doniol, II. 120-2.

lions from the king, who exacted only that the thing be kept secret.[29]

But if Vergennes thought thus to stop the mouths of the Americans, he soon learned his error. Congress' instructions did not at this date permit its envoys to offer France and Spain an alliance,—only treaties of amity and commerce.[30] On February 2nd, however, with the news before them of the preparation of Burgoyne's expedition in England, the commissioners resolved to break through this limitation and to offer the two crowns a pledge that, if they became involved in war with Great Britain in consequence of making a treaty of amity and commerce with the States, the latter would not conclude a separate peace.

[29] *Ib.*, 266; Wharton, II. 247, 250 fn., 404-5. It must be understood, of course, that until the declaration of the Treaty of Amity and Commerce, in Mar., 1778, all of the intercourse of the commissioners and the Foreign Office was guarded from publicity with the greatest care. Certain precautions were, in fact, taken against the Americans themselves, even after they were admitted to the general secret, for it was not impossible, of course, that France might eventually find it convenient to clear her skirts of rebellious associations. "No written proof of the least importance," says Deane, "was ever left in our hands. Even M. Gérard's letters appointing occasional interviews with us were always without any signature; though five hundred thousand livres were quarterly [in 1777] paid to our banker from the Royal Treasury, not the smallest evidence of the source from whence that subsidy came was permitted to remain in our power." *Deane Papers,* IV. 373.

[30] *Journals of the Continental Congress* (Ed. W. C. Ford, succeeded by G. Hunt, Washington, 1904 ff., 25 vols., covering the years 1774-82, still in progress), V. 768, 813, ff., the Instructions of Sept. 24, 1776.

This decision, moreover, was speedily confirmed by new instructions from Congress authorizing "any tenders necessary" to secure the immediate assistance of the Bourbon powers. The result was renewed activity on the part of the commission, and of a much more ambitious sort.[31] On March 18th Deane sent Vergennes a plan of triple alliance between France, Spain, and the United States looking to an immediate war against England and Portugal. Hostilities were to continue till Spain had conquered Portugal, till the United States had established their independence, and till France and the United States had expelled England from the North American continent and the West Indies; and peace was to be concluded only by the joint consent of the allies.

A few days later Franklin laid a similar scheme before Aranda.[32] The Spaniard was enthusiastic, Vergennes cold. "Considering," the latter inquired of the former, "the condition of lassitude and division in which this people is at present, what security could we have that our diversion would not produce their defection, especially if, as no doubt would be the case, they were offered their independence?"[33] Meantime Lee, having at the instigation of Aranda set out for

[31] Wharton, II. 257, 260 and footnote; Harrison *et al.* to the Commissioners, Dec. 30, 1776, *ib.,* 240.

[32] Doniol, II. 319-22; *Deane Papers,* II. 25-7; SMSS., No. 659.

[33] Vergennes to Aranda, Apr. 10, Doniol, II. 325.

Madrid with the idea of approaching the Spanish court directly, had been met at Burgos by Grimaldi and turned back, though with pledges of further monetary aid, some of which were ultimately redeemed.[34] Of this phase of the episode the British ambassador was, however, of course ignorant. Seeing only that a rebel envoy had been denied the hospitality of Spanish soil, he promptly made the fact a theme for obvious comparisons unfavorable to France.[35]

But in less direct ways too did the American commissioners daily contribute to rendering the French government's equivocal position more and more precarious. The mere fact that they were in Paris created an ever thickening cloud of speculation as to American prospects and English and French designs. It also brought thither the spies and secret agents both of the British government and of the Whig opposition, whose business it was to watch the Americans, the French ministers, and each other.[36] The quite normal precipitate of such an atmosphere was all sorts of startling rumors, many of which were concerned with an alleged pending agreement between representatives of the British government and the American commissioners, granting the Colonies their independence and providing for the inevi-

[34] *Ib.*, 195-6, 265-6; Wharton, II. 280-3. *Cf.* ib., 148.
[35] Vergennes to Ossum, Apr. 12, Doniol, II. 268.
[36] See Wharton, I. Chs. 21 and 22.

table joint attack upon the French West Indies.[37] Vergennes received these rumors with a
measure of scepticism. "We appreciate," he wrote,
"how little probable it is that the English would
confide so dangerous a secret into the keeping of
their enemies as that of their hostile views toward
France and Spain, and we are aware how great is
the interest of the insurgents to create suspicion."[38] At the same time he recognized that
France had not yet done enough for the Colonies
"to secure their gratitude,"[39] and he feared the
import of the armaments which England was preparing. Indeed, at no time during the Revolution do the hazards of France's equivocal position
appear more substantial than at just this period.
Yet at no time did Vergennes show himself more
bent upon keeping the peace, and that notwithstanding the still belligerent temper of France's
ally.

And meantime a fresh element of complexity
was introduced into the situation through Franklin's activity in encouraging American privateers
to resort to French harbors. Vergennes had from
the first foreseen that difficulties would arise when
American "corsairs" began seeking the hospitality of French waters and he had determined to

[37] Doniol, II. 319, 335-8 and fn., and 368-70.
[38] *Ib.*, 257.
[38a]*Ib.*, 341.

restrict them to the universally recognized right of asylum, that is the right to take refuge from adverse elements. But this meagre concession, which signified only that the French government did not accept the British view that they were pirates, was little satisfactory to the American vikings. What these individuals demanded was the right to equip, arm, and supply themselves in French ports, to bring their prizes there and sell them, to arm and equip once more and sally forth, —in short, the right to make the French coast a base of operations against English shipping. In vain did Vergennes point out how entirely incompatible such demands were, not only with His Most Christian Majesty's treaty obligations, but with the Law of Nations itself; for these were a thick-skinned gentry, who well understood that hard words break no bones and with whom measures to be effective had to be drastic. The resultant dilemma personified itself in the bland Franklin and the insistent Stormont. Franklin professed to accept Vergennes' legal principles but was endlessly resourceful in concocting delays to blunt their practical application. Stormont was unremittingly vigilant of results.[39]

[39] In general, see Hale, *Franklin in France*, I. ch. 7. Also, the correspondence between the English and French government; Doniol, II. 334-5, 478-9 and 504-19; and between Vergennes and the commissioners, *ib.*, 520-22 (translated in Wharton, II. 364-6). See also index to SMSS. under "Conyngham," "Wickes," "Dolphin," "Lexington," "Reprisal."

By the middle of July, the "corsair" issue had become so acute that it was clearly necessary for the French government to cease drifting and take its bearings once more. Meantime, and this was the one material result of the policy of delay, the French marine had reached a plane from which substantial parity with the British marine was within easy reach. In a memoir communicated to the king on July 23rd, Vergennes, contending that the moment had arrived when France must resolve "either to abandon America or to aid her courageously and effectively," pronounced with eloquence and fervor for a close alliance with her. The document is worthy of a brief *résumé*.[40]

The primary question, Vergennes declared, was whether France and Spain could afford to see the colonies return either directly or indirectly to British control; and that question turned on the further one, whether it was sound policy to contribute to the strength of an enemy when opportunity offered to enfeeble that enemy. England was the natural rival of the House of Bourbon. Mistress again of North America and its immense resources of all sorts, she would be a menace to the possessions of the two crowns in that part of the world. It followed that the re-union of North America and Great Britain, in whatever manner brought about, could not be indifferent either to the security, the prosperity,

[40] Doniol, II. 460-69.

or the glory of the two crowns and that no pains must be spared to prevent it.[41]   Secret aid had been well enough in its day, but it was no longer sufficient to prevent the reconciliation of the colonies and the mother-country, especially since the charge was now made by the English that the policy of France and Spain was to destroy England by means of America and America by means of England. It was necessary, in short, that the assistance rendered the Americans be sufficient to assure their total separation from Great Britain and their gratitude to the House of Bourbon. Open assistance undoubtedly meant war.   But war was probably imminent anyway, since if Great Britain failed in the current campaign to reduce the rebels, she would make an accommodation with them and then with their assistance would fall upon France and Spain.[42] No doubt the magnanimity and religion of the two monarchs made repugnant to them the thought of profiting by the circumstances in which England found herself to give her influence a mortal blow. But in diplomacy self-interest was the major force, and in politics the same maxim held as in war, that it was better to anticipate than to be anticipated. Besides, let their majesties consider whether their flags were respected, their commerce free, whether, in fact, their vessels were

[41] *Ib.*, 461.
[42] *Ib.*, 462-3.

not subject from the moment they left home waters, to humiliating visitations, odious seizures, unjust confiscations.[43] What the situation called for was a close offensive and defensive alliance with the Americans, all parties to which should be bound not to abandon the war without the consent of the others. The American commissioners should be informed of the intentions of the two crowns at once; but at any rate decisive steps could not be delayed later than January or February, when the British Parliament would meet to determine the fate of the present ministry. Fortunately, the European situation was in every way favorable to a joint enterprise by the two crowns against England. Spain's difficulty with Portugal was on the way to settlement, and a war on the sea would not spread to the Continent. From such a war, it was possible that the two crowns would not derive every advantage they could hope for, but to succeed in breaking the chain between England and America would forever be an immense advantage.[44]

The memoir was approved by the king the same day, and three days later was despatched to Ossun, Louis' ambassador at Madrid, to be submitted by him to the Spanish crown.[45] Why then, the question at once arises, was not the

[43] Ib. 464-5.
[44] Ib., 467-9.
[45] Ib., 469.

course it recommended promptly entered upon, at least by France? The answer is to be found in the altered attitude of Spain. Spain's desire for war during the latter half of 1776 and the early months of 1777 had rested almost altogether upon the prospect of having Portugal for her quarry. By July 23rd, however, as Vergennes himself noted, the *contre-temps* between the two Iberian courts was practically at an end. With a new monarch on the Portuguese throne, the warlike Pombal had fallen from power; and meantime the Spaniards under Ceballos had trounced the Portuguese forces along La Plata soundly.[46] But another factor, too, in bringing about the pending settlement had been Vergennes' constant opposition to the idea of Spain's overrunning her neighbor; and, as was now to transpire, he had therein overshot his mark. For with Portugal out of the calculation, Spain had no wish to fight England, and least of all in behalf of American independence. On the other hand, even Louis' assent to the program of July 23rd was only a conditional one, *the condition being Spanish coöperation. Until, therefore, either Spain could be brought to the support of this program or Louis could be persuaded that it was perilous for France longer to wait upon her ally, decisive action was impossible.*

[46] *Ib.*, 432.

CHAPTER V

Notwithstanding a close coincidence of race, religion, and economic interests, and the fact that they were ruled by the same House, the two branches of which were bound together in presumably indissoluble alliance, the French and Spanish peoples of the eighteenth century were strongly disposed to mutual antipathy, not to say antagonism; while between the Spanish and English, particularly of the governing classes, there seems always to have been a considerable measure of reciprocal understanding and sympathy.[1] So long as Grimaldi, a Genoese by birth, had remained at the head of affairs at Madrid, Vergennes had not encountered the anti-Gallican prejudices of the court circle of the Escurial. But in February, 1777, Grimaldi had fallen from power and had been succeeded by a Spaniard of

[1] See François Rousseau, "Participation de l'Espagne à la Guerre d'Amérique," *Revue des Questions historiques*, LXXII. 444 ff. Note also Jay's observation: "They [the Spanish] appear to me to like the English, hate the French, and to have prejudices against us," Jay to the President of Congress, May 26, 1780, Wharton, III. 733.

Spaniards, Don José Moniño, the Count de Florida Blanca.[2] To be sure, the new minister promptly volunteered the assurance that he would base his policy on the maintenance of the Family Compact, and "the most perfect harmony" between the two crowns;[3] but he also soon made it clear that in interpreting the alliance between France and Spain, he would treat the interests of his own country as of quite as much importance as those of France and, furthermore, that he regarded these interests as strictly material.[4] Accordingly, whereas Grimaldi had accepted Vergennes' contention that Spain as well as France had "much to gain from breaking down British power by effecting the complete and radical separation of the colonies,"[5] Florida Blanca considered "the abasement of England" as without substantial interest to a nation whose Continental rôle was no longer worth restoring.[6] Nor yet did Vergennes' notion of "a durable peace" to follow upon England's undoing appeal more strongly to him. These were "moral objects," and he frankly characterized them as "quixotic."

However, Vergennes also urged it as an argument for his program that the total separ-

[2] Doniol, II. 24-7, 197-8.

[3] Ossun to Vergennes, Feb. 24, 1777, *ib.*, 227-8.

[4] See the correspondence cited in note 59, *supra.*

[5] Grimaldi to Aranda, Feb. 4, *ib.*, 192-3.

[6] *Ib.*, 703. *Cf. ib.*, 567.

ation of the American provinces from Great
Britain would make for the security of French
and Spanish colonial possessions in the Western
Hemisphere, and he contended further that, inasmuch as Spain's colonial empire in this part of the
world was vastly more valuable than the few
islands that still remained to France, Spain's interest in bringing about the separation in question
was proportionately greater than France's.[7]
Again the Spanish minister's views diverged
widely from those of his respondent. For while
he was ready to admit that British sea-power was
more or less of a menace to Spain's holdings in
the New World and also that this power was sustained to an important extent by England's
mastery of North America, he was not ready to
conclude that therefore the independence of England's North American provinces would, so far as
Spain was concerned, remove the danger. On the
contrary, he held that it would, if due precautions
were not taken, actually increase it. We are thus
brought to a subject that must be of very controlling interest in the pages following.

One of the earliest advocates of a French-
Spanish-American alliance was the Count
d'Aranda, the Spanish ambassador at Paris.[8]
Unhappily for the Colonies, Aranda was less a
representative of his government than a Themis-

---

[7] *Ib.*, 461, 643-4; III. 50-1, 140.
[8] See his memoir on the subject, *loc. cit.*, II. 210-8.

tocles in exile,—a former chief-minister whom
the existing régime at Madrid found it convenient
to devise any plausible expedient to keep remote
from the seat of power. So long as Grimaldi was
Charles III's chief-minister, Madrid had been
quite willing that Paris should make its own arrangements with the rebellious provinces, but
even he had not favored Spain's doing more than
to contribute secretly certain funds to the American cause, of which he dexterously made France
the almoner. And after Long Island his attitude
became still more aloof. Writing Aranda as he
was about to leave office, he admonished his too
enthusiastic subordinate thus:

> The king our master, who possesses in the Indies
> domains so vast and important, should be very backward
> in making a formal treaty with provinces which as yet
> can only be regarded as rebels, an inconvenience that
> would not exist should the colonies succeed in really
> throwing off the yoke and constituting themselves an
> independent power. The rights of all sovereigns to their
> respective territories ought to be regarded as sacred,
> and the example of a rebellion is too dangerous to allow
> of His Majesty's wishing to assist it openly.[9]

How a little later he met the American Lee and
turned him back at the Spanish frontier has already been told.

And if Grimaldi saw cause for alarm on Spain's
part in the rebellious example of the Americans,

[9] *Ib.*, 192.

the Marquis de Castejon, a member of the Spanish royal council, saw it no less in their actual power and their supposed ambitions. "Spain," said Castejon, writing also in February, 1777, "is about to be left alone, face to face with one other power in the whole of North America,—a power which has assumed a national name, which is very formidable on account of the size of its population and the ratio of increase thereof, and which is accustomed to war even before it has begun it. I think that we should be the last country in all Europe to recognize *any* sovereign and independent state in North America." Such a state would develop more rapidly than a colony, would have its resources immediately at hand, would be uninfluenced by the Balance of Power, and so, careless of the good will of Europe, would be able to push its own designs with the utmost aggressiveness. Furthermore, even assuming the English colonies in America to have become independent, "the English and American powers would still be of one nation, one character and one religion, and would so form their treaties and compacts as to obtain the objects they both desire." In such a contingency "the kingdom of Mexico would be compromised, in fact lost."[10]

But indeed the Foreign Office had been forced to meet and allay opinions of this sort even from French sources from the very outset of the Revo-

[10] Sparks MSS., CII. The date of the document is Feb. 3, 1777.

lution. Thus in the *Réflexions* of November, 1775, Gérard had recited: "But, they say, the independence of the English colonies will prepare a revolution in the new world; they will hardly be at peace and assured of their liberty than they will be seized with the spirit of conquest, whence may result the invasion of our colonies and of the rich possessions of the Spanish in South America." In answer to these objections Gérard had urged two considerations: first, that the existing war would fatigue the colonists for a long time to come; and secondly, that if they became independent, the colonists would have a republican form of government and would be united with each other only in a loose confederacy. The dominant spirit of the new community, he had therefore concluded, would be one of trade, industry, and peace; and he had added: "Even supposing that the colonists should encroach upon the Spanish possessions, that is far from proving that this revolution would be prejudicial to France."[11]

In July, 1777, however, Vergennes had before him the direct task of reassuring Spanish opinion; and it is entirely evident that he had underestimated its difficulty. There are those, he wrote in the memoir of July 23rd, who hold that the time will come when America will be "a formidable

[11] Doniol, I. 245. See also a passage in the "Considérations," *ib.*, 274. For further arguments against Spain's favoring American independence, forthcoming from English sources, see Wharton, III. 727-31.

power even to her benefactors." The danger
surely was greatly exaggerated. Doubtless
America would in time become a considerable nation, but certainly never "a terror to be armed
against." For one thing, their constitution stood
in the way of such a consummation. For they
were held together only by a confederacy of thirteen members, each of which reserved its powers
of internal administration. Furthermore, the interests of the several provinces were as diverse as
their climate; and particularly striking were the
differences between North and South. The South,
with its sparse population and with the cultivation
of its soil abandoned to negroes, was bound to
have commerce for its informing principle. The
North, it was true, furnished with abundant population living in frugality, might well breed a
spirit of emigration and conquest; but its attention in turn would be occupied with Canada,
which to that end should remain in the hands of
the English. Also

many years, not to say ages, must pass, ere the New
Englanders have occupied effectively all the lands which
still remain for them to cultivate and before therefore
they will have a superabundant population which they
will want to be rid of; and ere that time shall have come
our vices will have been introduced among them by more
intimate intercourse, with the result of having retarded
their increase and progress.[12]

[12] *Ib.,* II. 466.

The argument was ingenious but to Florida
Blanca, who participated to the fullest extent in
the apprehensions that had been voiced by Castejon, it was quite unconvincing. The Spanish
minister's program, while the dispute with Portugal was still unsettled, had been that the struggle
in America should be kept going till the parties to
it were exhausted; meantime France and Spain
should increase their forces in the West Indies;
then when the moment arrived, they should intervene between England and her rebellious provinces, with the object of filching from the occasion
such profits as might be available, perhaps the
Floridas for Spain and Canada for France.[13]
And in August, 1777, the Spanish minister was of
opinion that the time was not yet at hand for any
course of action likely to precipitate war with
England, and he was especially averse to the suggestion of an alliance with the Americans: For
one thing, the Spanish treasure fleet from Mexico
would not arrive until spring, and it would never
do to tempt British cupidity with that. For another thing, for the two crowns to declare themselves in behalf of the Colonies would be to
furnish England with the best possible argument for coming to an accommodation with them
at once. Finally Spain had not yet had an opportunity to build up a sufficient *casus belli* against
the English, to give, that is, her multiplied causes

[13] *Ib.*, 264, 273-4.

of complaint that fair appearance of consistency that decency demanded. Meantime, however, it would be pertinent, with a view to preventing the reconciliation of England and the Colonies, to persuade the latter, through Franklin and Deane, and also through envoys to the Congressional chiefs, that any accommodation with the mother-country would be useless which was not guaranteed by France and Spain. "We can assure the deputies at the outset that we would not sanction anything contrary to the liberty and advantage of the Colonies, and that they would be protected in these respects, without saying more for the present." Surely the Americans could not withstand such an inducement.[14]

Obviously balked in his own design by the specious intransigency of the Spaniard, Vergennes, in his despatch to Ossun, of August 22nd indicated the willingness of Paris, for the nonce at least, to follow in the wake of Madrid: "We admit, Monsieur, without abbreviation, the hypothesis of the Spanish minister, that before thinking of a rupture we should make sure of the return of our own fishermen and of the fleet from Mexico." Meanwhile, it would be appropriate for the two powers to send secret envoys to America, charged with "brief, indirect hints" as to the advantage

[14] "Traduction du Mémoire de la cour d'Espagne du 8 aoust 1776 [sic] servant de reponse à celui de la cour de France, envoyé le 26 Juillet même année," ib., 490-3.

that the colonies would gain if, when procuring England's recognition of their independence, they should also obtain "the recognition and guaranty thereof of the European states most interested in sustaining it." True, it did appear somewhat improbable that the American deputies in Paris could be brought round to this view. "Ready enough to enter into the closest kind of union if the two crowns would consent to war, they are apparently determined to decline any other sort of diplomatic connection," and "I have had more than one occasion to observe that their art looks not only to interesting us in their cause, but also to compromising us with England." "Still, I will throw out some words to them of a guaranty, and if they refuse to nibble at that bait, I have another idea . . . namely, to make them comprehend that it would not be enough to obtain from England a recognition of their independence without taking steps at the same time to establish its permanence," and that the measure best calculated to that end would be treaties of amity and commerce with the powers most interested in seeing them free and prosperous.[15]

But before any action could be taken along this line, opportunity presented itself for Vergennes to press afresh for open war with England. The very day the French secretary penned his despatch to Ossun, an unaccredited agent of the

[15] Vergennes to Ossun, Aug. 22, *ib.*, 500-3.

British government named Forth announced to
Maurepas the intention of his government to oblige France, under pain of war, to return to their
British owners all prizes brought into French
ports by American vessels.[16] The day following
Vergennes presented the king a memoir vigorously protesting against compliance with such a
demand. To do so, he argued, would be tantamount to stigmatizing the American privateers,
and their countrymen as well, as pirates and sea-
robbers; and the result of that would be to arouse
resentment in America that would lead at once to
reconciliation with England and "a desire for
vengeance that ages perhaps would not diminish."
It would be in entire accord with his dignity for
the king to make some concessions, and policy
demanded it on account of the absence of the
Spanish treasure fleet. The orders against the
admission of American privateers and their
prizes to French harbors except in "absolutely
urgent cases" could be renewed, and such privateers as were already in port could be sent
away, without however the time of their departure being fixed. But more than this could not
be conceded. "A great state can undergo losses
without suffering in its reputation, but if it sub-
scribes to humiliations, it is undone." As to "an
assurance of the possessions of the two crowns
in America,"—for apparently Forth had sug-

[16] *Ib.*, 525-6.

gested some such idea,—that would be both un-
profitable and useless. "It would tie our hands
so that we should be unable to put ourselves in a
state of defense" and arm our enemy with a club
with which he could always extort some new
compliance.[17]

The memoir received the approval both of king
and council the same day, and three days later a
second despatch was sent Ossun to acquaint him
with the new turn of affairs. It was accompanied
by a letter in Vergennes' own hand to Florida
Blanca, which, recounting that "a new order of
things" had most surprisingly intervened since
the previous communication, indicated the opinion that it was touch and go as between war and
peace, but promised that every precaution which
wisdom could suggest would be taken "to avoid
if possible that the first blow should be too sensible."[18] Four days later, the secretary wrote
Noailles, at London, that "the British ministry,
despairing of subjugating the Americans . . .
will seek to direct the passions of the nation
against an object more capable of inflaming them,
which object can only be France and Spain."[19]

But again the complexion of affairs suddenly
altered. Not only did Stormont fail to back up
Forth's representations, but what is more to the

[17] Ib., 527-9; SMSS., No. 706.
[18] Ib., 534-5.
[19] Ib., 536-7. See also ib., 526-9, 533-5.

point, the news now came to Paris of Burgoyne's capture of Ticonderoga.[20] As after Long Island Vergennes' anxiety as to the ultimate intentions of the British ministry underwent notable surcease. Florida Blanca was quick to detect the French secretary's vacillation and the opportunity offered for a homily against American wiles. The shaft struck home, for with the advance of Burgoyne through northern New York, further disconcerting intelligence had come from London. His despatch of September 26th shows the secretary of state in full retreat, though with an arrow or two still in his quiver: The Spanish minister had rightly judged that Forth's mission was not to be taken seriously, but what then was to be expected of a government that lent itself to such pranks in the midst of a civil war! France would give the preference to peace, of that Spain could be assured, and the more so as the moment had passed when by striking at England she could have guaranteed success to the revolution in America. No doubt the attention of France and Spain ought to be directed to winning the confidence of the Americans without entirely forfeiting that of the English but the task would not be an easy one, especially since the English government at least was well aware of what it was for the *interest* of the two crowns to do, while the Americans on

[20] *Ib.*, 537, 572 fn., 628.

the other hand were inconsiderately disposed to look at everything from the point of view of their own advantage.[21]

And what precisely was the attitude of the Americans at this juncture? Earlier in the year it had been their tactics to keep before Vergennes the possibility that, unless France promptly espoused their cause, the Colonies, "dispirited by bad success,"[22] might be forced to accept terms from England that would be to the serious disadvantage of France.[23] But these methods, if they had not actually injured the American case by making the secretary sceptical of the substance and durability of the Revolution,[24] had at least netted nothing, and after Ticonderoga the commissioners discarded them. Evidence of this fact is to be seen in their letter of September 25th to Vergennes and Aranda, to beg a subsidy of the two crowns or their friendly offices in a negotiation for peace, with a view to saving to America her "liberties with the freedom of commerce:"

[21] *Ib.*, 551-4.

[22] See Carmichael to Vergennes, SMSS., No. 647. The date is illegible save for the year, 1777, but it was clearly written before the news of Saratoga.

[23] See Wharton, II. 280-3; *Deane Papers,* I. 434-42, II. 52-6, 66-9; and the memorial prepared early in 1777 by Franklin, Deane, and the Abbé Niccoli, SMSS., Nos. 149 and 150. This document was communicated to Lord Suffolk by the British spy Wentworth and was later quoted by Pownall on the floor of Parliament. See SMSS., No. 182, and *Parliamentary History,* XIX. 930 ff.

[24] See p. 67 *supra.*

They [the commissioners, the letter proceeds] can assure Your Excellencies that they have no account of any treaty on foot in America for an accommodation, nor do they believe there is any. Nor have any propositions been made by them to the court of London, nor any the smallest overture received from thence which they have not already communicated; . . . and the commissioners are firmly of the opinion that nothing will induce the Congress to accommodate on the terms of an exclusive commerce with Britain but the despair of obtaining effectual aid and support from Europe.[25]

On October 3rd Vergennes proposed that France and Spain should each pledge the Colonies three millions *livres* on condition that they should enter into no negotiation with Great Britain without the joint approval of the two crowns. *Raisons de finance,* he admitted, were apparently opposed on this occasion to *raisons de politique,* but, he contended, in appearance only, since if England were enfeebled by the loss of America both France and Spain would enjoy peace for many years.[26] But Florida Blanca was not to be persuaded; and on November 7th, Vergennes an-

[25] SMSS., No. 1698. See also Lee's "Journal" in R. H. Lee's *Life of Arthur Lee,* I. 354. On November 27, Deane proposed that the commissioners demand "a categorical answer" from France. "Dr. Franklin," Lee writes, "was of a different opinion: he would not consent to state that we must give up the contest without their interposition, because the effect of such a declaration upon them was uncertain. It might be taken as a menace, it might make them abandon us in despair, or anger. Besides, he did not think it true." Lee agreed with Franklin.

[26] See Doniol, II. 564, 570, 575-8.

nounced that Louis had determined to give the United States three millions outright, to be paid quarterly.[27]   Some days later, the Foreign Office instructed one Holker to proceed to America to sound Congress on the question of a French-Spanish guaranty along the lines originally suggested by Madrid. The instructions were never carried out. On November 30th, the news of Burgoyne's surrender at Saratoga reached Nantes, and M. Holker became the first emissary to America of a new and decisive policy.[28]

[27] *Ib.*, 579-80. But word of this decision was apparently not communicated to the commissioners till after November 30, as no mention is made of it in their report to Congress of that date, Wharton, II. 433-6. And *cf. ib.*, 445.

[28] *Ib.*, 615-6 and notes; SMSS., No. 1748. Holker late became the first French consul at Philadelphia.

CHAPTER VI

VERGENNES, ALARMIST AND PROPAGANDIST

Vergennes' first reaction to the news of Saratoga was that it meant American independence and that the problem presented to France by it was whether she could beat Great Britain out in according recognition of the fact. "The power," he wrote Montmorin, "that will first recognize the independence of the Americans will be the one that will reap the fruits of this war."[1] Later he revised this estimate: *Absolute independence* would probably cost the pride of the British monarch too much, but even so, what guaranty was

[1] Vergennes to Montmorin, Dec. 11, Doniol, II. 632; SMSS., No. 1769. The words are taken from Beaumarchais' extremely alarmist letter of the same date to Vergennes: The ministry, he writes, are denounced in London, the opposition triumphs, secret councils multiply, Ireland prepares to rise. What is the meaning? "It is that of the two nations, England and France, the first who recognizes American independence will alone gather from it all the fruits, whilst the independence will be certainly fatal to the one that allows its rival to take the lead": SMSS., No. 1768. The letter will also be found in Doniol, II. 684. Vergennes' recognition of the decisive character of Saratoga was delayed somewhat on account of the exultant tone assumed by the British government and its ambassador over the news of Howe's capture of Philadelphia and Washington's defeat at Brandywine: *op. cit.*, 620-4, and footnotes.

there that the Americans, wearied by the war
and discouraged by the indifference of Europe, would not consent to waive the name if
they were given the substance? At any rate,
some sort of reconciliation of the mother-country
and her rebellious provinces impended and with
it the menace of a joint attack by the English
and Americans on France and Spain. The succor given the insurgents by the two crowns would
furnish from the British point of view a sufficient pretext and the rehabilitation of the French
and Spanish navies a sufficient grievance. In
such a war, New York would furnish the English
a port of embarkment for the French possessions; the American corsairs would enrich themselves by falling upon French and Spanish commerce; the exclusive navigation of the Mississippi
would be a powerful lure to the Americans, and
in their hands would render the possession of
Mexico precarious, because, protected by the
British navy, the colonists would have nothing to
fear from the vengeance of France or Spain on
the American continent. There could not be the
least doubt in the world that such a program
would be carried through were it not for His
Britannic Majesty's squeamishness in the matter
of independence. Thanks to that, the House
of Bourbon had its opportunity.[2]

[2] Vergennes to Montmorin, Dec. 27, Doniol, II., 665-6; "Mémoire
lû au Roi," Jan. 7, 1778, ib., 724-5; Vergennes to Montmorin, par
l'Epine, Jan. 8, ib., 719-20; SMSS., Nos. 1805, 1824, 1826.

A question touched upon at the beginning of this volume becomes at this point of renewed interest, that of Vergennes' intention in urging the above argument for his crown's intervention in the American revolt. Immediately, of course, his intention is to present the war which this act of intervention will probably bring in its wake as essentially a war of self-defense on France's part, rather than one of aggression, or, to use his own terms, as "a war of necessity" rather than "of choice"; and were he thus making, for a policy already determined upon, the usual concession to "the decent opinion of mankind," his words would call for little comment. But in fact he is doing something quite different. He is arguing for the adoption of a proposed policy, and on that account it becomes important to inquire with some particularity whether this argument was a sound one, whether it was probable, was sustained by credible evidence, was consistently adherred to. In the pages immediately following I shall canvass these questions.

Certainly the theory that England, defeated in America, would attack France and Spain had not gained in intrinsic probability in the three years that had elapsed since it was first broached. Then the weakness of the French and Spanish fleets had presented British naval aggressiveness an obvious temptation; now, by the statement of Vergennes himself, this weakness had been repaired and Bourbon naval power had become

matter for alarm on England's part.[3]   Then the
name of Chatham and his monumental hatred of
the House of Bourbon had given viability to the
most disturbing speculations; now it was recognized by the French Foreign Office itself, as at
least highly probable, that the North ministry
would continue as the instrument of His Britannic Majesty's American policies.[4]   Then it was
plausible to argue that the colonies could yet be
drawn off from their pursuit of independence by
the ancient lure of an attack on France, and the
anticipated assault upon the French Antilles had
accordingly been pictured as the first step to
reconciliation between England and America.
Now it had to be conceded by all that independence was the paramount objective of the Americans, with the result that this hypothetical assault
had to be presented as the outcome of reconciliation.[5]   But in this connection, Vergennes is fur-

[3] See also Vergennes' comments quoted *infra* on Lord Sandwich's review in Parliament of the British naval situation; note,
further, the following words in the *Exposé des Motifs* of the
French government (1779): "It is notorious that the armaments
of France were in a condition to act offensively long before those
of England were prepared," *Annual Register*, XXII. 394.

[4] There was no possibility of Chatham's being called to power at
this period.   Even after France had declared the Treaty of
Amity and Commerce with the United States, we find George III
asserting that "nothing shall bring me to treat personally with
Lord Chatham"; and again, that "no consideration in life shall
make me stoop to Opposition."   Donne, *Correspondence of George
III*, II. 149, 153.

[5] See especially Doniol, II. 664 and 727.

ther citable for the admission, as we have just observed, that England would not even yet offer the Americans complete independence, that she would insist upon retaining at least a nominal sovereignty over them. The question thus emerges whether it was reasonable to suppose that the Americans would consent, in return for less than independence, to join in an assault on the possessions of France and Spain. It was not improbable that the Colonies, weary of war, would finally content themselves with less than independence, if France did not come to their aid, but it was most unlikely that they would do so with any great alacrity or precipitancy; and just in proportion as the necessity of peace was a motive with them was it unlikely that they would embark upon war in another quarter for a comparatively minor object, and particularly when, in the pursuit of such object, they would alienate the only powers that had befriended them and whose enmity would leave them henceforth to face alone a still wrathful mother-country.[6]

Nor when I pass in review the evidence offered by Vergennes in support of his alarmist theory,

[6] Vergennes himself admitted that any arrangement between England and America would "not be the affair of a day," *ib.*, 738-9, fn. In his despatch to Montmorin of Dec. 13, the secretary gives it as his own opinion that the commissioners prefer a coalition with the two crowns to a reconciliation with England: *ib.*, 639. See also the Congressional resolutions of Nov. 22, 1777, and the commissioners' letter of Dec. 8 to Vergennes, Wharton, II. 425-6 and 444-5; also, pp. 117-9, *supra*.

am I better convinced of its substance. First I shall consider some items of a comparatively trustworthy sort that bear on the question of what terms England would be likely to offer America and America be likely to accept. Then I shall turn to some items that demand more careful scrutiny.

Vergennes knew from his confidential agents of the visit to Franklin of an Englishman named Hutton, reputed to be a friend of the English king;[7] and he observed that Franklin remained reticent about the matter.[8] This circumstance, however, was plausibly explained to him by Chaumont, one of the above-mentioned agents, as due to Franklin's reluctance to prejudice an old acquaintance with the English court,[9] and we find the secretary himself testifying at this very time to his confidence in Franklin's loyalty and good faith.[10] Again, he had before him two letters which had been shown him by the American commissioners and which he considered so important that he forwarded copies of them to Madrid. In the first of these, the writer, a citizen of Boston, seems to have advanced the idea that unless France and Spain evinced a disposition to come to the assistance of the colonies, at least in a *financial* way, Burgoyne's victory could be turned

[7] Doniol, II. 771-2.
[8] *Ib.*, 718.
[9] See Note 113, *supra*.
[10] Vergennes to Noailles, Dec. 27, Doniol, II. 657, footnote.

to best account by getting as favorable terms as possible from England.[11]   In the other one, which had been sent from London to a secret agent of the commissioners named Bancroft, the anonymous writer foreshadowed the intention of the North ministry to bestow something like autonomy on the colonies for their internal affairs, while retaining control of their external relations, political and commercial.[12]   Lastly, he knew from Deane that an Englishman named Wentworth had visited this commissioner and, suggesting a truce for America, had proposed that the envoys send one of their number either to England or up into the Netherlands, to meet there an Englishman of high rank and negotiate a reconciliation on the basis of a qualified dependency; but he knew also that Deane had met these propositions with a demand for unconditional independence, and that the Englishman had in turn pronounced the latter demand unallowable.[13]

But obviously this evidence is quite insufficient to justify Vergennes' assertion in the memoir of

[11] Vergennes to Montmorin, Dec. 11, *ib.*, 634. The content of the letter is further revealed by Florida Blanca's comments upon it in his despatch to Aranda of Dec. 23rd, *ib.*, 769.

[12] SMSS., Nos. 1787 and 1805; Vergennes to Montmorin, Dec. 27, Doniol, II. 664-5. For some interesting speculations as to Bancroft's real character, see Wharton, I. 621-41.

[13] Vergennes to Montmorin, Dec. 19, *ib.*, 661-2; SMSS., No. 1786. See also Beaumarchais to Vergennes, Doniol, *loc. cit.*, 685-6. Wentworth was a spy and stock-jobber in whom George III professed small confidence, Donne, *Correspondence*, II. 109.

January 7th, which immediately preceded the king's sanction of an alliance with the United States, that the English government "already . . . displays to them [the American envoys] the certain advantages of a coalition against France and Spain,"[14] and still less, if possible, does it prove that the English government was likely to achieve anything by such tactics. It is true that, in making this assertion, the secretary pleads that "the particulars are too long to detail," though he says the king knows them.[15] But the fact is that both on this occasion and on earlier ones Vergennes does cite numerous "particulars,"[16] which it is fair to conclude are the most cogent ones for his purpose; and while, of course, we do not know what matters Vergennes reported orally to the king,[17] we do have both the elaborate memoir upon which the royal council based its decision in favor of an American alliance and also the extended correspondence with Madrid at this

[14] Doniol, II. 723. The statement is repeated in the "Précis of Facts relative to the Treaty of Friendship and Commerce," which was read to the Council Mar. 18, SMSS., No. 1904.

[15] *Ib.*, 724.

[16] The fact of the matter is that he straightway contradicts the words just quoted, in his confidential letter of the day following to Montmorin, where he writes: "J'espère que ce prince [the king of Spain] nous jugera favorablement lors qu'il aura pézé les raisons exposées dans le mémoire et la dépêche que vous recevrez par ce courier." Doniol, II. 736. For the memoire and despatch referred to, see *ib.*, 717-38.

[17] "Ie Roi . . . a entendu mon raport particulier, a gardé les piéces, a examiné le pour et le contre": Vergennes to Montmorin, "Privé," Jan. 8: *ib.*, 736; SMSS., No. 1828.

period; and we may, I submit, reasonably believe that the evidence intended for the eyes of the Spanish king and for the critical scrutiny of the Spanish minister was at least as convincing in character as that which, supplemented by the personal presence and eloquence of the French secretary, persuaded the well-intentioned but stupid Louis of "the moral certainty of peril."[18]

We turn, then, to consider this additional evidence, if "evidence" it may be called; and first we note the kind of sources from which it issued. So far as is discoverable, Vergennes' informants, with the single exception of the French ambassador at London, were either professional alarmists whose practical interests were already enlisted with the American cause—men like Beaumarchais, Chaumont, and Grand—or the mere anonymous voices of rumor,—as witness his repeated *"on dit."* From such sources as these it is that the statement finds its way into the secretary's despatches, that the Howes have been instructed to open negotiations with Congress,[19] that a

[18] "Ce n'est point l'influence de ses ministres qui l'ont décidé; l'évidence des faits, la certitude morale du danger et sa conviction l'ont seuls entrainé," *loc. cit.* To the same effect is the letter of Louis to Charles, Jan. 8, *ib.,* 713-4.

[19] Vergennes to Montmorin, "P.S., Dec. 15, *ib.,* 649: "Ce qu'on [N. B.] a recueilli de plus positif est, que des instructions ont été envoyées aux frères Howe pour entamer une negociation en Amerique." But compare with this the cautious tone of his despatch to Noailles five days later: "Des ordres de réconciliation *doivent* avoir été envoyés très récemment à M. Howe," *ib.,* 704. For

special courier has been sent to America,[20] that
Lord George Germaine's secretary is in Paris to
treat with the commissioners,[21] that Franklin's
attitude of silence with reference to Hutton is
matter for suspicion,[22] that the first steps have
been taken in London toward the formation of a
coalition ministry of which Chatham and Shelburne are to be members,[23] that at Passy "they
are negotiating briskly"[24] and finally, that "one
formal proposition is to unite cordially and fall
upon us."[25]   Ordinarily, it is true, the secretary discloses through what channels he obtained his information; but that fact does not
hinder his arguing on the basis of it without allowance for its source, nor yet from sinning
against the light shed by more reliable sources.

a later rumor that General Howe had arrived at terms of reconciliation with Washington, see Wharton, II. 483. This rumor was
of too late date to find a place in the despatches.

[20] Doniol, II. 647.

[21] Vergennes to Montmorin, Dec. 13, "au soir" *ib.*, 645, footnote
2: "D'une autre part le Lord Germaine . . . envoye, dit on
[N. B.], ici son secrétaire pour traiter avec les Américains."

[22] Same to same, Jan. 8, *ib.*, 718, following Grand's alarmist
account of the matter, *ib.*, 771.

[23] Same reference as note 21, *supra*.

[24] Same reference as note 22. The source of this item, which
Vergennes himself says did not influence his decision, was Frank-
lin and Deane's landlord at Passy, who was in Vergennes' pay.
Sparks MSS., LXXVIII. p. 139.

[25] Doniol, II. 649. The "inconnu" was Wentworth, whose prof-
fers were reported by Deane to Vergennes a day or two later as
impossible, since they did not include *unconditional* independence,
supra, p. 127.

The person best entitled, both by length of official experience and by first-hand knowledge, to claim something like authority for his conclusions was the Marquis de Noailles, Louis' ambassador at the court of St. James, and indeed Vergennes himself pays striking tribute to the reliability of Noailles' reports.[26] Yet it is plainly not the policy of the secretary to put forward the ambassador's communications except so far as they can be wrought into the fabric of his own alarmist theory. Thus Noailles points out that there can be no binding negotiations between the British executive and the Americans till Parliament shall have repealed certain statutes. Vergennes, without citing Noailles, repeats the observation in his despatches to Montmorin but accompanies it with the conjecture that it will be the policy of the British ministry to solicit overtures from the Americans as a basis for propositions to be laid before Parliament. Again, Noailles always implies that the North ministry will survive. This conclusion, too, Vergennes seems generally to accept; but he pits against it the contention that North and his associates now participate in the Opposition's way of thinking.[27] Again, Noailles assures his government that North will not and

[26] Same reference as note 21.

[27] Unfortunately, what "the Opposition's way of thinking" was is by no means clear. See note below. As used by Vergennes this phrase signified what was for the most part a figment of his imagination—or calculation.

cannot offer the Americans their independence. That is quite probable, rejoins the secretary, but the real danger lies in the possibility that the Americans will take less. At this point, however, the divergence between the secretary and the ambassador becomes flat contradiction, for Noailles, like Florida Blanca and Montmorin, is confident throughout that the Americans will never take less.[28]

Vergennes is determined, in short, that everything shall be grist to his mill. Unfortunately, there are times when his heroic endeavors to make it such hedge perilously upon dereliction. Thus on the authority of the *Courier de l'Europe,* he erroneously attributes to Lord Sandwich the remark that "the time will come perhaps when complete reparation will be had of France and Spain for their insults," though the version of Sandwich's speech which the scrupulous Noailles had forwarded him contained no such menacing passage.[29] Again, on no apparent authority at all,

[28] See Noailles to Vergennes, Dec. 12, 23, 26, SMSS., Nos. 1772, 1793, 1803. *Cf.* Vergennes to Montmorin, Dec. 19 and 27, Jan. 8, 16, and 23, SMSS., Nos. 1786, 1805, 1827, 1838, 1847.

[29] Vergennes to Montmorin, Dec. 3, Doniol, II. 589. *Cf.* SMSS., Nos. 1743 and 1772; also *Parliamentary History,* XIX. 479. Even in quoting the above remark attributed by the *Courier* to Lord Sandwich, Vergennes is forced to add the Englishman's admission that "it would be folly to propose war against the House of Bourbon." But he underscores the more alarming sentiment. The *Courier de l'Europe* was evidently somewhat disposed to sensationalism. See *Last Journals of Horace Walpole,* II. 181.

he attributes to Lord North the idea of a frater-
nal union with America and a new family compact to confront that of the House of Bourbon,
though Noailles' report of the same debate quite
correctly credited this idea to Lord Richmond,
a Whig advocate of American independence.[30]
Indeed, as late as January 13th, that is nearly a
week after the royal council had sanctioned an
alliance with the United States, a memoir from
the Foreign Office repeats the assertion that England is disposed to sacrifice her supremacy in
America for "a sort of family compact, *that is to
say,* a league against the House of Bourbon."
This seems to be a distinct reference to the sentiment which, Vergennes must have known, had
been wrongly attributed to Lord North.   It is,
moreover, the only reference in the document,
direct or indirect, to any evidence whatsoever
supporting the charge that a coalition between
England and America, hostile to France, im-

[30] Vergennes to Montmorin, Dec. 13, Doniol, II. 640 and 645 fn.
2.   *Cf.* Noailles to Vergennes, Dec. 12 and 23, SMSS., Nos. 1772
and 1793; also *Parliamentary History,* XIX. 591 and 609. The fact
of the matter is that the Parliamentary debates during the period
between Burgoyne's surrender and the declaration by France of
the Treaty of Amity and Commerce were singularly free of hostile
flings at that power. The government wanted France's support,
the Rockingham Whigs advocated unqualified independence for the
colonies, Chatham, opposed to independence, had not yet further
indicated his course. The fact that the only two citations which
Vergennes made at this time of the debates were the two spurious
ones considered above is significant of their general tone toward
France.

pended![30a]   But even where the secretary's deflections from the most scrupulous methods of propagandism are more venial, they are frequently not less instructive; and it is interesting to observe conjectures which have the form of positive statement in a despatch to Madrid assume, in a despatch of the same date to London, the more modest form of interrogation.[31]

And not less illuminating is the constant habit of the secretary in his despatches of dropping the note of alarm for that of confidence. Examples might be multiplied, but one will suffice, that furnished by his comments upon Lord Sandwich's review in Parliament of the British naval situation:

But why should we look only on the dark side of things? According to Lord Sandwich himself, England has thirty-five ships of the line ready and with some effort could increase the number to forty-two. That then is all she can rely upon to guard the Channel, to observe our fleet at Brest, the Spanish fleets at Cadiz and Ferrol, to protect her establishments and her commerce in the Mediterranean and secure the defense of her islands in America. Even she does not count greatly upon the naval forces which she has in North America. These consist of such ancient vessels, with such impoverished and dilapidated equipment, that they could lend

[30a] The memoir is given in Appendix III. It represents an effort to bring together every possible argument for the American alliance.

[31] *Cf.* SMSS., Nos. 1805 and 1807, bearing date of Dec. 27, 1777. See also note 19 above.

little assistance to inferior forces. All of which, as you see, Monsieur, is not calculated to discourage the two crowns if they know how to take their time and strike at the proper moment.[32]

How badly these words comport with Vergennes' supposed anxieties for the French Antilles is obvious. But what is equally to the point, the inconsistency thus exemplified is much more than a characteristic of the secretary's argument; it also projects itself into his policy in the most vital way, if we are to regard that as designed primarily for the defense of the Antilles. The only feasible method of either attacking or defending the Antilles was with a fleet; but the United States, though they had ports of embarkment, had no fleet capable of such an enterprise, while Spain, pledged to come to France's assistance at the first hostile blow, had both a fleet and ports of embarkment that opened directly on the Caribbean. Yet Vergennes deliberately put in jeopardy the alliance with Spain in order to get an alliance with the United States; and in so doing, moreover, made war with England a certainty![33]

[32] Vergennes to Montmorin, Dec. 27, Doniol, II. 666; SMSS.; No. 1805. See also to same general effect Vergennes to Montmorin, Jan. 30, Doniol, II. 789-90; SMSS., No. 1853. Note, too, the secretary's complacent survey of the defenses of the West Indies, in his "Project de Reponses," to Florida Blanca's questions, which was read to the king Jan. 28, Doniol, II. 782.

[33] Of course, if it was assumed that America reconciled with England, would be the one to instigate the attack on the French

Nor does inconsistency stop short always of contradiction. For the fact of the matter is that Vergennes himself is quotable for the contention that the defense of the French Antilles was not a leading, or even a considerable object with his government. Thus, early in the volume I drew attention to a despatch penned shortly after the news of Saratoga in which he wrote: "The interest of Spain is at least tenfold our interest; our islands are little designed to tempt the cupidity of the English; they already have enough of that sort of thing; what they want is treasure, and that is to be got only from the continent."[34] And the alliance having been consummated, he expressed himself even more to the point:

West Indies and that England would not otherwise make such an attack, then the above argument would fail. But Vergennes suggests America's interest in such an attack in only one passage and that put in the form of an interrogation. Thus, in his despatch of December 27th to Montmorin, he writes: "Les Américains nous proposent de conquérir les isles angloises et de leurs y accorder un commerce libre. Si *vice versâ* les Anglois font la même proposition, ne sera t'elle pas ecoutée, sera t'elle rejettée?" Doniol, II. 665. It is true that he represents the Spanish colonies as also presenting certain temptations to the Americans, *e.g.,* the navigation of the Mississippi, but he also constantly assures Spain that the Americans will be very peaceable neighbors, quite different from the avaricious English. As we have seen repeatedly, it is upon the proverbial cupidity of England and the desire she will have to retrieve her losses that Vergennes bases his whole alarmist argument. As to the Spanish alliance being put in jeopardy, the memoir given in Appendix III proves that the Foreign Office was quite ready to face the possibility, in January, 1778, that Spain would remain neutral throughout the war. *Vd. ib.*

[34] *Ib.,* 643.

It is not, I assure you [he wrote Montmorin, April 3, 1778], without something of pain and effort that the king and those of his ministers who enjoy his closest confidence have brought themselves to adopt a different course with reference to American affairs than that of the Catholic king and his ministry; but indeed, the interest of Spain herself has had greater weight in our decision than our own interest. The latter is comparatively feeble, if we measure it by our possessions, for these are hardly of a nature to whet the desires of the English, since they have none of the precious metals for which the English are so famished. It is rather toward the Spanish mainland that their eyes are turned, and I demand if England, mistress of the industry and resources of North America, and capable of fructifying these with her own wealth, would not be a neighbor more inconvenient, more formidable than the United States could probably ever become, given over as they are to the inertia which is the very essence of democratic institutions?[35]

Now, of course, it is quite true that these passages both occur in despatches intended for Madrid and designed to persuade that government that its interest lay with France and America, wherefore it may be argued that they are not to be taken too seriously as a revelation of the way of thinking of the French Foreign Office. Let the argument be granted to the fullest extent: what, then, is the implication as to utterances designed primarily for another forum and showing imminent peril to French possessions? Be-

[35] *Ib.,* III. 50-1.

sides, it does not appear very precisely how, supposing there had been a *reasonable* degree of likelihood of France having to come to the defense of her possessions, Vergennes' plea in extenuation of her course, addressed as it was to France's ally, was strengthened by disparaging that fact. Palpably, the very contrary is the case.

However, it may be urged from another angle, that the material feature of the passages under consideration is the assertion of France's concern for the safety of Spanish America, and that since this feature constantly reappears both in papers intended for Madrid and those intended for his own court, it is to be taken as expressing a serious objective of his policy. Let this too be granted: the question then confronts us, Why was this so? It will hardly be contended, I suppose, that the French government was moved to any great extent by altruistic considerations, and especially since the course it took was extremely disagreeable to the only possible beneficiary of its altruism. And by the same token, the terms of the Family Compact can scarcely be cited to furnish the required explanation. One explanation, then, and only one, remains: The very keen interest that France felt at all times in preventing a British conquest of Spain's holdings in America sprang from considerations connected with the doctrine of the Balance of Power, the idea being that, since England and France were rivals, any accession of new resources to the former would

put the latter at a correlative disadvantage in the
field of rivalry. Yet the moment these considerations are made premises of the discussion,
France's vast interest in promoting the separation of Great Britain and North America looms
before us. And which of the two contingencies,
this separation or a British conquest of Spanish
America, must have appeared the more imminent
after Saratoga, and therefore as furnishing the
more calculable basis of policy, is hardly a matter
for serious doubt.

*"The interest of separating the English colo-
nies from the mother-country and of preventing
their reunion at any time in any manner whatsoever is so primary a one that if the two crowns
should purchase it at the price of a war a little
disadvantageous, yet if they brought this separation about, it would seem that they ought
not to regret the war whatever its outcome."*
Thus wrote Vergennes in December, 1777, while
American recognition was still under debate.[36]
And why should France desire this separation?
The answer is supplied from another despatch
written after the cause of recognition had triumphed, in these words: *"That which ought
to determine and indeed has determined her
[France] to join with America is the great enfeeblement of England effected by the subtrac-*

[36] *Ib.*, II. 644. To the same effect is the memoir given in Appendix III.

tion of a third of her empire."[37]   And why should France desire the enfeeblement of England? This question is answered in a third despatch, written with reference to the appearance of the Bavarian Succession question, at the moment the American alliance was in the act of consummation. *"England is our first enemy, and the others never had any force or energy except from her."*[38] But with these and like passages before us,[39]

[37] Vergennes to Montmorin, June 20, 1778, *ib.,* III. 140.

[38] Vergennes to Noailles, Jan. 17, *ib.,* II. 745-6 and fn.; SMSS., No. 1839.

[39] See Ch. I, note 21. "Ou est, pourra t'on me dire, la sûreté que cette guerre nous sera heureuse? Je repons d'abord: est elle de choix ou de necessité. Si elle est de la derniere espèce, comme tout en fait la démonstration, il faut donc s'y soummettre avec resignation et courage. Mais supposons qu'elle soit malheureuse, ce qui est bien problématique. *Si l'independance de l'Amérique en est la consequence, si cette independance est absolue; si elle ne produit pas un pacte de fraternité qui reindentifieroit les deux peuples et n'en feroient plus q'un,* les deux Couronnes n'auront elles pas infiniment gagné d'avoir procuré une separation aussi considerable et diminué d'autant la puissance de leur ennemi inveteré?" Vergennes to Montmorin, Dec. 27, Doniol, II. 666. Florida Blanca thus epitomizes the arguments of the French despatches: "La cour de Versailles a pensé de son côté qu'il convenoit à sa gloire, à la bonne politique et aux intérêts les plus essentiels de la monarchie françoise de gagner de vitesse l'activité du cabinet britannique, et de ne point laisser échaper une occasion aussi favorable (et qui ne se présentera plus jamais) de convertir en avantages immenses pour la maison de Bourbon les mêmes moyens dont les Anglois avoient imaginé pouvoir se servir pour sa ruine,' *'ib.,* 749. "L'objet principal des ministres du roi était d'assurer l'independance des Etats-Unis et d'enlever ces treize riches provinces à l'Angleterre," Ségur, *Mémoires ou Souvenirs et Anecdotes* (Paris, 1844, 3 vols.), I. 166. Ségur was a friend and confidant of Vergennes.

it becomes evident that the substance of Vergennes' concern in the period following the news
of Saratoga was not, primarily, the security of
the French West Indies; that, indeed, the anxieties which he at times professed on this score, at
other times minimized, are not to be regarded too
seriously. His real concern, a concern that finds
repeated utterance in his despatches and again
through Gérard, in the latter's negotiations with
Franklin, Deane, and Lee, was of a reconciliation
between England and America which, however
devoid of belligerent intent toward the House of
Bourbon, would yet pave the way for the final
restoration of British dominion over the military,
industrial, and commercial resources of America,
and especially of the last.[40] In other words, his
concern was the obverse of his desire, and, with
the evidence that Saratoga afforded of the real
dimensions of the Revolution, of his *hope,* that is
to say, the hope of seeing England and America
permanently separated. The way, however, to
make that *sure,* he argued, was for France to
espouse the cause of American independence;
for then the Americans would persist till inde-

[40] See Doniol, II. 633-4, 638, 640, 655-6 fn., 665-6, 738 fn., and 837;
SMSS., Nos. 1831 and 1847. "We must now either support the
colonies or abandon them. We must form the alliance before England offers independence or we will lose the benefit to be derived
from America, and England will still control their commerce."
Vergennes to Montmorin, Phillips, *op. cit.,* 73 (citing the Archives
des Affaires Étrangères, *Espagne,* 588, No. 17).

pendence was in fact won and, when won, would use their liberty of action in ways beneficial to France. But before, of course, he could put this program into effect he had either to persuade his own king and the king of Spain to join in accepting it, or to persuade Louis to take a line of his own. He soon found that the latter alternative was the immediately feasible one, though not so easily feasible; whereas, in so important a matter as this one of intervention, involving the certainty of war, no half-way conversion of the king to the ministerial program would at all suffice. The somewhat abstract argument showing the large but rather intangible advantages to flow from England's loss of North America and its resources, had, therefore, to be supplemented by an argument of a more imperative sort, showing a danger immediate and concrete.

The notion that French possessions in the West Indies were menaced by a pending English-American coalition played an important part in bringing France into the War of Independence. It was this suggestion, supported by the somber name of Chatham, which first drew Vergennes' infra-Continental gaze to what was taking place on the other side of the Atlantic. It was with the same notion that Vergennes himself was able to counter Turgot's argument against secret aid, that it invited war. Lastly, it was with this notion that Vergennes overcame

Louis' reluctance to part company with his royal uncle for the sake of some rascally American rebels. Yet, when all is said, the theory in question throws little, if any, light on the nature of the principal advantage which the secretary expected that France would derive from intervention. And clearly, his statement at the moment of the royal council's decision in favor of an American alliance, that it was "not the influence of his ministers that decided the king" but "the evidence of facts, the moral certainty of peril," should be taken with a saving allowance of salt. No doubt Louis *was* convinced by the "facts" as they were represented to him; but if the monarch was unable to discern the flimsy texture of hearsay and guess-work beneath the ministerial varnish, the secretary was not so unaware of the quality of his own elaboration, as his constant admissions attest. Nor does "the evidence of facts" from American sources assist his effort thus to bridge the gap between remote possibility and calculable probability. Not a single statement of either Franklin, Deane, or Lee is on record showing either that they ever heard the word "coalition" from any British agent, or that, after Saratoga, they ever hinted such an idea to the French government, or that they supposed the French government to be alarmed on that score. The argument from silence is not always the most convincing, but its concurrence with more positive considerations, as in this instance, is at least reassuring.[41]

[41] The theory of an impending hostile English-American coalition having played its part in bringing the king into line for an American alliance was next utilized to exonerate France's conduct to legitimist Europe. The original form of the French government's apology for recognizing the independence of the United States is to be found in the "Précis of Facts relative to the Treaty of Friendship and Commerce," which was read to the Council, March 18, 1778, (SMSS., No. 1904). Several months later a more extended apology was put forth in the form of the *Exposé des Motifs, etc.* (translated in the *Annual Register*, XXII. 390 ff.). In the latter document the following statement occurs: "The French treaty defeated and rendered useless the plan formed at London for the sudden and precarious coalition that was about to be formed with America and it baffled those secret projects adopted by His Britannic Majesty for that purpose." This document was answered for the British government by Gibbon the historian in a paper of vast ability, entitled *Mémoire justicatif*, etc., and written in French. (For translation, see *Annual Register*, XXII. 397 ff.) Gibbon taxes the French government with having rendered the Colonies secret aid—"the court of Versailles," he says, "concealed the most treacherous conduct under the smoothest professions"; with having revived old quarrels reaching back, some of them, to before the Peace of Utrecht; and with claiming the privileges of a belligerent while professing the character of a neutral. Coming then to the coalition charge, he writes: "When an adversary is incapable of justifying his violence in the public opinion, or even his own eyes, by the injuries he pretends to have received, he has recourse to chimerical dangers. . . . Since, then, that the court of Versailles cannot excuse its procedure but in favor of a supposition destitute of truth and likelihood, the king hath a right to call upon that court, in the face of Europe, to produce a proof of an assertion as odious as bold; and to develop those public operations or secret intrigues that can authorize the suspicions of France that Great Britain, after a long and painful dispute, offered peace to her subjects with no other design than to undertake a fresh war

against a respectable power with which she had preserved all the appearances of friendship." The author of *Figaro* was now set to answer the historian of the *Decline and Fall*. His answer, entitled *Observations sur les Mémoire justicatif*, etc., in its original form practically ignored Gibbon's challenge. The bulk of it consists of an excited review of cases of seizures of French vessels by the British on the charge of carrying contraband, and the coalition idea appears in a single paragraph near the end of the document. See *Oeuvres Complètes* (Paris, 1835), pp. 530-42. The work was unsatisfactory to the Foreign Office, however, and was recast, presumably by Rayneval, Vergennes' secretary. (See Appendix IV and bibliographical data there given.) In the form in which it received official sanction the *Observations* rehashes Beaumarchais' review of British seizures, stoutly denies Gibbon's charge of secret aid, asserts that the Americans were independent in fact when France recognized them, and devotes considerable space to the coalition charge, but without very convincing results. Thus Gibbon's demand for proof is met by the assertion that naturally the British government was not so imprudent "as to leave direct marks of its darksome manouvre" and by the reputation of the king of France for probity. *"It was natural,"* the document continues, "for the British ministry, unable to subdue her Colonies, to seek to be reconciled with them." "In this situation," the query is put, *"ought it not to be supposed* that, the moment the British ministry perceived the necessity," etc. Finally, it is added: "Moreover, *although the king had not had certain proof of the hostile views of the court of London, it would have been sufficient to have had probable grounds to suspect that they existed,"* etc. In other words, if the fact did not exist, it at least behooved the French government to imagine that it did. Later passages in the document defend France against the charge of having entered the war for the purpose of *crushing* England: her purpose was only *to diminish British power,* and in this endeavor she represented the interests of Europe. See Appendix IV; also the following note. For the more general considerations supporting the conclusions of the above chapter, see chapter I, *supra.*

NOTE

Just as the page proof of this book is coming in I receive my April number of the *American Historical Review*, in which Professor C. H. Van Tyne reasserts the notion that the French government's decision to enter into alliance with the United States after Saratoga was determined by the fear that otherwise it would be confronted with a hostile English-American coalition which would pounce on its West Indian holdings. The printer has kindly put space at my disposal for some comments on this article, and I avail myself of the opportunity the more gladly as in doing so I can perhaps make my own position somewhat clearer: 1. To begin with, Professor Van Tyne is in error in stating that this explanation of France's action has heretofore escaped American writers. Pitkin (*History*, I. 398-400), Otis' Botta (II. 423-39), Perkins (*France in the American Revolution*, pp. 231-2), and Laura C. Sheldon (*France and the American Revolution*), *passim*, all note this argument for the alliance. And see further *American State Papers*, "Foreign Affairs," I. 569-71. Indeed, so far from the idea in question being at all "elusive," as Professor Van Tyne suggests, it is quite impossible for one perusing the documents to escape it, the only question being, *what weight, when all the evidence is compared, ought to be assigned it in explanation of the alliance.* So also, Doniol places the "coalition" argument alongside the "enfeeblement" argument as explanatory of the alliance, without however making any effort to assess the relative value of the two as representative of French motives or to distinguish between the point of view of the Foreign Office and that of the king. See *ib.*, II. 624-5. As to the French writers whom Professor Van Tyne cites as voicing his own view, it may be conjectured that they got the idea from widely circulated *Observations* described above. But it is to be noted that later writers, like Lavisse and Sorel both of whom have investigated the origins of Bourbon diplomatic policy and both of whom had Doniol available, give the "coalition" argument no weight whatsoever. 2. Professor Van Tyne would draw a hard and fast line between the policy of secret aid and the policy of alliance. But as he himself shows, the "coalition" argument was urged no less in behalf of secret aid than in that of the alliance.

*Indeed, it is altogether obvious that the reasoning by which the
Foreign Office supported its policy from start to finish was all of a
piece, and that the American victory at Saratoga—and, consequently, the situation which it produced—was the consummation,
exactly, which secret aid had from the first been intended to
bring about.* 3. Professor Van Tyne brings forward what he calls
a "key-document" to the motives of the French government in
entering into alliance with the United States in 1778. I fail to see,
however, that this document has any significance whatsoever,
save that it may have been the source from which Professor
Van Tyne himself first derived his idea of French motives. Thus,
on the point under discussion, it merely repeats several earlier
documents (see previous note) and brings forward not one iota of
additional evidence, except that it apparently endeavors to represent North's conciliatory propositions, which post-dated the alliance, as having been known to the French government at the time
of its decision. Again, it was written more than five years after the
events which it narrates. Finally, it was written with the purpose of silencing the very bitter criticism which, after Grasse's
defeat in the West Indies, was visited on the ministry's American
policy. Vergennes' tactics, it seems clear, are to remind the king
of his own responsibility for this policy and so to fasten on his
critics the charge of *lèse-majesté*. See Doniol, V. 186-7 and fn.;
Revue d'Histoire diplomatique VII. 528 ff.; Jobez, *La
France sous Louis XVI* (Paris, 1881), II. 492-506. 4. Nor is
Professor Van Tyne's citation of one or two other documents in
support of his thesis beyond criticism. Thus the Carmichael
memorial cited by him on p. 538 of the *Review* was written before
Saratoga and is in no wise applicable to show the attitude of the
American commissioner at the later date. See p. 118, *supra*.
Again, the Broglie memoir, cited at p. 537 of the *Review*, makes
distinctly against the thesis it is brought forward to support.
For while Broglie argues that England must in an endeavor to
preserve her rank, try to recoup her losses at the expense of
France and Spain, he rejects the idea that the Colonies will accept
a coalition with her or anything less than independence. And it
may be fairly said that while it is insisted that England will, from
the very desperation of her case, fall upon the Antilles, the whole
trend of the argument is that she has already lost her opportunity,

together with her naval superiority. Finally, Broglie opposes an alliance with the Americans, contending that a commercial connection will answer all purposes. See Doniol, II. 674 ff. All of the other material which Professor Van Tyne cites that is relevant to his contention will also be found in Doniol, and is sufficiently discussed in the above chapter. 5. At the close of his article Professor Van Tyne writes thus: It seems "clear that Vergennes did not invent this motive for the alliance—the idea that France was confronted by the dilemma of war with England anyway . . . merely . . . to get the consent of the king and the other ministers to the plan he wished to pursue. But whether it is his conviction or his device, the idea of this terrible dilemma remains the reason for the decision of the French cabinet." These words avoid the real issue on several accounts: The "terrible dilemma" with which Vergenes confronted the king was not of a war with England simply—for that France, backed as she would have been by Spain, was quite ready (see following chapter)—but of a hostile English-American coalition. Again, the attitude of the cabinet was assured from the first (see pp. 78-9, 85 *supra*), and it is the conversion of the king alone which Vergennes finds it worth while to explain—in terms meant for the ears of the Spanish court—in his despatch of January 8. See Doniol, II. 736. Finally, since the American alliance was the work of Vergennes, it is the underlying reason for *his preference* that we really need to know. Does this reason connect itself primarily with the history of French-English rivalry for colonial dominion in the Western Hemisphere, or with the history of French-English rivalry for influence on the Continent of Europe? That is the interesting question. See further, the data in chapter XVI, *infra.*

CHAPTER VII

THE TREATY OF ALLIANCE AND OUTBREAK OF WAR

The steps by which the fascinated monarch approached the decision that was ultimately to cost him his crown and his life are visible in the stages by which the Foreign Office and the American commissioners came to terms. On December 6th the king authorized advances to the Americans looking to a good understanding between the new republic, on the one hand, and France and Spain, on the other,—but nothing more definite.[1] In the audience that he accorded the commissioners, six days later, in consequence of this authorization, Vergennes emphasized the fact that the common policy of France and Spain made it impossible for the king to agree to a negotiation without the concurrence of his uncle. The Americans in turn indicated their preference for a simple treaty of amity and commerce and renewed an argument they had earlier made, that such an engagement would not involve the two crowns in war. But to this con-

[1] *Ib.*, 625-6. For further details of this interview and of the ensuing negotiations, see Lee's "Journal" in R. H. Lee's *Life of Arthur Lee,* I. 357-89.

tention Vergennes demurred strongly, urging
that if they were to treat at all "it must be in
good faith" and on such foundations of justice
that the resulting ties "would have all the solidity
of human institutions."[2]

Mid-December came the rumor that Lord
Germaine's secretary was in Paris, and Vergennes at once authorized Gérard to go to
Passy and "make glitter before his [Deane's]
eyes, as consented to in advance, everything
necessary to keep the legation in the lap of
France."[3]   On December 17th, accordingly,
Gérard brought to Passy the news that the
king had decided to acknowledge the independence of the United States, to enter into a treaty
of amity and commerce with them, and to sustain
their independence by all the means at his disposal without exacting any compensation for the
risks he took, "since, besides his real good-will to
us and our cause, it was manifestly the interest
of France that the power of England should be
diminished by our separation from it."   Of an
active alliance, however, Gérard said not a word.
On the contrary, according to the united testimony of the three Americans he stated explicitly
that the king would "not so much as insist that, if
he engaged in a war with England on our account,
we should not make a separate peace," the only

[2] Doniol, II. 637-9.
[3] *Ib.,* 647.

condition being "that we, in no peace to be made with England, should give up our independence and return to the obedience of that government."[4] In other words, while recognition of American independence had been decided upon, the question of an alliance was still in abeyance.

There now ensued a fortnight's delay while word from Madrid was being awaited. It came the last day of the year and was unfavorable.[5] A further delay of a week was set against the gout of the aged chief-minister. Meantime, the Americans were pressing for a more indicative sign of the course that France was to take, and the date of the British Parliament's reassembling, January 20th, was drawing nigh. At last, on January 7th, a royal council, convened at Versailles, declared unanimously for a treaty of amity and commerce with the United States, and a treaty of alliance which should embody the following features: first, it should become operative only upon the outbreak of war between France and Great Britain; secondly, it should have for its end to secure the "absolute and unlimited independence of the United States"; thirdly, it should stipulate a reciprocal guarantee of the possessions of the two powers in North America and the West Indies; fourthly, it should allow the accession of either party to it to a treaty of peace

[4] Wharton, II. 452-3.
[5] Doniol, II. 706, footnote, and 765-70.

with the common enemy only upon the consent of
the other; lastly, it should provide, in a separate
and secret article, for the right of Spain to join
the alliance.[6]

The next evening Gérard made a second visit
to Passy. Pledging the Americans to secrecy,
he began by repeating much of what he had said
on the earlier occasion, inveighed strongly
against a curtailed independence, especially as
to matters of commerce—saying that "clear-
sighted people had perceived this to be a commercial war from the outset"—and urged that
the deputies at once forego every appearance of
negotiating with their enemy. Franklin, inter-
rupting, inferred that war would be begun at
once by the king upon England, but Gérard
answered that such was not the king's plan, that
that was out of the question. He then asked what
the deputies would consider a sufficient inducement to make them reject all propositions from
England which did not include full independence
in matters of trade as well as of government; also
what terms would evoke a like response from the
American Congress and people. To the first
question the envoys returned answer on the spot:
the immediate conclusion of a treaty of commerce
and alliance would close their ears to all proposals not providing for the unqualified independence of the United States both political and

[6] *Ib.*, 729-30.

commercial. Gérard now announced that he was authorized to say that the king would conclude such an arrangement at once, in the form of two treaties, one a commercial treaty, which should go into effect upon ratification and should be strictly reciprocal, and the other an eventual treaty of alliance. He then referred to the possible conquest of the American continent by the United States, Deane having told him that Franklin was eager for this and indeed found in it the principal reason for an alliance with France. But Gérard indicated that he was uncertain how far His Most Christian Majesty would engage to coöperate in such an enterprise. He also let them know that he now spoke for France alone and not for Spain, with whom, he implied, they would have to come to terms separately,—an announcement which disappointed Franklin greatly.[7]

Three days later the commissioners, through Deane, returned Gérard an answer to his second question. It was a demand for "an immediate engagement" on the part of France "to guarantee the present possessions of the Congress in America, with such others as they may acquire on the

[7] Gérard's Narrative, Jan. 9, 1778, SMSS., No. 1831. Note that on this occasion, as on that of his earlier visit to the commissioners, Gérard's chief concern was to make sure, not that the Americans would not come to terms with England before making a treaty with France, but that they would not come to terms with her at any time on any other basis than that of *complete independence.*

continent during the war, and either to enter into a war with England or furnish Congress with the money" to do so, until "all that the English now possess on the continent shall be conquered" and the English fisheries be secured "to the United States and their allies."[8] From this time forward the principal point of difference between the envoys and the Foreign Office was whether the alliance should go into effect at once or be contingent upon the outbreak of war between France and Great Britain, the desire of the Americans being to see the guaranties stipulated by the treaty effective at once. Though they eventually gave way, they showed themselves, according to Vergennes' unexpectedly pertinacious; and actually, as we shall soon see, their concession was immaterial.[9] The first drafts of the treaties had been handed the commissioners by Gérard on January 18th; the final drafts were signed February 6th.[10]

[8] *The Deane Papers,* II. 313-4; SMSS., No. 796.

[9] See Vergennes to Montmorin, Jan. 16 and 30, Doniol, II. 774 and 791; SMSS., Nos. 1838 and 1853; and Lee's "Journal," in Lee's *Lee,* I. 388.

[10] The text of the Treaty of Alliance is given in Appendix I. During the final stages of the negotiation, the Foreign Office received two memoirs that may have had some part in inducing the king to take the final plunge. One of these came from Broglie, who, arguing that England "without colonies and commerce" would be without a marine and without a marine would be "henceforth only a third-rate power" but that she must none the less now concede American independence, concluded from these

From the negotiations between the Foreign Office and Passy we turn to those that were proceeding synchronously between the Foreign Office and the Pardo; for though the general result of this correspondence has been anticipated, some of the details, too, are of interest. Partially misled perhaps by Aranda's enthusiasm for a French-Spanish-American alliance, which was redoubled by the news of Saratoga, partially misled too, it may be, by his own enthusiasm for

premises that she would, simply in an effort to preserve herself, attempt to appropriate the French Antilles and portions of Spanish America. The fact that Broglie was averse to any but a commercial connection with the United States may have given his argument additional weight. Doniol, II. 673-82. Beaumarchais' memoir is in characteristic vein. One of its principal arguments is the assertion that Chatham and Shelburne would probably join the Tory ministry before February 2nd. Then would follow, it was possible, American independence and a British-American attack on the French West Indies, and France would be the laughing-stock of Europe. To meet this situation, the king should at once declare openly that he recognized American independence. The document thus foreshadows the action taken early in March, in declaring the Treaty of Amity and Commerce, in which connection it should be compared with Vergennes' despatch of January 23rd to Montmorin, written the day following the presentation of the memoir. The memoir will be found in Doniol, II. 841-7, and SMSS., No. 1814.—A circumstance tending to prolong the negotiations was the difficulty that arose between Lee and the Foreign Office over the XIth and XIIth articles of the Treaty of Commerce. It was eventually agreed that Congress should pass upon these articles separately; and Congress exercised its option by rejecting them. See J. T. Morse, *Benjamin Franklin* (American Statesmen Series), 277 ff.; also Wharton, II. 477-85 *passim*.

the enfeeblement of England, but also finding it
the better policy to show a confident front on this
question that was quite in contrast with his pessi-
mism in the matter of British intentions, Vergennes professed to believe, as long as he could
plausibly do so, that His Catholic Majesty could
be brought into line quite promptly with whatever policy toward the Americans His Most
Christian Majesty should adopt for the security
of the House of Bourbon and its possessions.

The aged Ossun, who had long since shown
himself quite unable to hold his own with Florida
Blanca, had now been superseded at Madrid by
the Count de Montmorin, a personal friend of the
king and admirer and confidant of Vergennes.
Privately the secretary tried to stir the ambition of the young diplomat by a portrayal of the
unique opportunity offered by the existing
situation. It was an opportunity that could not
often recur, especially since, "if we come out of
it successfully I hope we shall have quiet for a
long time."[11] "Take for your motto," he accordingly exhorted, "and make them adopt it:
Aut nunc aut numquam." "Let Spain give her
word and the *good* word and we shall anticipate
England." If, however, contrary to all expectations, we should neglect "the most interesting
conjecture that heaven could present us, the
reproaches of the present generation and of the

[11] Same to same, "Privé," Dec. 13, SMSS., No. 1775.

generations to come will accuse us forever of our culpable indifference."[12]

To all such pleadings the astute Spaniard turned a heedless ear. He was willing to give abundant money succor to the colonies under "the express condition of an inviolable secrecy"; also to offer them "protection" should they need it, "provided they conducted themselves with loyalty and prudence"; and he admitted that an alert attention ought to be given to the current vicissitudes of the various English parties, especially so far as these might affect the American question.[13] For the rest, however, he was as intractable as ever: The existing British ministry would never incur the odium of proposing independence for the Americans and the Americans would now never take less. There was, therefore, no danger of an English-American coalition unless the British should be spurred to extreme measures by the efforts of France to win over the Americans. For France and Spain to recognize American independence was quite unnecessary, since their interest attached the insurgents to the two crowns anyway. His Catholic Majesty had an unconquerable repugnance to recognizing American independence and the prejudices of a man of sixty-two were not easily uprooted. The

---

[12] Doniol, II. 644-5.
[13] Florida Blanca to Montmorin, Dec. 23, *ib.*, 695, fn. 2.

abasement of England was no object to Spain.[14]

Coming to the Pardo one day late in December, Montmorin was informed that a despatch just received from Aranda showed the government at Versailles to be already in negotiation with the Americans. Montmorin had not received word to this effect and believed that the information was false, but he decided not to contradict it at first because he wanted to see what the effect would be if the case really were as Aranda had stated. He soon discovered, for the Spanish minister, in a mounting rage, denounced the folly, inconsiderateness, and precipitancy of France's policy to his heart's content. When the storm had a little abated, the young Frenchman said: "You will be astonished to learn that far from having begun with the Americans, despite the urgency of the case . . . the king awaits . . . the advice of his uncle." For a moment Florida Blanca was taken aback, but soon recovered sufficiently to resume his reproaches: Only the year before Spain had been ready for war and France had backed down. Again, it was France that had left Spain in the lurch in 1762. To treat with the Americans was equivalent to declaring war on England. However, if Spain did enter the war she "would not be the first to ask for peace." "Before asking for it she would sell her last shirt,"

[14] Florida Blanca to Aranda, Dec. 23, *ib.*, 765-70; Mortmorin to Vergennes, same date, *ib.*, 700.

to which Montmorin rejoined pleasantly that he hoped it was the English who would have to sell their shirts.[15]

But if the young ambassador thought that he had drawn his enemy's fire against the day when he would have to tell the whole truth about his government's policy he was much mistaken. Louis' decision to ally himself with the Americans was communicated to Charles in a note from the royal hand under date of January 8th,[16] which Montmorin transmitted nineteen days later,—a delay that is to be credited to the *finesse* of the French secretary, who, it may be conjectured, did not wish news of the Pardo's reaction to Versailles' decision until the latter had been put beyond recall. The Spanish minister's reception of the news was most dramatic. The intensity of his emotion displayed itself in both countenance and gesture. To contradict or oppose him was in vain. "He trembled in all his body and had the greatest difficulty in the world in expressing himself." "You think," said he finally, "this moment a most auspicious one for the two crowns; I think it the most fatal for Spain; but it would be the fairest day of my life if the king would let me retire." Next day Montmorin visited the king who, he soon perceived, shared his minister's feelings to the full. His Majesty voiced in solemn tones

[15] *Ib.,* 696-9.
[16] *Ib.,* 713-4.

his affection for his nephew and his concern for
the peril in which Spain found herself.[17]

Yet in the days following both monarch and
minister recovered something of their equanimity
in apparent resignation to accomplished fact.
They were, moreover, counting on the ostensible
disposition of France at the moment not to anticipate events further. Vergennes' original program had been to secure Spain's assent to the
general principle of an alliance with the United
States and then to leave the two powers ample
time to make their own terms with one another.[18]
This course he had indeed abandoned when he entered upon negotiations with the Americans, but
the Treaty of Alliance itself still carefully safe-
guarded in Spain's interest the margin of time between its signature and the anticipated outbreak
of war with Great Britain.[19] Furthermore, as
Florida Blanca analyzed the motives probably
governing the British cabinet, this interval was
not unlikely to be a considerable one, provided
only the initiative were in future left with that
body. Thus guaranteed, as he thought, the spa-
cious tomorrows so dear to the Spanish heart, His
Catholic Majesty's minister began early in February gradually unfolding the expectations of

[17] Montmorin to Vergennes, Jan. 28, *ib.*, 750-2. See also Florida
Blanca to Aranda, Jan. 27, *ib.*, 748-50.

[18] "Les epoques de l'Espagne seront les notres," Vergennes to
Montmorin, Dec. 11, *ib.*, 636. See also *ib.*, 637-8 and 644.

[19] See the separate and secret article in Appendix I.

Spain. "The Spaniards," wrote Montmorin in comment, "are a little like children. They can be interested only by presenting shining objects to their gaze." The Spaniard on the other hand complained that France's moderation had hopelessly prejudiced his case from the outset. He did, however, venture to indicate the restoration of the Floridas and a share in the Newfoundland fisheries as possible objects of ambition to Spain.[20]

But while Florida Blanca was just beginning his bidding in a game which he evidently expected to be a leisurely one, Vergennes was coming to the conclusion that by France and England at least all cards must soon be boarded,—a conclusion to which he was undoubtedly assisted by an interview he had with the British ambassador on January 22nd. Stormont initiated the conversation by taxing the secretary with reports in circulation about Paris of active military preparations going on at certain French ports. Vergennes, showing embarrassment, disavowed any knowledge of these, whereupon Stormont brought forward the report, which "gains ground every day," of a treaty or convention with the rebels or "at least" of France's "having accepted some proposals from them." Vergennes now became more embarrassed than the Englishman had ever seen

[20] Montmorin to Vergennes, Feb. 2, 5, 9, 16, 26, paraphrased in Doniol, II. 795-8.

him, "played with his fingers and remained quite silent," whereupon the relentless Stormont proceeded: "Your Excellency, who was so long a foreign minister . . . certainly knew how to observe the silence as well as the language of those you treated with. You will allow me to follow that example." He then cited an interview of the previous month in which the secretary had met a similar report with a hearty denial, which was no doubt truthful. But on the present occasion, he continued, being unwilling "to stoop to falsehood . . . [you] did not answer a single syllable." Vergennes now sought retreat behind a distinction between "Lord Stormont" and "the British ambassador": when the former had jocularly questioned "the Count de Vergennes" about the current rumors of an American treaty, "the Count de Vergennes" had been free to respond with candor, but when "the British ambassador" seriously questioned "the secretary of state" on so important a matter, the latter before answering must first obtain the views of his royal master.[21] Certainly, a rather lame evasion. But what was even more ominous, though "Lord Stormont" continued malignantly to pester "the Count de Vergennes" with unwelcome questions, "the British ambassador" carefully refrained from pressing inquiries "a categorical answer to

[21] Stormont to Weymouth, Jan. 22, SMSS., No. 1846; Vergennes to Noailles, Jan. 24, Doniol, II. 792-3.

which . . . would probably lead to the most serious consequences."[22]

In other words, not only was it evident that the British government took it for granted that a treaty existed between France and America, but also that it desired to conceal the fact; and, of course, the inference was inevitable that, if concealment was calculated to promote England's plans, it could not be a good thing for France.[23] Moreover, the unsatisfactory answer that the American envoys had, on January 11th, returned to Gérard's second question had, naturally, not been forgotten; while the fact that, if the Treaty of Alliance was eventual as to France it was the same as to Congress also, could not be ignored. Lastly, Vergennes, recalling no doubt some of his own experiences with legislative bodies on the Continent, began to apprehend the possible ef-

[22] Stormont to Weymouth, Jan. 28, SMSS., No. 1851; Vergennes to Montmorin, Jan. 30, *ib.,* No. 1853.

[23] Wentworth, had written, as early as Dec. 29, in the most positive terms, of the decision of France *and Spain* to support American independence (SMSS., No. 722), but this was obviously mere guesswork on his part; and little credence seems to have been given by George III to his reports (Donne, II. 109, 121). As late as Jan. 13 George is still confident that the French ministers want peace (*ib.,* 118), but by Feb. 9, he has changed his opinion (*ib.,* 133) and has come to recognize, in consequence, the need of offering some measure of conciliation to America, a thing he had previously opposed, apparently. In a letter of Feb. 23, Gibbon says that treaties were signed at Paris with the Americans on the 5th of the month.

fect of British gold on the loyalty of Congress.[24]

Vergennes' determination to force developments is made clear in his despatch of January 23rd, and again in that of January 30th.[25] In the latter he gives renewed assurance of the secrecy of the French government and the American commissioners, but argues that as soon as the treaties reach America the news of them will speedily become public. From this he concludes that it will be necessary for the king to proclaim the Treaty of Amity and Commerce by the end of April or the first of May, that is, several weeks before the Mexican fleet will have reached Spain. He accordingly offers Spain the loan of ten vessels of war for her Cadiz squadron and to make sure the safe return of the treasure fleet.

Not only, however, did the Spanish minister sulkily decline the proffered war craft, he also showed himself quite determined not to quicken his pace in negotiation,[26] thus stressing anew the precarious situation in which France now found herself, with the old love off and the new one not yet securely on. True, the Treaty of Amity and Commerce constituted a pledge of American friendship, but so long as Spain remained aloof, something more than this was wanted; while, on

[24] Vergennes to Montmorin, repeating a rumor that the English government was sending 500,000 guineas to America to pave the way for a negotiation, Doniol, II. 802, footnote.

[25] Ib., 738-9, footnote, and 789-92; SMSS., Nos. 1847 and 1853.

[26] See note 11, above.

the other hand, England, now aware of the existence of a treaty between France and the United States, might at any moment offer the latter their independence, which offer the Americans were still free to accept, and then withdraw from the war.[27] On February 17th Lord North introduced his plan of conciliation into Parliament. It undoubtedly fell a long way short of according the colonies independence, but there was, of course, the constant possibility of its being further modelled on that idea.[28] The same day, moreover, a colloquy occurred in the House of Commons between Fox and Grenville on the one hand and Lord North on the other which furnished additional evidence that the British ministry was well informed of the subsisting relations between France and America but preferred to keep the matter hidden for the time being.[29]

[27] See art. I of the Treaty of Alliance.

[28] *Parliamentary History*, XIX. 762 ff.; "Instructions to the Earl of Carlisle," etc., Apr. 12, 1778, SMSS., No. 440. "Upon the subject of commercial regulations," runs this document, "the prevailing principle has always been to secure a monopoly of American commerce." If these ancient restraints were to be abolished, then certain new ones must be stipulated in their place. That, however, was a matter for Parliament, but before it was considered, representatives from the colonies would be admitted to that body. Evidently there was no intention of surrendering the old commercial system without a further struggle. See further SMSS., Nos. 359-63 and *Parl. Hist.*, XIX. 379, 577, and 942.

[29] *Parliamentary History*, XIX. 769, 774-5. There was also in-

On March 7th Louis approved a declaration of
the Treaty of Amity and Commerce between
France and "the independent States of America,"

creasing tension between the two governments at this time on
account of certain of England's naval measures. In Vergennes'
despatch of Feb. 21st occurs the following passage that has an
obvious pertinency to recent questions between the United States
and certain of the present European belligerents: "Vous lui [Lord
Suffolk] ferez sentir . . . que le droit des gens, les traités et
surtout la dignité de la Couronne de France ne sauroient dépendre
des circonstances ou peut se trouver la Grande-Bretagne." Doniol,
II. 806. Vergennes was evidently now coming around to the view
that England meant to attack France first, or to force France to
attack her, and then press negotiations in America, *ib.*, 744 fn.
2, and 803-5. Another circumstance that may have influenced
Vergennes in deciding to precipitate developments with England
is the belief which he may have formed at this time that Arthur
Lee was acting the spy for the British government. Doniol gives
a paper said to be in Vergennes' own hand and endorsed thus:
"Extrait d'une lettre de M. Arthur Lee à Md. Shelburne, écrite
immédiatement après la signature du traité entre la France et les
Etats-Unis de l'Amérique." The passage in question informs
Shelburne that the treaty is about to be signed and that England
will have to make haste if she is to prevent the alliance of France
and the United States. Doniol, III. 169; Wharton, I. 639. The
letter referred to was probably the work of Lee's secretary Thorn-
ton, who was undoubtedly a British spy; see data in Wharton, I. 659-61 (§ 207). Again, it may not have been known
to Vergennes as early as March 7, 1778. But in this connection,
the memoir of Beaumarchais to Vergennes of March 13, 1778,
is important. An early paragraph of this document contains the
following charge: "Son plan [Lee's plan] ayant toujours été
de préférer, entre la France et l'Angleterre, la puissance qui le
ménerait plus sûrement à la fortune, l'Angleterre, a pour lui des
avantages reconnus; il s'en a souvent expliqué dans les soupers
libertins," *Deane Papers*, II. 392. For Beaumarchais' interest in
attempting to discredit Lee, see Moncure D. Conway in the *Athe-*

which Noailles deposited with the British foreign office six days later.[30] The purpose of the move was threefold; first, to forestall any tampering with Congress by British agents, by making the American public aware that France had recognized American independence; secondly, to

naeum for 1900, I. 305. Lee's loyalty to the Alliance is, in fact, above suspicion. See Wharton, I. 525-50; also Ballagh's *Letters of R. H. Lee,* II. 132-42; also Lee's own "Journal." But the matters above detailed go, of course, to explain the distrust henceforth manifested by Vergennes and his representatives toward Lee, and to a less extent toward his relative, R. H. Lee. See *infra.*

[30] Doniol, II. 820-6. See also Vergennes to Montmorin, Mar. 6 and 10, for statement of motives, *ib.,* 810-2 and 813-8. In the latter we find Vergennes reiterating the argument that, whatever course France took, war was inevitable: "Je pense . . . que quelque parti que nous prennions, de moderation, de force, ou même de foiblesse, nous ne pouvons plus éviter la guerre. Ce ne seront ni nos engagemens avec l'Amérique ni les secours que nous pouvons lui avoir données qui nous la procureront; c'est la déroute de Burgoyne qui l'a préparée et décidée. Le ministre anglois a senti au moment même ou cet evénement a éclatté que la continuation de la guerre pour soumettre les Américains devenait impossible, mais pour détournér l'animadversion de sa nation de dessus sa mauvaise conduite, il nous a destinés deslors à être les objets de la haine nationale et de sa vengeance particulière." However, he continues thus: "Je crois bien qu'il la suspendroit volontiers pour peu de tems jusqu'à ce qu'il eut celui terminer avec les Etats-Unis . . . ; pourvû toutefois que nous consentions à dévorér dans le silence les afronts multiplies . . . ; mais independam't que ce sistème passif et honteux ne peut être celui d'une grande puissance, fermerons nous les yeux à l'intérêt majeur que nous avons d'empecher et prévenir une réconciliation et une coalition entre l'Angleterre et l'Amérique qui uniroit ces deux nations dans un même sistème de paix et de guerre?" Such is the final form of the secretary's apology for his program: *ib.,* 816.

hasten the breach between France and England which it was felt the former's recognition of American independence must produce, with a view to making the Treaty of Alliance operative; thirdly, to associate America in an act flouting British dignity in a way to anticipate and prevent any proffer by England of independence to the United States.[31] Fearful that the British government would still endeavor to conceal the insulting intelligence, Noailles was also instructed to drop a hint of it in private conversation.[32] On March 19th, Stormont left Paris and Noailles London;[33] and the American commissioners, after being presented at court, dined with Vergennes.[34] Nine days later, Louis, addressing

[31] In this connection see Chatham's words in the House of Lords, May 30, 1777, *Parliamentary History*, XIX. 319. Also, compare the attitude of the Rockinghams and that of Chatham when the French-American treaty became known. The former wished to grant independence immediately, but the latter contended that national honor forbade. See his last speech, that of Apr. 6, 1778. So long of course as it was not generally known that the British government *knew* of the French-American treaty, North was free to offer America what terms he chose. And anyway, even if England should choose to pocket her pride and recognize American independence, she would plainly have done so because France had forced her to it and the latter power would have America's gratitude. Doniol, II. 815.

[32] *Ib.*, 826.

[33] "The French message was deemed so ironic and insulting that at night orders were sent to Lord Stormont to leave France directly without taking leave, and M. Noailles was acquainted with that step, that he might retire too," *Last Journals of Horace Walpole*, II. 224. See also Doniol, II. 828-38.

[34] See Gérard to the Commissioners, Mar. 17, Wharton, II. 516.

two letters to his "Very Dear and Great Friends
and Allies," informed Congress, in the one, that
he had appointed M. Gérard "to reside near you
in quality of our minister plenipotentiary"; and
in the other, that he was sending a fleet under the
Count d'Estaing "to endeavor to destroy the
English forces upon the shores of North America."[35]   The first hostile blows were passed on
the evening of June 17th between a French fri-
gate and two English vessels off Ushant.[36]

Thus step by step did Vergennes lead his halt-
ing monarch into war in behalf of American independence.   Yet even before the American treaties
had been drafted, the Continental peace upon
which the success of the design hinged had been
brought into jeopardy by the appearance of the
question of the Bavarian Succession.[37]   For our
purposes it is sufficient to know that upon the
death of the Elector Maximilian Joseph, his successor made a treaty in January, 1778, recognizing certain claims of Austria to lower Bavaria and
upper Palatinate, and that Frederick II had
promptly interfered in the name of other heirs to
the lands involved to prevent this treaty's being
carried out.   France was thus confronted with a
difficult alternative.   Her traditional policy and

[35] *Ib.* 521-2.
[36] Doniol, III. 147-8.
[37] See Vergennes to Noailles, Jan. 17, Doniol, II. 745-6 and footnotes; SMSS., No. 1839.

her position as guarantor of the Treaty of Westphalia required that she should side with Prussia.
But if she did this she ran the imminent risk of
throwing Austria into the lap of England once
more, which would be the first step, perhaps, in
producing a Continental conflagration. Nevertheless, Vergennes decided to follow the line dictated by the *Système de Conservation* and to
throw France's weight in with the lesser claimants.
Fortunately he was able to count on the peaceful
inclinations of Maria Theresa and to draw the
czarina to France's side. The Treaty of Teschen
(May, 1779), which excluded Austria from all
but a small district of Bavaria and yet left the
Treaty of Versailles intact was a great triumph
for the secretary's diplomacy and should be regarded as signalizing the restoration of France
to something like her former influence in Continental affairs.[38]

And while he was thus saving one situation,
Vergennes was creating another, more propitious
one. In asserting the right of France to receive
American vessels in her ports because of the belligerent character of the provinces in revolt
against Great Britain, and of the right of French
merchants to send goods to America and to receive them thence, Vergennes had had occasion to
revive and to define with new precision those

[38] Lavisse, *Histoire de France,* IX.¹ 98-100, 109-10; Doniol, III.
Ch. 3.

principles of the Law of Nations which the neutral states of Europe had long pitted against the harsher rules that England supported; and in articles XXIII-XXVIII, of the Treaty of Amity and Commerce, the opportunity had been seized to give these principles formal and summary statement. Here one will find asserted the principle that "Free ships make free goods"; also, rules restricting the belligerent right of visit and search within narrowest compass; also, a stipulated contraband list confining, for the most part, the prohibitions imposed in the case of such goods, to munitions of war. Then on July 28th, the French government issued a *Règlement* which to a reiteration of the above principles added the principle that a blockade to be binding must be effective. These principles, neutral states were informed, France voluntarily agreed to observe for the ensuing six months for the benefit of all neutral states, and thereafter, for the benefit of all such states as were prepared to force England to observe the same principles with reference to themselves. The declaration was, in other words, a clever bid for neutral pressure upon Great Britain to force her to surrender her more aggressive rules. But neutral states were wary, and until 1780 the declaration met with only a very qualified success. Early in this year, however, the czarina, angered by the seizure of some Russian vessels by the Spanish, issued a declaration of her own which followed very closely the lines of its French predecessor; and let it be known, moreover, that she was prepared to back up her principles by force of arms. At Vergennes' instigation both the French and Spanish governments immediately announced their acceptance of this declaration, while the English government held back. The czarina who had hitherto lent her sympathies to England, now transferred them to the Bourbon powers. The result was the First League of Neutrals, which, comprising practically all the neutral powers of Europe, announced its intention of supporting for the benefit of its several members the principles of maritime warfare which had found formulation in the *Règlement* of July, 1778. To the war which began as a war for American nationality and French prestige was thus imparted the more universal character of a war for the freedom of the seas.[39]

[39] Lavisse, *loc. cit.*, 111-12; Doniol, III. Ch. 12; IV. Ch. 8; Paul Fauchille, *La Diplomatie française et la Ligue des Neutres* (Paris, 1893). For the Czarina's Declaration and the responses to it of the courts of London, Paris and Madrid, see the *Annual Register*, for 1780, pp. 347 ff.

CHAPTER VIII

SPANISH MEDIATION AND THE CONVENTION
OF ARANJUEZ

To have affixed to France's assault upon the
British Empire a character that was ultimately
to attract the moral support of all Europe and
to have preserved the indispensable condition of
success for France, peace on the Continent, were
notable achievements for Vergennes' diplomacy.
Even so, so long as Spain remained a mere on-
looker of the struggle, the secretary regarded his
war program as lacking a vital element. For one
thing, he must show Europe that French and
Spanish policy still marched abreast; for another
thing, the condition of the royal finances counselled a quick, decisive war. To Florida Blanca's
frank notification that Spain would never shoulder the risk and expense of war merely for the
intangible and highly speculative benefits to flow
from the enfeeblement of England and a read-
justment of the balance of power he had, as we
have seen, lent a heedful ear for some time. Unfortunately, before it had been possible for the
Foreign Office "to penetrate Spain's desires,"

the situation had developed which had forced France to break with England; and the result of this step, in turn, was a new obstacle to Spanish coöperation that was quite as formidable as any of those which it reinforced.

The keynote of French-Spanish negotiations throughout the spring and early summer of 1778 is furnished by the ever recurrent reference in Montmorin's despatches to "the wounded *amour-propre*" of the Catholic king. Louis had taken action vitally affecting the joint interests of the two crowns not only without awaiting the assent of his uncle, but even without making a plausible show of consulting him. Darkly ruminating this fact Charles concluded that his nephew had come to regard Spain as standing in some sort of vice-royalty to France, from which it followed that Spain's first duty was to herself, to demonstrate her independence and dignity.[1] Whether Florida

[1] Doniol, III. 10-25. Charles had of course been greatly offended to begin with by the French-American treaty. See *ib.*, II. 747-57. Florida Blanca sketched his monarch's character thus: "Caractère mal connu en France, rempli de la plus exacte prohibité, plein dè tendresse pour sa maison, mais défiant, soupçonneux, très attaché à ses opinions; on a offencé son amour-propre, il a cru qu' on le considérait comme un viceroi d'une province de France devant prendre ou quitter les armes suivant les ordres qu'il recevait; cette idée l'a humilié et dès ce moment il a conçu le projet de prouver qu'il était libre; d'ailleurs, n'étant plus jeune, très pieux toute sa vie, des scruples viennent à présent l'assaillir, le souvenir de ses disgrâces passées le rend timide, tout concourt à lui inspirer le désir d'éviter la guerre; il faudrait pour le décider lui présenter quelque succès brillant qui flattât son amour-propre;

Blanca felt the same degree of alarm that Charles professed, lest the younger branch of the House of Bourbon should suddenly find itself in a position of tutelage to the older, may well be doubted, but at any rate his royal master's resentment was too good grist to his mill to be turned aside. Not only did it fend off all danger that an untimely appeal by Louis to the Family Compact would succeed, but it furnished a further argument for that delay which, the wily Spaniard early discovered, was bound to whet France's appetite for greater aid than the Family Compact stipulated for and which must, therefore, be purchased on Spain's terms.[2]

There was one respect, moreover, and that an important one, in which both monarch and man were in genuine accord in reckoning France's

je le connais; quoique dévot l'amour de la gloire le touche et il voudrait illustrer son régne, *ib.,* III. 495. To much the same effect, is M. Bourgoing's characterization in his letter to Rayneval of May 25, 1778, *ib.,* 40.

[2] See *infra.* M. Bourgoing's letter, referred to in the above note, contains many acute observations upon the principal persons and factions then at the Spanish court. Of Florida Blanca he writes: "Discret, dissimulé même, il a le talent rare de bien cacher quand il veut ce qu'il sait, ce qu'il sent." Comparing him with Aranda, Bourgoing says further: "Les deux principaux traits de dissemblance entre ces deux ministres sont que l'un est aussi ferme que l'autre étoit foible et facile à conduire; que l'un se dissimule au point qu'on ne sait guères qui il hait, qui il aime ni en qui il met sa confiance, au lieu que l'autre se livroit sans retenue à ses animosités et ne voioit presque rien que par les yeux de . . . M. de Campo:" *ib.,* 42, 45. —. For an interesting analysis of Florida Blanca's policy, see *ib.,* 559, 576, and 583.

precipitancy a substantial grievance to Spain, and that was its tendency to put the question of the American peril out of reach of a satisfactory solution. In March Florida Blanca's views on this subject were still very much "in the vague": The Americans ought first to be allowed to weaken themselves and then left in anarchy akin to that of Germany.[3] Four months later he was forthcoming with a more definite remedy: "Seeds of division and jealousy" must be sown between the new republic and its former mother-country; to which end the latter must be left Canada and Acadia.[4] The suggestion fell in well with Vergennes' own program, and he at once answered that, while independence "implied the free possession of all parts of the Thirteen States," it had not been guaranteed by France for "other English possessions which had not participated in the uprising."[5] And by November, the Spanish court's view of the American question had received yet further clarification from America it-

[3] Montmorin to Vergennes, Mar. 30, 1778, *ib.*, 20.

[4] Same to same, Oct. 15 and 19, *ib.*, 556-9. In the latter despatch Montmorin makes the good point, that to leave "seeds of dissension" between England and America was to leave the seeds of a fresh war for which, very probably, France and Spain would not be so well prepared as for the present one. He also deprecated the idea that danger could result from the prosperity of the United States. That danger, said he, is "fort eloigné et même incertain."

[5] Vergennes to Montmorin, Oct. 30 and Nov. 2, *ib.*, 561-2.

self.[6] "There is no concealing the fact," wrote Montmorin at this time, "that the interest they feel here in the Americans is not very tender." "Spain regards the United States as destined to become her enemy in no remote future, and consequently, far from allowing them to approach her possessions she would omit no precaution calculated to keep them off, and especially from the banks of the Mississippi."[7] Florida Blanca would "drive both the English and the Americans from the banks of the Mississippi." "He would render forever impossible the accession of the Spanish colonies to the United States, whom he more distrusts than he does the English."[8] These words, be it noted, do not compromise an appeal from Spain to France, or anything like it. They are reported by Montmorin on his own initiative and quite casually. Why, then, the question suggests itself, did Spain not make such an appeal? Plainly, because she recognized that the discussion now touched interests with regard to which

[6] See ch. XI, *infra*.

[7] Montmorin to Vergennes, Nov. 12, *ib.*, 575-6. To this Vergennes answered: "Il est bien étrange qu'on s'obstine à voir dans les Américains un voisin plus dangereux que ne le seroient les Anglois. Il ne faudroit pour se désabuser qu'examinér avec réflexion les constitutions . . . que les Etats-Unis se sont données. Leur République, s'ils n'en corrigent pas les vices, . . . ne sera jamois q'un corps foible et susceptible de bien peu d'activité . . . . Je vous avoue que je n'ai q'une foible, confiance dans l'énergie des Etats-Unis:" *ib.*, 581. Vergennes was apparently somewhat disappointed in the new ally.

[8] *Ib.*, 585.

France was already committed; and this being so, Spain must keep a free hand to deal with the American question in accordance with her own interests.

Thus the problem of getting Spain into the war tended to become more and more complicated. At the same time, Vergennes' impatience to bring the thing about became more and more intense. In a memoir addressed to the king on June 20th, he had declared his belief that the temporizing policy of Spain, if persisted in, spelt disaster for both crowns: There could be no doubt, of course, what the choice of His Catholic Majesty would be when it was once made, but delay alone might easily prove fatal to Bourbon hopes. France ought to stand ready, in order to spur her ally to action, to promise aid in recovering Gibraltar, in casting off certain distasteful commercial arrangements that had been foisted on her by England, and in conquering Jamaica, a portion of the Newfoundland fisheries, and the mastery of the Caribbean.[9] And the Spanish ambassador was not less urgent, though for rather different reasons. From the first a confident prophet of American independence, he was now convinced that the triumph of France and America over England was near at hand. If then Spain wished to be in at the killing, she must

[9] "Réflexions sur la conduite à tenir dans les circonstances présentes relativement à l'Espagne," *ib.*, 159-63.

make her election without delay. "It is only a dolt," he declared sententiously, "who armed *cap à pie* will consent to stand guard over others comfortably eating their dinners." Spain could not rely indefinitely on any efforts save her own. "When the sowing is late the harvest is usually meagre."[10]

[10] Aranda to Florida Blanca, Dec. 28, 1777, April 11, Aug. 4, and Nov. 1, 1778, Sparks MSS., CII. Other characteristic expressions from these despatches are the following: "There is not much to be read in this despatch, but a great deal to be thought and not slept over." "Spain alone is the party that will be exposed [to danger] unless she takes heed. . . . They [the Americans] will have no other neighbors than Spain,—they close at hand but we afar off, they increasing in population and flourishing and we the contrary." "Let us confess that a like opportunity will not present itself in centuries for Spain to right herself in several particulars." "Spain has treasures which she must redeem. . . . This chance will hardly return while the world shall last." Writing on May 2, 1779, with reference to the still pending project of mediation, Aranda declared that if it succeeded, he would "weep tears of blood, that Spain should have taken care of the business of others and neglected her own." Florida Blanca expresses the point of view of the Spanish court in his despatch to Aranda of April 19, 1778: "All the considerations that Your Excellency so wisely sets forth are less important than that of the king's ceasing to be sovereign and making himself the subject of another in the great matters of peace and war." In a report on the French navy, of Aug. 4, 1778, Aranda says that by November it will be, with the naval aid stipulated for by the Family Compact, "in condition to subjugate England without [further] assistance." "This crown," he continues, "wants nothing but the disposition; its immense population, its adventurous spirit, its great wealth permit everything." He predicts the success of France's enterprise and resulting "tranquility for many years." Evidently, he had become thoroughly indoctrinated in Vergennes' viewpoint.

But was Spanish aid really worth waiting for? Would it—considering the sulky humor of Charles and the palpable self-seeking of his minister—be worth the price that would have to be paid for it? Young Montmorin was sceptical. "The moderation affected to-day," he wrote, "will to-morrow make way for an ambition that will cause more embarrassment than Spainish assistance will pay for."[11] Vergennes, however, for the reasons already suggested, gave the warning less weight than, in the light of subsequent events, it may seem to have deserved. His answer was that assurance could not be made too sure, that another campaign must see the two nations acting together, if it was humanly possible to bring the thing about.[12]

The road by which Spain finally took her leisurely way into the war was the edifying one of mediation. There were several reasons why it seemed good to Florida Blanca to dress his monarch up as the champion of peace and capable in

Further correspondence between the two men is taken by Sparks from D. Antonia Ferrer del Rio, *Historia del Reinado de Carlos III en España,* III. pt. V., ch. I., pp. 256-67. Aranda in a postscript had quoted Maurepas as saying that evidently "Spain hoped, by her mediation, to pick something from the cracks." This makes Florida Blanca extremely angry. "It is a malicious invention," he says, but continues that if "England is hard picking for us, we shall not be less so for those gentlemen." Sparks MSS., XCVII.

[11] Report of June 22, Doniol, III. 473.
[12] See *ib.,* 481-5, 486, 526-32, etc.

its interest of dispensing an even justice between France and her ally on the one hand and Great Britain on the other. For one thing, the proposal gave His Catholic Majesty that independent rôle which his affronted dignity demanded. Again, it furnished a new reason for delay. Lastly, in the form it finally assumed, it promised Spain an opportunity to curtail American independence.

The great difficulty was to get the idea launched under proper auspices. For France, whose act had precipitated the war, to solicit Spain's good offices at the outset would have been ridiculous; while England on the other hand, entirely apart from her natural distrust of the connection between France and Spain, was of no mind to accept peace on any terms that did not leave her free to deal with her rebellious colonies as she saw fit. A round-about hint from Florida Blanca in April that His Catholic Majesty's services were available to England and France, which was accompanied by some absurd by-play designed to conceal the manner of its origination, was met with a blunt snub from London. Florida Blanca vented his chagrin on the British ambassador, and for the moment it looked to Montmorin as though Spain might enter the war without more ado.[13] But so incon-

[13] For these and other details with reference to this abortive effort at mediation, see *ib.*, 56-80, *passim*.

tinent abandonment of the cause of his affronted
dignity was hardly to be expected of the quixotic
Charles. Four months later, however, His Catholic Majesty had begun to relent somewhat, and
the English government, alert to the fact and
eager to keep Spain out of the autumn campaign,
did, in September, convey a very definite intima-
tion to the Spanish ambassador at London that
His Britannic Majesty hoped to see "the war
ended by the mediation of Spain" and "had no
doubt that she would be able to save the honor of
Great Britain without lessening that of France."[14]
From the point of view of the necessity of placat-
ing Charles this event may well be regarded, as
M. Doniol indicates, as decisive. On September
28th, Florida Blanca sent a note to Almodovar
stating the moral obligation that Spain would
be under if England did not submit propositions
along with the king of France, and ten days
later Vergennes also, conformably with a hint
from Montmorin, wrote the Spanish ambassador formally accepting Spanish intervention.[15]
Charles' gratification expressed itself in a variety
of attentions to the French ambassador, while
Florida Blanca, though ostensibly sceptical of
peace, professed to be not less satisfied on that
account. He now predicted to Montmorin that
the following spring would find Spain in arms
alongside her ally.[16]

[14] Ib., 513. See also ib., 497-9.
[15] Ib., 515 and footnotes.
[16] Ib., 516.

From this point on, though Spanish policy continues as devious as ever, the course of events becomes comparatively straightforward. The British answer to the Spanish note of September 28th was delayed some six weeks, and when it arrived, it laid down the impossible condition that mediation must be preceded by the withdrawal of the French fleet from American waters and the cessation of French aid to the Americans.[17] The obvious incompatibility of these conditions with those that had already been laid down by France ought, it would seem, have at last given the mediation project the bare bodkin.[18] But the obstinacy of the Spanish monarch, who now had the scent of a great rôle in his nostrils, and the subtlety of his minister, who still saw profit in delay, were equal to the occasion. On November 20th Charles himself addressed Louis a note accompanied by a "confidential declaration" in which, while France's obligation to secure independence for the United States was fully recognized, it was pointed out that the demand for

[17] *Ib.*, 524.
[18] The French conditions are laid down in the "Articles à proposer pour la Paix" of Oct. 17, *ib.*, 551-4. The first paragraph reads: "Le roi d'Angleterre avouera l'indépendence absolue des 13 Etats-Unis de l'Amérique septentrionale pour le politique, le civil, et le commerce et les reconnoitra pour Etats souverains et parfaitement libres. S. M. B. s'engagera de retirer immédiatement toutes les forces de terre et de mer qu'elle tient dans aucune partie des dits Etats-Unis et de leurs remettre toutes les places, territoires, et isles en dépendans."

a direct and formal recognition of it would be a serious offense to British pride. Why then, it was argued, should not the procedure that had been taken in the case of the Low Countries be followed again? In that case France, supporting the liberty and independence of Holland against Spain herself, had been content with obtaining, in the first place, a long truce in favor of her protégé, and then, when Holland had wished to make a definitive treaty with Spain, had merely stipulated that this should not be ratified without her consent. Peace, the Spanish court further urged, was necessary to America herself, wherefore there was always the danger that England might seduce the United States into accepting a separate treaty,—a poignant argument at the moment, as we shall presently appreciate. The conclusion was inevitable that some sacrifice in form was advisable to secure peace at once, though no sacrifice of real obligation.[19]

It is perhaps hardly necessary to point out how entirely this proposal of a truce for a term of years for the Americans in lieu of a permanent peace met Florida Blanca's problem of neutralizing American independence as far as possible. Such an arrangement would abound in opportunities for "sowing seeds of discord" between the English and Americans and, by the same

[19] *Ib.*, 622-3.

token, in opportunities for making the latter feel the necessity of a guaranty of their independence from the Bourbon crowns. And such a guaranty need not, of course, be accorded gratuitously. It might well be made to bring a substantial price in terms of American territory along the Mississippi.

But though fully awake to the possible advantages to Spain of peace in America on such a basis, the Spaniard was not over-credulous of its ever coming about, nor blind to the necessity of keeping the door hospitably ajar to the other alternative. The royal communication and memoir were accompanied to Paris by a characteristic product of the minister's own pen, addressed to Vergennes: His Catholic Majesty was still genuinely hopeful of peace, but at the same time he was well aware of the possibility that negotiations might fail. He accordingly still continued his preparations "with the greatest activity and trusted that his nephew was doing the same." Indeed, the king was "of the opinion that without the greatest dissimulation up to the very moment of striking no advantage could be got of England." Meantime, it became pertinent to inquire what *advantages Spain might obtain, and how and in what terms France might bring herself not to listen to any proposition without assuring them to" her.*[20]

[20] *Ib.*, 619-21. The last sentence quoted above is underscored in the translation of the document by Vergennes.

Before, however, Vergennes could deal with this most significant inquiry, he had to settle the more exigent question posed by the royal communication, whether France could, harmoniously with her engagements with the United States, accept for them a truce in substitution for a permanent peace. His first opinion was plainly adverse. "The Peace of Vervins," he wrote Montmorin, December 1st, "was unavailable as a precedent in the case of the Americans," for the situation of France and her engagements with the United State were of "quite a different character to those which Henry IV and his predecessors had contracted with the Dutch."[21]   But as it happened, Franklin's English friend Hartley was at this very moment urging much the same idea from the British point of view.   When accordingly Franklin, making a confidant of Vergennes, showed the latter Hartley's letter, it was not difficult to elicit from the American the sentiment that

provided France and Spain were ready to accord the United States their good-will and protection, independence, whether recognized as a matter of right or only as one of fact, would be a very good thing for them, in that it would secure them, along with the sweets of peace, or of a truce, the time and opportunity to perfect their political arrangements and internal order.[22]

[21] Vergennes to Montmorin, Dec. 1, *ib.*, 583, footnote.   See also note 18, above.

[22] Same to same, Dec. 4 and Dec. 24, *ib.*, 595 and 599.

In his despatch of December 24th to Montmorin, Vergennes, though still insisting that the
Peace of Vervins afforded no precedent, yet indicated that France would be willing to consent,
either to the Americans "treating directly and
alone with England, under the express condition,
however, that the treaty shall keep pace with
our own and that each treaty shall be null and
void until the other is concluded"; or, to a long
truce between Congress and Great Britain which
should leave France at liberty to make a definitive treaty. In either event the negotiations
should proceed under the mediation of the Catholic king, and England should treat with the Americans as if they were independent and should at
once withdraw her forces from "all parts of the
American continent comprised in the Confederation"; and the truce, were there one, should run for
from twenty to fifty years and be guaranteed by
France and Spain, or at least the former.
Franklin, Vergennes added, had been prepared
for "an imperfect recognition of the independence of his country" but not his associates, for in
them "I do not have the greatest confidence."[23]
The day following Vergennes wrote Gérard, the
French representative at Philadelphia, to prepare
Congress for a truce and indirect recognition.
The matter was to be handled "with dexterity"
and the unalterable disposition of the king to

[23] The despatch of Dec. 24, *ib.*, 596-9, 602-3.

sustain all his engagements was to be unremittingly insisted upon.[24]

Thus was the first concession registered at the expense of His Most Christian Majesty's engagements with the United States to the program of getting Spain into the war, and others were to follow. There was now of course no question of bringing Spain into the autumn campaign, for that had long since closed, but Vergennes, who was already finding the Americans disappointing allies, was now becoming fearful that even the spring would find the Escurial still balancing and undecided. On December 5th the secretary presented the king a second memoir on the subject nearest his heart:

If it is a fact [he wrote] that Your Majesty cannot *alone* long sustain a contest with the English on equal terms and that the war unduly prolonged would involve both Your Majesty's commerce and finances in ruin, . . . then it necessarily follows that everything advises our risking something in order to bring this ally to the desired point of reunion with us. I do not conceal the fact, Sire, that the pretentions and expectations of Spain are gigantic, but it is necessary to consider that the time one would employ in opposing them would be lost for the establishment of that concert of operations which cannot be effected too promptly.[25]

Three weeks later, in the same despatch in which he announced to Montmorin the French govern-

[24] *Ib.*, 613-5.

[25] *Ib.*, 588-90. For Vergennes' view of the Americans at this date, see note 7, above.

ment's willingness to accept a truce for the United States, Vergennes wrote further that, despite the vast difference between the general situation as it existed at the opening of the war, when England would have been fairly "at the knees of the two crowns," and now when she had had time to fortify all her possessions, His Majesty "approved in advance all that the king his uncle should deem it right and fitting to exact."[26]

But a vague disposition of concession was not what Florida Blanca was after,—this must precipitate itself in a shower of definite, concrete stipulations, and particularly must the objects be named for which France would fight *to the end*. And what is even more important, with the possibility of a truce between England and the Americans to be guaranteed by France and Spain, the mediation project was still worth coddling for its own sake. In his despatches of January 12th and 13th, Montmorin told Vergennes that he had sought in vain to secure Florida Blanca's views in detail of the advantages which France and Spain might expect to obtain from the war with England. "At that point the prime minister had placed his lever, there he had anchored solidly." "His Catholic Majesty," the Spanish minister's own plea had run, "wished to show his nephew the same measure of confidence that the latter had shown him. He accordingly

[26] *Ib.*, 607-8.

desired that His Most Christian Majesty should
be the one to specify the conditions *without which
he would promise not to consent to peace."*
Montmorin's own opinion was that a convention
guaranteeing Spain the possession of Mobile and
Pensacola, the expulsion of the English from
Honduras, and the restitution of Gibraltar would
be signed promptly if mediation failed, and that
Jamaica was no longer an object. At the same
time he noted that, according to Florida Blanca
at least, the king still preferred peace and that
consequently it still remained necessary to "allay
the scruples that were to be anticipated from a
conscience at once so delicate and so timorous."[27]

But all things end, and the term of Spain's
vacillations—always more apparent than real—
was at last nigh at hand. On February 12th
Vergennes sent Montmorin the desired draft of a
convention together with full powers to agree "to
any modifications or additions that might seem
needful."[28] The keystone of the project was its
third article which reiterated the stipulation of the
Family Compact that neither party should make
peace without the consent of the other. The
fourth article further pledged both parties not
to make peace till Great Britain should recognize American independence. The fifth declared

[27] *Ib.*, 641-3. See also the letter from Florida Blanca to Vergennes, of Jan. 13, 1779, *ib.*, 681-3.
[28] *Ib.*, 685.

certain additional objectives of a successful war
that would be of interest to France, including the
restoration to His Most Christian Majesty of the
right to build such works at Dunkirk as he chose
and the expulsion of the English from Newfoundland. The sixth article pledged France, in
case she should regain Newfoundland, to admit
Spanish subjects to the fisheries there. The
seventh enumerated the objects of interest to
Spain, to wit, those that Montmorin had listed in
his report.[29]

Florida Blanca's reception of the proposed
convention was at first apparently cordial but he
soon developed numerous criticisms, and particularly against the fourth article; and finally he
proposed that he be allowed to draw up a project
of his own.[30] Spain's policy, wrote Montmorin,
is "to exact everything and accord nothing"; yet,
he added, it is only by adopting her terms that we
can bring her in. "I have need of patience
a-plenty."[31] Vergennes in reply professed some
surprise at the attitude taken by the Spanish
minister toward "a work that was in some sort
more his own than ours," yet he continued: "We
are literally committed to omitting nothing that
may appear to enlist the interest of Spain." Some
of the difficulties that had been raised he was dis-

---

[29] *Ib.*, 803-10, left hand column.

[30] Montmorin to Vergennes, Feb. 28, 1779, *ib.*, 665-7.

[31] Same to same, same date, *ib.*, 662.

posed to attribute to Florida Blanca's faults of
temper, on which he heartily commiserated the
young ambassador. Nor was he greatly astonished at the repugnance which the Spanish minister had expressed against recognizing American
independence at present: "From Spain nothing
is to be got for nothing: we have from her directly that she wishes some advantages from the
Americans as well as from us, and we will not
oppose her."   At the same time, Vergennes
thought some reference ought to be made to the
secret article of the American treaty; for even
though the convention with Spain would also be
secret when entered upon, yet in time it would see
daylight, and then "the glory and honor of the
king would suffer if it appeared that he had neglected this ally, and that in order to gain the
powerful protection of the crown of Spain."   In
short, any proposition would be approved of
provided that "by the general tenor of the act we
have not neglected the interests of this republic."[32]

On April 12th, 1779, the secret Convention of
Aranjuez was signed by Florida Blanca and
Montmorin. The first article declared the intention of the Catholic king, in the event that His
Britannic Majesty rejected the ultimatum of the
third of the month offering Spain's friendly offices for the last time, of making common cause
with His Most Christian Majesty against Great

[32] Vergennes to Montmorin, Mar. 19, *ib.*, 670-2.

Britain. The third, fifth, sixth, and seventh articles were essentially the same as the corresponding articles in Vergennes' project. The fourth article, on the other hand, was very different. Diligently recording the fact that the king of France had "proposed and demanded that the Catholic king should from the day when war should be declared against England recognize the independence and sovereignty of the United States and offer not to lay down his arms until that independence should be obtained," it reserved to the Catholic king the right to conclude for himself a treaty with the Americans to govern "their reciprocal interests," the sole condition being that, to any treaty made by Spain with or affecting France's ally, Louis should also be a party. The article was well understood on both sides to be mere banality. More than a fortnight before this Florida Blanca had confided to Montmorin, who in turn had confided it to Vergennes, that the Spanish monarch, fearful of the "example he would give his own possessions," would "not recognize the independence of the United States until the English themselves should be forced to do so by a treaty of peace."[33] Finally, article IX of the convention read thus:

Their Catholic and Most Christian Majesties promise to make every effort to procure and acquire for themselves all the advantages above enumerated and to con-

[33] *Ib.*, 753 for ?

tinue their efforts until they have obtained the end which they propose to one another, mutually pledging themselves not to lay down their arms nor to make any treaty of peace, truce, or suspension of hostilities without having at least obtained . . . the restitution of Gibraltar and the abolition of the treaties relative to the fortification of Dunkirk, or in default of this last some other object to the taste of His Most Christian Majesty.[34]

[34] *Ib.*, 803-10.

CHAPTER IX

THE TWO ALLIANCES COMPARED

Spain was at last committed—conditionally! We may then, without anticipating much that is to follow, proceed to consider the question already suggested, of how far France was forced, in the interest of bringing Spain into the war with England—and later, of keeping her there—to modify her obligations with the United States as defined by the Treaty of February 6th, 1778. The most interesting phase of this question is that touching the direct clash of interests of the United States and Spain along the Mississippi river, and this we reserve for fuller treatment in the chapters to follow. At the moment we have to review some lesser consequences of the necessity which Vergennes finally found himself under, of yoking his government to two more or less antagonistic allies instead of, as he had originally hoped, to governments themselves allied.

The question of the shape which British recognition of American independence should take has already been touched upon. By the Treaty of February 6th British recognition was to be either formal or tacit, but in either case it was to be by a *peace ending the war*.[1] By the Spanish proposition, however, which Vergennes, after some hesitation, finally adopted and transmitted to Gérard with orders to obtain Congress' assent to it, a truce to run for a term of years and to be accompanied by the actual withdrawal of British forces from the territory of the United States was to count as a fulfilment of the purpose of the alliance, provided that France continued to guarantee American independence or that France and Spain jointly guaranteed it. In point of fact Gérard received the orders referred to at an embarrassing moment and in consequence presented his case so feebly that Congress in its Instructions of August 14th, 1779, made no declaration on the subject of a truce.[2] Not till June, 1781, in circumstances to be reviewed later, did Congress formally declare its assent to the idea of a truce which should be accompanied by a British evacuation of all territory of the United States.[3]

[1] Treaty of Alliance, art. VIII.

[2] Indeed, by the Instructions of this date "The commissioner to be appointed to negotiate a treaty of peace with Great Britain" was ordered "to make it a preliminary article to any negotiation that Great Britain shall agree to treat with the United States as sovereign, free and independent." *Journals of the Continental Congress*, XIV. 956.

[3] *Op. cit.*, XX. 652. "If a difficulty should arise in the course of the negotiation for peace, from the backwardness of Britain to make a formal acknowledgment of our independence, you are at

The concession demanded of Congress in the matter of British recognition owed its origin, though not its later repetition, to the necessity that France thought herself under at the end of 1778 of supporting Spanish mediation. Inducements more directly designed to bring Spain into the war against England were, first, the promise by France in the Treaty of Aranjuez, in the event of the conquest of Newfoundland from Great Britain, of a share in the fisheries there, and secondly, the listing of the Floridas as objects of Spanish ambition. Though the Floridas, in significant distinction to "the northern parts of America," were not specifically mentioned in the American treaty, it was acknowledged by Vergennes in his instructions to Gérard of March 29th, 1778, that they entered "into the plans of conquest of the Americans." Gérard was accordingly instructed more than a year before the Treaty of Aranjuez was signed, in view of Spain's well-understood desire to restore her monopoly over commerce on the Gulf of Mexico, "to prepare them for an eventual withdrawal"; or, if he was not able to obtain this—and it was recognized that the matter was one that would "require all the dexterity of M. Gérard"—he should at least "exert himself to obtain Pensacola

liberty to agree to a truce, or to make such other concession as may not affect the substance of what we contend for; and provided that Great Britain be not left in possession of any part of the thirteen United States."

and the parts of the coast which will be estimated
to be of the greatest value to the court of Madrid."[4]   Gérard did as he was told, but again his
efforts met with little success, as meantime the
Florida and Mississippi questions had become
merged.   Eventually, in 1780 and 1781, Spain
went ahead and conquered the British posts in
Florida for herself,—without American aid, it
is true, but also without American protest.[5]

The reason for the French government's taking the United States into its confidence with
reference to the Floridas is to be found in articles VI and XI of the Treaty of Alliance.   Under
the latter, if the United States had conquered
this region and obtained its cession from Great
Britain, France would have been bound to guarantee them in its possession.   By the former, His
Most Christian Majesty had "forever renounced
possession of any part of the continent of North
America" which had previously belonged to Great
Britain, a stipulation which naturally carried

[4] Mémoire pour servir d'Instruction au Sr. Gérard," etc.,
"Approuvé," Mar. 29, 1778, Doniol, III. 153-7: see pp. 155-6,
See also Montmorin to Vergennes, Oct. 15, ib., 556. From the
latter document it appears that Florida Blanca was willing at this
date to see all of the Floridas go to the Americans except such
part as was necessarily for the security of Spain's "navigation in
the Gulf of Mexico," i.e., probably for the security of Spain's
monopoly of trade on the Gulf.

[5] Other phases of the Florida question are treated of in the
chapters following, in connection with the Mississippi question
and Jay's residence in Spain.

with it the further idea that His Majesty was not free to tender, even contingently, any portion of this continent to another power in consideration for a treaty therewith. But if this was the case with the Floridas, then why was it not also the case with Newfoundland? Yet in article V of the Convention of Aranjuez "the expulsion of the English from the island and fisheries of New-foundland" is listed as one of the advantages which France sought by the war, while in article VI it is agreed that if His Most Christian Majesty "succeeds in becoming master and acquiring possession of the island of Newfoundland, the subjects of His Catholic Majesty are to be admitted to the fisheries." Evidently the Foreign Office interpreted the term "continent" of article VI of the Treaty of Alliance rather strictly, although it does not seem to have taken Congress into its confidence in the matter. And while the representatives of the French government at Philadelphia frankly combatted the idea from the first that the Americans were entitled of prescriptive right to continue to enjoy that participation in the fisheries which was theirs as British subjects, they always did so on the ground that France ought not to be asked to assume fresh obligations the discharge of which might delay peace.[6]

[6] But while the French government did not inform Congress of its views in this matter, it probably did so inform the American

And from the fisheries one turns readily to Canada and Nova Scotia, to which the self-denying ordinance registered by France in article VI of the Treaty of Alliance bore especial reference.[7]

commissioners. Thus Lee records in his "Journal" that, in view of the ambiguity of the word "continent" in article VI, he, with the approval of Franklin and Deane framed an additional clause by which France was also to renounce the right to all conquests "in the islands of Newfoundland, Cape Bréton, St. John's Anticosti, and the Bermudas." Lee's *Lee,* I. 378-9, 383. In the final treaty the Bermudas alone are mentioned in this connection. It ought to be recalled that by the Peace of 1763 Spain had lost her share of the Newfoundland fisheries, while France had retained hers.

[7] See Vergennes to Guines, Aug. 7, 1775, with reference to the instructions to be given Bonvouloir. One point that he should be clear about, says the secretary, is to reassure the Americans "contre la frayeur qu'on cherchera sans doute à leur donner de nous. Le Canada est le point jaloux pour eux, il faut leur faire entendre que nous n'y songeons point du tout." Doniol, I. 156. See also his comment on Miralles' suggestion that, while Spain recovered the Floridas, France should seek to recover Canada: "Vous savez que nous sommes d'une opinion contraire, parceque nos possessions sur le continent de l'Amerique ne seroient propres qu'à inspirer de la méfiance aux Américains et qu'à les raprocher insensiblement de la Grande-Bretagne." Vergennes to Gérard, Oct. 26, 1778, *ib.,* III. 570. Earlier Vergennes had offered the same objection to Florida Blanca's plan of intervention, the purpose of which for France was to be the recovery of what she had lost in 1763: "La France a des colonies dans la proportion qui convient à sa population et à son industrie. Plus seroit une charge plutôt q'un benefice. Si la perte du Canada a été sensible elle doit la moins regrettér depuis que l'abandon qu'elle a été obligée d'en faire est devenu le signal de la revolte des provinces angloises sur le continent. Si nous tentions de nous y reintegrer nous reveillerons les anciennes inquietudes et jalousies qui faisoient le gage de la fidelité et de la soumission de ces mêmes provinces à l'Angleterre; leur veritable façon de pensér est

Indeed, by article V of the same treaty, as I have just mentioned, the expectation of the United States to attempt the reduction of what British power remained in "the northern parts of America" is formally recorded. From the very outset, nevertheless, the French government was determined, if not to thwart, at least to discourage in every way possible, this expectation on the part of its ally. Vergennes' own plan for Canada and Nova Scotia originally was to expel the English thence and establish there a free "agricultural and commercial state which should govern itself under the protection of France" and enjoy reciprocal naturalization and commercial privileges with it. In this way, he argued, the country would be peopled by the French themselves and "by any who choose to go there," and a national spirit, grounded on similarity of language, customs, and national character and kept alive by constant intercourse, would be created substantially identical with that of France herself. Thus would France raise up to herself an ally which, without being burdensome to her

découvert dans les propositions qu'elles nous ont fait parvenir: elles ne s'efforcent pas de secoüer le joug de leur patrie pour s'exposér à subir celui de toute autre puissance." Letter to the king of Apr. 26, 1777, *ib.*, II. 274-5. See also *ib.*, III. 62-3 and 527, where France's indifference to territorial acquisitions of any sort is insisted upon. It is interesting to regard article VI of the Treaty of Alliance as a sort of forerunner of that phase of the Monroe Doctrine which declares that "the American continent is no longer subject to colonization."

would yet avail to protect the French interests in the Newfoundland fisheries and to check the new republic to the south.[8]

But this apparently was the dream of a moment.[9] At any rate, by the beginning of 1778 Vergennes had come to believe that, to furnish the necessary make-weight to the United States, Canada and Nova Scotia should be left with Great Britain. In Gérard's instructions we accordingly read that, though Congress has much at heart the project of a conquest of Canada, Nova Scotia, and the Floridas and would like to obtain an agreement with France looking to the carrying out of these projects, the

king has come to the conclusion that the possession of these three countries, or at least of Canada, by England would be a valuable source of uneasiness and vigilance to the Americans, that it would make them feel the need

[8] Aranda to Grimaldi, Oct. 10, 1776, Sparks MSS., CII. Aranda also quotes Vergennes as saying that France herself "would not again occupy anything more than the islands to the north of the St. Lawrence."

[9] See, however, Estaing's "Addresse à tous anciens François de l'Amérique septentrionale" of Oct., 1778: "I shall not urge a whole people that to join the United States is to secure their own happiness; since a whole people . . . must know their own interest; but I will declare and I now formally declare in the name of His Majesty . . . that all his former subjects in North America who shall no more acknowledge the supremacy of Great Britain may depend upon his protection and support." *The Continental Journal and Weekly Advertiser* (Boston), Dec. 3, 1778. See further, Doniol, III. 417-25.

they have of the friendship and alliance of the king, and that it is not to his interest to destroy such a feeling.[10]

In the views thus expressed Vergennes was fortified in the course of the months following by the similar views communicated in Spain's behalf by Montmorin.[11] As it chanced, however, at this very time La Fayette was perfecting in conjunction with a committee of Congress a plan for a joint campaign in Canada by the allies. Commenting upon the plan, Vergennes wrote Gérard thus: "I will confide to you, but to yourself alone, that the opinion of Spain is that it will be advantageous to reserve Canada and Acadia to Great Britain, and you feel yourself that we ought to be far from contradicting her. . . . But, I repeat, it is for circumstances to confirm or modify our views."[12] The final disposition of

[10] *Ib.,* III. 156-7. Note also the extracts furnished by the Count d'Estaing from his Instructions, to Gérard: "7° chef—Requis que je dois faire de contribuer à la conqueste du Canada autrement que par une croisère et par des attaques des posttes. . . . 3° chef . . . chaque expression désigne la répugnance que le Roy a pour cette enterprise." *Ib.,* 237-9. See also Vergennes to Montmorin, Oct. 30: "Nous ne désirons pas à beaucoup près que la nouvelle république qui s'élève demeure maîtresse exclusive de tout cet immense continent." Accordingly Canada and Nova Scotia should remain with England in order to make the Americans feel the need "de s'assurér des garants, des alliés, et des protecteurs." *Ib.,* 561. See also SMSS., Nos. 872 and 891.

[11] *Ib.,* 557 and 616.

[12] Nov. 18, 1778, *ib.,* IV. 43 footnote 3; and to same effect is *ib.,* III. 616. See also Adolphe de Circourt, *Histoire de l'Alliance et de l'Action commune de la France et de l'Amérique* (Paris, 1876,

the question was somewhat curious. The plan mentioned having been referred to Washington, the commander-in-chief reported against it. Officially and publicly he based his objection upon the impossibility of furnishing sufficient forces for the expedition, but in a confidential letter to the president of Congress he also voiced the fear of offering France the temptation of reëstablishing her power in a country filled with the memory of her, whose customs, morals, religion, habits of government, everything, recalled her, and the possession of which would be valuable to her in many ways, especially in the facility it would afford "of controlling these states, the natural and most formidable rival of every maritime power in Europe."[13]

But after all, Canada, the Floridas, the fish-

3 vols.). The work is a translation of vol. X of Bancroft's *History,* of the edition of 1874, with added notes and documents. Here, vol. III. pp. 263-4, Vergennes, writing Gérard under date of Dec. 25, 1778, says: "You have done wisely to elude the overtures made you concerning Halifax and Quebec. Your instructions embody the king's way of thinking upon this subject; and His Majesty has changed the less because he has reason to believe that it enters into the policy of Spain as well as in ours, to maintain the English in possession of Nova Scotia and of Canada." M. Doniol would make Spain originally responsible for the idea of leaving Canada in England's hands, but in this he is clearly mistaken.

[13] Washington the President of Congress, Nov. 14, 1778, *Writings of Washington* (Ed. Sparks, Boston, 1834, 12 vs.), VI. 106-10. Later, however, Washington changed his opinion on this subject. See Doniol. IV. 565: also ch. XIII, *infra.*

eries, and even the form that British recognition should take, are matters more or less by the way. For either France did not transgress her engagements with the United States with reference to them, at least to any very easily definable extent, or else she candidly took the United States into her confidence and asked their coöperation. The one point, and the only one, at which there was flat incompatibility, technically at least, between the Treaty of February 6th, 1778, and the engagements subsequently incurred by His Most Christian Majesty with Spain was the stipulation by the secret Convention of Aranjuez, that France should make no peace without the consent of Spain, which was fortified by the further and more definite stipulation that the war should continue until His Catholic Majesty had obtained Gibraltar. Thus was the purpose of the war, in which the United States were already bound to remain to the end, altered and enlarged, not only without their consent, but without their knowledge.[14] Having failed in her efforts to ally with one another the powers with which she herself was allied, France bound the two to one another's fortunes by conditioning peace-making in all cases upon her own consent, but while the relation thus created between France and the United States was known to Spain, the analo-

[14] That it was the purport of Florida Blanca's program to "alter the object of the war" is stated by Montmorin, *ib.*, III. 487.

gous relation between Spain and France was
unknown to the United States.

And this discrepancy, of which the United
States were contingently the victim, is thrown
into even higher light when we turn to the
history of M. Gérard's early months at Philadelphia. Here Louis' representative found upon
his arrival a widespread belief that the United
States could make peace at any time with England, provided only they did not renounce their
independence.[15] The source of the idea is not
far to seek. It was the commissioners' letter of
December 18th, which was written at the period
when the French government was negotiating
for the amity and commerce of the Colonies, but
not their active alliance. But the later treaty,
which however in July had not yet been published in America, proceeded of course along
quite different lines. As soon, therefore, as Vergennes learned the state of belief in the United
States on the subject of peace-making, as he did
from some American newspapers even before
Gérard had reached Philadelphia, he penned the
latter a despatch ordering him preëmptorily to
"destroy an opinion . . . which would reverse
the whole system upon which our Treaty of Alliance rests."[16]

This despatch reached Gérard early in August.

[15] *Ib.*, III. 277-84.
[16] *Ib.*, 284. See further *ib.*, 399-401, and IV. 17-34.

At the same moment, with the arrival of Deane in Philadelphia, whither he had been summoned by Congress, the famous Deane-Lee controversy broke forth, over the question whether the Colonies were under any obligation to pay for the supplies that had been furnished them through Hortalez and Company. Deane, who had made a contract with Beaumarchais guaranteeing payment, contended that Congress was bound to live up to this agreement, while Lee asserted that these supplies had been intended by the French government as gratuities and that Hortalez and Company had been a mere device to conceal French assistance under the guise of commerce, and further insinuated that Deane and Beaumarchais were in conspiracy to defraud Congress.[17] The merits of the controversy are divided. Lee was certainly right as to the supplies purchased with the money that had been contributed by the Bourbon kings,[18] but was quite

[17] For references on this topic see Chapter III. notes 27 and 42; also *Letters of Richard Henry Lee* (Ed. J. C. Ballagh, N. Y., 1911-4, 2 vols.), I. 373-5, 457-63, II. 1-203, *passim*.

[18] Note in this connection the following words from Louis' letter to Charles, of January 8, 1778: "Je ne parle pas des secours d'argent et autres, que nous leurs avons donnés, le tout étant passé sur le compte du commerce." Doniol, II. 713. The king's intention, therefore, with reference to the million livres which were entrusted to Beaumarchais in June, 1776, seems clear: he meant it as a gift to the Colonies. Vergennes, on the other hand, was perhaps not unwilling that Beaumarchais should have it, in return for his services to the Foreign Office. See Wharton, I. 376-84; also, M. D. Conway in the *Athenaeum*, 1900, pt. I. 305-7.

unwarrantably suspicious of Deane's motives, while Deane was right as to the balance of the supplies, which was a considerable one. The French government, however, which at this very moment was defending itself before Europe against the indignant charges of the British government, of having clandestinely aided the Colonies while the two powers were still ostensibly at peace, could not afford to admit that Lee was right to any extent. The result was that Gérard soon took up the cudgels for Deane, with the natural result of offending Lee's brother, Richard Henry, who revenged himself by blocking all the envoy's attempts to get a declaration from Congress on the subject of a separate peace.[18a] Fortunately for Gérard, early in January Thomas Paine, who was secretary of Congress, published some articles in the *Pennsylvania Packet,* sustaining Lee's case with citations from official documents, which action forced Congress to declare its position on both issues at once. On January 12th, accordingly, it passed a resolution disavowing Paine's lucubrations and declaring

[18a] For Lee's change of opinion of Gérard in consequence of the latter's intervention in behalf of Deane, *vd.* his *Letters,* I. 423, 427, II. 114, 119-20, and 124. Gérard's endeavor, however, to fasten upon Lee the stigma of disloyalty to the alliance falls flat in light of the evidence. See especially Lee's letter of December 16, 1778, to the *Pennsylvania General Advertiser, ib.,* 457-62, where he satisfactorily explains his relations with the British agent Berkenhout and his sentiments on the subject of a separate peace.

itself convinced "by the most indisputable evidence" that the supplies furnished by Hortalez and Company "were not a present" and that "His Most Christian Majesty . . . did not preface his alliance with any supplies whatever sent to America"; and two days later it disavowed explicitly the notion of a separate peace.[19]

In other words, it was settled, and by the strenuous insistence of the French government itself, that Congress could agree to no peace or truce

[19] *Journals of the Continental Congress*, XIII. 54-5, 62-3. "Whereas it hath been represented to this House by the Hon. Sieur Gérard, minister plenipotentiary of France, 'that it is pretended the United States have preserved the liberty of treating with Great Britain separately from their ally, as long as Great Britain shall not have declared war against the king, his master'; therefore, *Resolved, unanimously,* That as neither France or these United States may of right, so these United States will not, conclude either truce or peace with the common enemy, without the formal consent of their ally first obtained." It will be noted that the advocates of a separate peace finally based their case on the fact that there had never been a formal declaration of war upon France by Great Britain. The resolution which Gérard had desired to see adopted reprobated the condemned opinion very strongly, but it was superseded by the resolution just quoted, p. 62. The action of Congress, nevertheless, elicited some criticism. Thus a writer in the *Pennsylvania Packet* of Mar. 18, 1779, while denouncing the Lees as men of "base principles," charges that M. Gérard has altered the Treaty of Alliance from its original form. The charge is repeated in the same journal of Apr. 8, where great disfavor is expressed with the treaty with France as compared with the one published "in our papers" nine months earlier. "In the first treaty, by one of the articles America had the right to withdraw herself from the war, provided she did not relinquish her independence."

with Great Britain—though it might "listen to overtures"—*without the consent of France;* while three months later, France agreed, in turn, that she would not consent to such a peace or truce till Spain would do the same, or at any rate, till Spain had obtained Gibraltar. Nor is M. Doniol's contention that the two developments were quite unconnected in the conscious intention of the French government necessarily sound simply because the Congressional interpretation of the Treaty of February 6th came first, since Vergennes was well aware from a much earlier date that Spain would enter the war only on condition that her objectives be made a *sine quâ non* of peace. And that the two developments were connected in practical effect is obvious.

But, then, did the French government by acceding to the Treaty of Aranjuez commit anything worse than a merely *technical* breach of its engagements with the United States? Did it not, on the contrary, take a step that was actually beneficial to the United States in forwarding the cause of independence? For though Spain herself was not allied with the United States, yet once she had entered the war her forces were turned against the common enemy. To begin with, I think it highly questionable whether, all things considered, Spanish aid really paid for itself. Thus the opportunities of the campaign

[19] Doniol, III. 762, fn. 2.

of 1778, when American enthusiasm for the alliance was fresh and the new French marine was in the pink of condition, were frittered away to no small extent because of the French government's efforts to accommodate its course to the exigencies of the Spanish monarch's whimsy mediation.[20]   Again, the campaign of 1779 netted nothing, largely because France yielded again to Spain's views, which were for an invasion of England.[21]   Again, in 1780 Spain, save for the forces she maintained at Minorca, in the Floridas, and along the Mississippi, was practically out of the war.[22]   Only in 1781, when the siege of Gibraltar was formed, was Spain's assistance more than negligible, when indeed it was not worse.   In short, Montmorin's prediction that Spain's demands would be more embarrassing than her help was worth was substantially fulfilled.[23]

Waiving, however, the question of the value of Spanish aid, can it yet be contended that the Convention of Aranjuez signified any real danger to American interests?   Verbally the United

[20] See, for instance, Montmorin to Vergennes, June 22, 1778, *ib.*, 472-3; also *ib.*, 503-7 and 590.

[21] *Ib.*, IV. 322-4.   Florida Blanca was of the opinion that "it was possible to strike the English so they would feel it only in England," *ib.*, III. 674.   Charles III was convinced that the war must begin with a *grand coup* such as a descent upon England, *ib.*, 665.   See also Florida Blanca's plan of operations of Feb. 26, 1779, *ib.*, 688-91.   For La Fayette's connection with the plan of descent and the failure of the project, see *ib.*, IV. ch. V.

[22] The Spanish court was at this time engaged in informal and

States were bound by article VIII of the Treaty
of Alliance not to make peace till France gave
the word, but morally their obligation would be
fulfilled the moment Great Britain was willing
to accord them independence and their ally an
unconditional peace; and certainly Vergennes
himself must have foreseen that the Americans,
despite the secrecy of the Treaty of Aranjuez,
would not be easily hoodwinked into prolonging
the war once England manifested a disposition
to grant the terms just described. The real danger of the Convention of Aranjuez from the
point of view of American interests sprang from
its *secrecy* taken in connection with the fact that
France was to exert a powerful influence upon

unavowed negotiations with the English emissary Richard Cumberland, Lord George Germaine's private secretary. See ch. XII,
infra.

[23] For a rather more favorable estimate of Spanish participation
in the war, see Francois Rousseau in *Revue des Questions historiques,* LXXII. 444 ff. See also Florida Blanca's "Apology"
for his administration, William Coxe, *Memoirs of the Kings of
Spain* (London, 1813, 3 vols.), I. App., 331-44. Even in Congress,
which on the whole was not favorably disposed toward her, Spain
had one or two defenders. Thus we find Witherspoon of New
Jersey saying, in Aug., 1782: "Some gentlemen had underrated
the services of Spain. She had done much. She had entered into
the war with the common enemy. We had derived as much advantage from her exertions as if she had agreed to the treaty of
Alliance. . . . Besides this she had aided us with money, opened
her ports, and admitted us to trade to Havannah," *Thomson
Papers* (N. Y. Hist'l Soc. Cols., 1878), pp. 90-1. See also a
speech by Madison to much the same effect early in 1783, *Writings*
(Ed. Hunt), I. 418-9.

Congress in shaping the terms upon which that body would consent to peace. For at the outset it was a compensating consideration that, in proportion as Vergennes had insisted upon the indispensability of France's consent to America's making peace, so by the same token, he had insisted upon the indispensability of America's consent to France's making peace, and had therefore bound himself to give respectful heed to the American interpretation of the reciprocal engagements of the allies. Eventually, however, by the Instructions of June 15th, 1781, Congress surrendered outright to the French ministers the control thus given it over the final peace. There can be little doubt, I think, that Congress' ignorance of the Treaty of Aranjuez ought to be reckoned as one of the circumstances explaining this surrender.[24]

The issue thus finally becomes whether the Instructions of June 15th were in the circumstances a menace to American interests—and this issue can wait. For the moment, we turn back to review briefly the story of the ultimatum of April 3rd, 1779, upon the rejection of which by Great Britain the Convention of Aranjuez still left Spain's entrance into the war contingent.

Great Britain's answer to the suggestion of a

[24] See Chapter XIII, *infra.*

truce involving a tacit recognition of American independence and her evacuation of American territory did not reach Madrid till March 27th, but when it at last arrived it was found to be explicit to the point of insult: Great Britain could not recognize the right of France "to confound her own affairs with the pretended interests of those whom she affects to call her allies," or to dictate "in what manner His Britannic Majesty should exercise his liberty of reëstablishing his authority over his own dominions."[25] Yet notwithstanding this language, which he admitted was "hardly satisfactory," Florida Blanca, pleading as always the necessity of continuing the deception of England,[26] proceeded to draft the ultimatum just referred to. In essence, what this ultimatum proposed was a truce of indefinite duration in America during the continuance of which England should remain in possession of the territory she still held there, including New York City and Rhode Island.[27] Vergennes' dismay at these propositions, when he learned of them on April 12th, may be imagined: "The more we examine them and weigh them," he wrote Montmorin, "the less do we see any way of reconciling them with what the king owes himself or his new allies." Nor, unfortunately was this the worst of the matter, for by leaving the British forces mingled with the American population at

[25] Doniol, III. 746-8.
[26] Ib., 748-9.
[27] Montmorin to Vergennes, Mar. 29, ib., 798-9.

some of its most important centers, the Spanish proposals still kept open a way for England's conciliation of her alienated subjects. "Endeavor, I pray you," he continued earnestly, "to prevent any further condescensions of the sort, for they can only be fatal to the dignity of the king, and the humiliation resulting from them the king his uncle will necessarily share."[28] On April 12th, 20th, and 29th and again on May 14th, Vergennes gave vent to vehement and even bitter protestations against the action that the Spanish government had so unwarrantably taken, in the very face of its repeated promise "to guard the honor of France as it would that of its own crown and country."[29] But one thing Vergennes had not counted upon—the obstinacy of the king of England, who, blissfully unaware that he had been presented with the opportunity of shattering not only the French-American alliance but the Family Compact as well, still adhered to his resolution to bring his rebellious subjects to their knees. On May 17th, Montmorin, breathing a sigh of relief, wrote Vergennes that England had repelled the Spanish ultimatum and that the Spanish fleet would soon join the French. Yet Montmorin's despatch containing this welcome news sounded also the now familiar note of warning: "We ought however not conceal from our-

[28] *Ib.*, 767-8.
[29] *Loc. cit.* and pp. 770 and 801-3.

selves, Monsieur, how little interest Spain takes in the United States of America; we shall certainly have evidence of this in the course of the war but especially when the question shall arise of concluding peace."[30]

[30] *Ib.*, 771. Beaumarchais in writing Vergennes commented upon Spain's entry into the war in characteristic vein: "Si le livre est aussi fort que la préface a été longue, nous devons voir de belles choses de cette nation-là; mais, je ne sais pourquoi, j'ai toujours un petit glaçon dans le coin de ma cervelle étiqueté *Espagne*. J'ai beau faire, je ne parviens pas à échauffer cette idée-là," *ib.*, IV. 446.

CHAPTER X

THE MISSISSIPPI AND THE WESTERN LAND QUESTION

The claim of the United States during the Revolution to extend to the Mississippi was based upon both sentiment and interest. Rebels against the authority of the British Empire could not have taken an impoverished view of their future; and at the beginning of the war at least the spirit of Continentalism, forerunner of Manifest Destiny, was abroad in the land. The Earl of Cork had proclaimed that "the ball of empire was rolling westward and would stop in America" and the prophecy was now repeated, while in confirmation of it were cited "the growing millions of western world." That such a spirit should treat the idea of being "shut up within the Mountains" with impatience was inevitable.[1]

[1] The Earl of Cork's words are reminiscent, perhaps, of Bishop Berkeley's famous lines in his essay on *The Prospect of Planting Arts and Learning in America:*

"Westward the course of empire takes it way;
The first four acts already past,
A fifth shall close the drama with the day:
Time's noblest offspring is the last."

One of the earliest forecasts by an American of the "manifest

And the view that sprang in the first place from enthusiasm found ready support from sober calculation. The original belief seems to have

destiny" of this continent was that of John Adams, in a letter written in 1755: "Soon after the Reformation a few people came over into this new world for conscience sake. Perhaps this apparently trivial incident may transfer the great seat of empire into America. It looks likely to me: for if we can remove the turbulent Gallicks, our people, according to exactest computations, will in another century become more numerous than England itself. Should this be the case, since we have, I may say, all the naval stores of the nation in our hands, it will be easy to obtain the mastery of the seas; and then the united force of Europe will not be able to subdue us." *Life and Works of John Adams* (Boston, 1856, 10 vols.), I. 23. The prophecy of naval supremacy for America is strikingly like that of Vergennes twenty years later: *vd. supra,* ch. III, 67-8 and note. Less than three years after Adams, James Wolfe was writing his mother from Louisbourg, thus: "These colonies are deeply tinged with the vices and bad qualities of the mother country; and, indeed, many parts of it are peopled with those that the law or necessity has forced upon it. Notwithstanding these disadvantages, . . . this will, some time hence, be a vast empire, the seat of power and learning." Beckles Willson, *The Life and Letters of James Wolfe* (London, 1909), p. 395. The outbreak of the Revolution naturally enhanced the vision of imperial greatness entertained by the friends of America. In this connection various expressions in Dr. Richard Price's famous pamphlet entitled *Observations on the Nature of Civil Liberty and the Principles of Government and the Justice and Policy of the War with America* (London, 1776) are interesting: see pp. 21 ffg. Price concludes that, "It is probable that the Americans in fifty or sixty years will be double our number and form a mighty empire consisting of a variety of states, all equal or superior to ourselves." In the same connection an extract from the Antigua *Gazette* of Sept. 10, 1777, is interesting. In what purports to be a "Circular Letter" delivered by a ministerial messenger to the different foreign ambassadors resident at Lon-

been, at any rate it was the view of Franklin
and Deane, that the lands west of the Mountains
were subject to the disposal of Congress to meet
the expenses of the common effort.[2]   Later, with

don, warning is given that it is obviously "the common interest of
Europe to annihilate America," which is destined to rival all
countries in production, to undermine their commerce by means
of free navigation, and to draw off their population in the way of
emigration.   The British territory in America is estimated at
718,592,000 acres, capable of supporting 145,918,400 people, or
twenty-six million more than Europe.   The phrase above quoted,
"the growing millions of the western world," is from a letter in
the *Pennsylvania Packet*, No. 144, postscript.   See also in the
same journal, No. 147, an extract from a sermon by John
Lathrop, American pastor of the Second Church in Boston:
"America has every natural advantage. . . . A coast three thous-
and miles in length and a breadth as yet unexplored. . . . The
united wisdom of North America should be collected in a
general congress of all the colonies."   The date of the sermon was
June 6, 1774.   See also the Boston *Evening Post and General
Advertiser* of June 26, 1779: "We are now upon the stage of
America, have an arduous task to perform, we act not only for
ourselves but for remotest posterity.   The political misery or
happiness of millions unborn depends on the conduct of our
public measures at this day."   These words occur in a plea in
support of the right of Congress "to ascertain and fix the limits
of those states that claim to the Mississippi or South Sea."

   [2] The first form of the Articles of Confederation as reported to
Congress was in the hand of Franklin.   Article XI of this draft
provided that all purchases of lands from Indians were to be
made only with the consent of Congress, that Congress was to
have authority to determine Indian boundaries, and that "all
purchases from them [the Indians] by Congress [were to be] for
the general advantage and benefit of the United Colonies," *Complete Works of Benjamin Franklin* (Ed. Bigelow, N. Y., 1887-8,
10 vols.), V. 552-3.   Article XVIII further gave Congress the
power to limit "the bounds of those Colonies which by charter or
proclamation, or under any pretence are said to extend to the

the rise of the principle of State Sovereignty, narrower views obtained sway and the conviction became general that these lands were the property of particular states.   Yet even so, all states still retained an interest in having these lands kept open to settlement by their citizens and in seeing their frontiers secure, both of which objects would have been jeopardized had a foreign power obtained control of the region in question and of the Indian tribes there.   Finally, by yet another turn of the wheel of public opinion, from 1781 on the prospect developed that the states credited with the sovereignty and ownership of these lands would surrender their claims to the Confederacy at large.   Once more the interest of all states in seeing the American title established became what it originally had been.

What, then, was this title?   As I have just hinted, it was twofold: that of the American Peo-

South Sea."   This clause gave rise to a debate, Aug. 2, 1776, which marks the beginning of the struggle between the "landless" states, headed by Maryland, and the "landed" states, headed by Virginia, and which ended five years later in the acts of cession of western territory to the Confederacy.   Chase of Maryland "denied that any colony has a right to go to the South Sea." Harrison of Virginia thereupon inquired, "How came Maryland by its land, but by its charter," and added: "By its charter, Virginia owns to the South Sea."   Huntington of Connecticut was all against "mutilating charters."   Stone of Maryland contended for the right of the small colonies to "happiness and security," and that "they would have no safety if the great colonies were not limited."   The clause was stricken out in committee. *Life and Works of John Adams,* II. 501-2.

ple to the region in question, and that of certain states. True, these two titles were mutually conflicting, and true also, the peculiar titles of some of the states conflicted with those of other states; and doubtless, if the matter were one to be resolved dialectically, this fact would have serious consequences. The question raised, however, is not one of logic but of law; and it has accordingly to be remembered that in the analogous case of real estate, titles that conflict are often consolidated to produce a title that is unimpeachable. It is therefore not inconceivable that while, on the one hand, no state had a perfect title against either the United States or her sister states to western domain, yet, on the other hand, the titles of all parties combined exhausted the legal rights to the region.

The states that held individual claims to domain west of the Mountains were Massachusetts, Connecticut, New York, Virginia, the Carolinas, and Georgia. The claims of Massachusetts, Connecticut and New York were confined to territory north of the Ohio river; that of Virginia, the most sweeping of all, was to the whole of this territory, and also to the region south of the Ohio that today comprises the state of Kentucky; those of the Carolinas and Georgia were, roughly, to the lands lying between their present western boundaries and the Mississippi river. The foundation for these claims, save that of New York

who based hers on a pretended overlordship over
the Iroquois Indians and their conquests, was in
all cases furnished by the "sea-to-sea" clauses
of the colonial charters as curtailed by the Treaty
of 1763, which made the Mississippi river the
western boundary of British America.³ As I

³ As noted immediately below, England based her case against
France in the dispute leading to the last French and Indian war
partly upon the colonial charters, and undoubtedly this dispute more than anything else made the colonies aware and confident of their charter claims to the Mississippi boundary. Yet
it is interesting to observe that the English cartographer Bollan
complained that his predecessors, Popple (in 1732), Keith (in
1733), Oldmixon (in 1741), Moll (at several dates), and Bowen
(in 1747) had all been recreant to British interests, Winsor,
Mississippi Basin, p. 331. The rising dispute, however, soon
registered itself in the views of the mapmakers. Thus Bowen's
map of 1749 is entitled: "A Map of the British-American Plantations . . . including all the back settlements *in the respective
provinces as far as the Mississippi.*" The famous Mitchell Map
of 1755 also recorded British official pretensions, which in turn
were supported by citations of Mitchell's and Bowen's maps.
On the other hand, Evans' map of the same year set the western
boundary of Virginia at the Mountains; while as late as 1777,
French mapmakers applied the term "Louisiana" to the region
between the Alleghenies and the Mississippi. See generally
Winsor's *Narrative and Critical History*, V. 79-86, and 235. Certain other occurrences also, lying between 1754 and the outbreak
of the Revolution, tended to confirm Virginia's charter pretentions. Thus Governor Dinwiddie, in 1754, made promises of land
to the Virginia soldiers, while a convocation of the chiefs of
the Cherokee and Choctaw Indians at Charleston the same year
recognized the right of the Virginia and Carolina governments
to establish magazines among them, and certain other rights of
apparent suzerainty. The legal significance of the Proclamation
of 1763, restraining settlements westward of the mountains, is
doubtful (see *infra*), but the discussion concerning it was calcu-

have just pointed out, the fact that these claims in some instances overlapped was not necessarily fatal to them as against third parties. There were other obstacles to their admission, however, that were more formidable.

The two nations against whose pretensions it was requisite for the states to secure their claims were Spain and Great Britain. The latter power,

lated again to arouse public attention to the question of where the western boundary of the colonies lay. Also, the Proclamation was constantly being transgressed or officially waived. "I have had, my Lord," wrote Lord Dunmore in his Report to Lord Dartmouth of December 24, 1774, "frequent opportunities to reflect upon the emigrating spirit of the Americans since my arrival to this government. There are considerable bodies of inhabitants settled at greater and less distances from the regular frontiers of, I believe, all the colonies. In this colony, proclamations have been published from time to time to restrain them; but impressed from their earliest infancy with sentiments and habits very different from those acquired by persons of a similar condition in England, they do not conceive that government has any right to forbid their taking possession of a vast tract of country, either uninhabited or which serves only as a shelter to a few scattered tribes of Indians. Nor can they be easily brought to entertain any belief of the permanent obligation of treaties made with those people, whom they consider as but little removed from brute creation." R. G. Thwaites and Louise P. Kellogg, *Documentary History of Dunmore's War,* p. 371. See also *ib.,* pp. 369-70 and footnote 91, also p. 5, footnote 8, for data with reference to the Treaty of Fort Stanwix (1768) and the Walpole Grant of 1769, both of which transgressed the principle of the Proclamation of 1763. On the eve of the Revolution occurred Lord Dunmore's War which gave rise to an acrimonious dispute between Dunmore and the proprietary governor of Pennsylvania, John Penn, with reference to Virginia's western claims. It was the forerunner of later disputes, in the course of the Revolution, between the states with fixed western boundaries and

having urged the charter rights of the colonies in partial support of her own claims against France anterior to the Seven Years' War, was perhaps estopped from denying that those rights had been all that she had once asserted them to be. The Treaty of 1763, however, had been followed by the Royal Proclamation of the same year, forbidding the colonial governors to make further grants of land in the region west of the Alleghenies.[4] The question therefore arises whether

those claiming to extend to the Mississippi. Dunmore, in his Proclamation of Sept. 17, 1774, asserted that Virginia's "ancient claim" was "founded in reason, upon pre-occupancy, and the general acquiescense of all persons," but makes no mention of Virginia's charter rights, Force's *American Archives,* 4th series, I. 790-1. Finally, in the Virginia Constitution of 1776, it is provided that "the western and northern extent of Virginia shall in all respects stand as fixed by the charter of King James I in the year 1609 and by the public peace between the courts of Great Britain and France in the year 1763." For Virginia's championship of the charter claims and Maryland's opposition to them, see *Collections of the New York Historical Society,* 1878 (Thomson Papers), *passim.*

[4] The text of the Proclamation of 1763 is to be found in the *Annual Register* for that year, pp. 208-13, and in Force's *American Archives,* 4th series, I. 171-5. The salient clause is the following: "We do . . . declare it to be our royal will and pleasure . . . that no governor or commander-in-chief of our other colonies or plantations in America do presume for the present, and until our further pleasure be known, to grant warrant of survey or pass patents for any lands beyond the heads or sources of any of the rivers which fall into the Atlantic from the west or northwest; or upon any lands whatsoever which, not having been ceded to or purchased by us, as aforesaid, are reserved to the said Indians or any of them." The line actually drawn by Hills-

it was the purpose of the Proclamation to set a definite western boundary to such provinces as had thus far remained without one. The American advocates contended that this was not the case, that the intention of the Proclamation had been "not to take away but to restrain an existing right," of which therefore it furnished formal official recognition.[5] But this opinion, it seems clear,

borough in pursuance of the Proclamation made exception in favor of the Virginia settlements on the Great Kenawha. The ostensible purpose of the Proclamation was to pacify the Indians, but Hillsborough in 1772 admitted another motive, viz., to keep the populace under the restraint of the seaboard authorities. A third motive, possibly, was to discredit the colonial charters. Winsor, *Mississippi Basin,* 430-1. Winsor also implies that the Proclamation met with some contemporary protest. "The party of progress," he says, "called it a tyrannous check on the inevitable expansion of the race." I am rather of opinion, however, that such criticisms came later, when the general argument against England's American policy was being shaped up. This is certainly true of Burke's characterization of the Proclamation, quoted by Winsor as if contemporary, as an attempt "to keep a lair of wild beasts that earth which God, by an express charter, has given to the children of men." Both Washington and Franklin regarded the Proclamation to be, as its terms imply, a temporary measure, and this was probably the view generally held of it.

[5] Livingston to Franklin, Jan. 7, 1782, Wharton, V. 88. This important document is also to be found in the *Complete Works of Benjamin Franklin,* VII. 348 ff. Other important statements of the American argument on the territorial question are the "Instructions to Jay" of Oct. 17, 1780, in *Journals of the Continental Congress,* XVIII, 935 ff., and *Writings of James Madison* (Ed. Hunt), I. 82 ff.; and the "Facts and Observations in support of the several claims of the United States," presented

runs counter to the evidence. Thus in 1772, when Franklin and some associates sought a grant from the Privy Council of a tract of land on the Ohio and the argument was brought forward that the proposed grant contained "part of the dominion of Virginia to the south of the river Ohio," it was answered "that no part of the above tract is to the eastward of the Allegheny mountains and that those mountains must be considered as the true westward boundary of Virginia"; *and this arguments prevailed with the council.*[6] Two years later moreover the Quebec Act was passed with the proviso "that nothing herein contained relative to the boundary of the province of Quebec shall in any wise affect the boundaries of any other colony," notwithstanding which the southern boundary of the province was drawn along the Ohio.[7] We may admit the American contention that, since the Quebec Act was itself one of the causes of the Revolution, "to build anything upon it would be to urge one wrong in support of

to Congress, Aug. 16, 1782, *Journals of the Continental Congress,* XXIII. 471-524, and *Thomson Papers,* 102-41.

[6] *Complete Works of Benjamin Franklin,* V. 3 and 25-35. The opposition to the proposed grant was headed by Lord Hillsborough, President of the Lords of Trade. The authorship of the answer to Hillsborough's representations is usually ascribed to Franklin, but Professor C. W. Alvord contends that its author was Samuel Wharton of Philadelphia. See the *Nation,* XCIX. 220-1. Wharton may have stood sponsor for the answer and yet Franklin have been the author of it.

[7] Force's *American Archives,* 4th Series, I. 216-20.

another."[8] Nevertheless, the evidential value of the act as to the meaning of the Proclamation of 1763, the validity of which was never questioned, still remains.

And as against Spain the claims of the American states were weaker still. Spain desired, first, to keep the Americans back from her own possessions, and secondly, to restore her monopoly of trade on the Gulf of Mexico;[9] to both of which ends it was essential that she should withhold from the Americans the right, which in 1763 she had accorded the subjects of Great Britain,[10] of navi-

[8] Wharton, V. 88. In the debate on the Quebec Bill, Dunning contended that the measure was inconsistent with England's position in the Seven Years' War. "Consider," he said, "what it was for which you engaged in the last war: encroachments of the French upon our colonies. . . . You repelled force by force. They offered to you to withdraw from the south of the Ohio and retire to the north, making that river the boundary of the two colonies. No, you replied, the river of St. Lawrence is the boundary of Canada; . . . the tracts which you claim are parts of our colonies of Virginia, Pennsylvania, etc.; and we cannot grant away the certain and undoubted right of our subjects in such a manner." Yet this was precisely what Parliament was doing by the Quebec Bill: it was merging with Canada what England had always contended was no part of Canada. The Attorney-General, Thurlow, answered Dunning thus: "It is success in war that gives success in peace, and by no means the imaginary line drawn by a state in its colonies; nor have the limits now drawn anything to do with old Canada; . . . it is a new scheme, and by no means a restoration of those old limits the French once contended for." *Parliamentary History*, XVII. 1359 ff.

[9] See Chapter XIV.

[10] Art. VII of the Treaty of Feb. 10, 1763: "Provided that the

gating the Mississippi through Louisiana to its mouth. For by denying the Americans this right, so obviously essential to an agricultural population between the Mountains and the River, she would discourage the further immigration of Americans westward; while she would also be taking an excellent preventive measure against the appearance of American smugglers on the Gulf. And her desire to acquire the left bank of the Mississippi looked to the same ends. She had no use for the region simply as so much territory, but once it was hers, any question of American navigation of the Mississippi would be foreclosed.

But now be it noted that, in order to achieve her purposes in the Mississippi country, all that was necessary for Spain to do at the outset was to assert, not a title of her own to the left bank of the River, but merely that of her enemy, Great Britain, which thereupon of course she would be free to acquire by conquest if she could. She, therefore, no less than Great Britain, was able to plead in her behalf the Proclamation of 1763, while, unlike Great Britain, she was not estopped

navigation of the river Mississippi shall be equally free, as well to the subjects of Great Britain as to those of France, in its whole breadth and length, from its source to the sea, and expressly that part which is between the said island of New Orleans and the right bank of that river, as well as the passage both in and out of its mouth." Chalmers, *Collection of Treaties*, I. 467-83; Martens, *Recueil de Traités*, I. 104-21.

from contending that the British title to the West was itself founded on conquest. Indeed, this was a natural position for both herself and France to take, since in the Seven Years' War both had contested the British charter claims by force of arms, as France had previously done diplomatically.[11] And with reference to the navigation of the Mississippi the position of the Spanish government was still more advantageous. The American argument was that the British right in this respect had devolved upon the United States in their capacity as proprietors of the former British holdings along the River.[12] In other words, the American claim to this right depended at best upon the further claim, which Spain did not admit, of American proprietorship of the lands in question. But furthermore, the view that the British right to use the Mississippi within territory subject to Spain comprised a servitude for the benefit of all lands adjoining the Missis-

[11] An extended presentation of the French case is to be found in the *Mémoire historique sur la Louisiane* of 1802. See ch. I. 9-13 and note.

[12] This was so, it was urged, both because the grant of right made His Britannic Majesty by article VII of the Treaty of 1763 was intended to run with the soil, was, in other words, an easement, and also because it was in accordance with the Law of Nature and of Nations, that the dwellers along the upper reaches of a river should have access to the sea through its lower reaches. See *Journals of Continental Congress*, XVIII. 942-3; also *American State Papers*, I. 252-3, where the argument is renewed by Jefferson as Secretary of State, 1792.

sippi was rejected by Spain. The right which
British subjects enjoyed to pass down the Mississippi through New Orleans and Louisiana, she
contended forcefully, was a privilege granted by
His Catholic Majesty solely to His Britannic
Majesty and would therefore not be claimable by
the United States even though they should make
good their claims to territory touching the Mississippi to the northward.[13]

But the claim of the United States to extend
to the Mississippi was also presented as the right
of the American People. This argument rested
upon the following propositions: first, that "the
rights of the king of Great Britain to America
were incident to his right of sovereignty over
those of his subjects that settled America"; secondly, that, since with the Declaration of Indepen-

[13] See Vergennes' Instructions of July 18 and Sept. 25, 1779,
to La Luzerne, *infra;* also Doniol, IV. 92. There can be little
question that Spain's position in this controversy was the correct
one at International Law. Thus, after considering the question
"whether rights of navigation are possessed by states over rivers,
or portions of rivers, not within their territory," in the light of the
most important data, W. E. Hall concludes: "From the foregoing facts it appears . . . that where rivers flowing through
more than one state are now open, they have usually at some
time either been closed or their navigation has been subjected
to restrictions or tolls of a kind implying that navigation by
foreigners was not a right but a privilege; . . . and that the
opening of a river, when it has taken place, having been effected
either by convention or decree, has always been consistent with,
and has sometimes itself formed, an assertion of the paramount
right of property," *International Law* (5th ed., London, 1904),
139-40.

dence the right of sovereignty of the king of
Great Britain over the people of America was
forfeited, all rights founded in that sovereignty
were forfeited with it; thirdly, that one such right
was the right to the backlands of America.[14] The

[14] Wharton, V. 88-9; *Journals of the Continental Congress,*
XVIII. 936-7; *Collections of the New York Historical Society,*
1878, pp. 138-9. The last citation gives the argument in the
form in which it was presented on the floor of Congress, Aug. 16,
1782. Arthur Lee and Bland of Virginia at once attacked it
vigorously. "Congress," said the former, "had no authority but
what it derived from the states. The states individually were
sovereign and independent, and upon them alone devolved the
rights of the Crown within their respective territories." This
was the position of the charter states. The position of the "landless states" was presented by Witherspoon of New Jersey, who
first attacking the charter claims as mutually contradictory and
conflicting and altogether extravagant, proceeded: "The several
states were known to the powers of Europe only as one nation
under the style and title of the United States. . . . Whether the
uncultivated wilderness on the frontiers should belong to one
state or another was a matter of little concern to the European
powers. The only argument that would weigh with them was
whether it was necessary for the security of the United States that
other nations should be excluded from that country, and particularly Great Britain, the enemy of these states." On August 27,
a petition was reported to Congress from the inhabitants of
Kentucky, which, declaring that they considered themselves as
"subjects of the United States and not of Virginia" and that
"the charter under which Virginia claimed that country had been
dissolved, asked Congress "to erect them into a separate and
independent state and admit them into the federal Union," *loc.
cit.,* p. 146. Lee declared that the countenance that had been
given the petition was "an insult to Virginia." Madison characterized "the supposition that the right of the crown devolved on the
United States" as "so extravagant that it could not enter into
the thoughts of any man," to which Witherspoon rejoined that it

argument thus traversed the general opinion that it was not the American People but the American States that had succeeded to the sovereign rights of Great Britain, but by the same token it was the more accordant with the philosophy of the right of revolution, which is a right of populations and not of political units; and it also did justice to the claims of the "landless" states, of which Maryland was the unyielding champion.[15] Diplomatically, too, it had the advantage of avoiding the difficulties that had their origin from the conflict of titles based on the colonial charters. On the other hand, plainly, it was adequate to establish the American title only as against powers that had recognized American independence, and Spain had not yet done this.

The question of the abstract validity of the American claims in the West is, however, a matter, after all, of secondary importance both in our own interest and in fact. Our interest is in the policy of France, which in turn was shaped with reference to these claims quite indifferently to speculative considerations. To anticipate some-

evidently could, since it actually had entered into his own thoughts and also "the thoughts of the petitioners and into the thoughts of very many sensible men at the beginning of the present controversy," *ib.*, 149. See also J. C. Welling in *American Historical Association Papers*, III. 167 ff.

[15] See H. B. Adams, "Maryland's Influence upon Land Cessions to the United States," *Johns Hopkins University Studies*, III. pt. I.

what the results of the inquiry to follow: So long as it was a question of pleasing the United States alone, France, having herself no territorial ambitions on the American continent, accepted the American pretensions without demur. Later however arose, first, the problem of bringing Spain into the war and, secondly, the problem of securing peace with Great Britain, once that power was prepared to accord the main objective of the war, namely American *independence*. Also, it was always a part of French calculations not to allow the United States to become too strong. The claims, therefore, that it had at first admitted, the French government came eventually to repudiate. Several questions are thus raised: 1. Could France act thus consistently with her engagements with the United States? 2. Was her repudiation supplemented by open championship of the interests of Spain along the Mississippi? 3. What light does her final attitude thrown upon the peace negotiations of 1782? In the pages to follow I shall endeavor to answer these questions.

France's engagements with the United States touching the territorial possessions of the latter were defined by articles XI and XII of the Treaty of Alliance, which read as follows:

XI—The United States and France guarantee each to the other, the United States to His Most Christian Majesty his possessions in North America forever; His

Most Christian Majesty to the United States their liberty, sovereignty, and independence, absolute and unlimited, as well in matters of government as of commerce, and also their possessions, and the additions or conquests that their Confederation may obtain during the war from any of the dominions now or heretofore possessed by Great Britain in North America, conformably to the 5th and 6th articles above written, the whole as their possessions shall be affixed and assured to the said states at the moment of the cessation of their present war with England. XII.—In order to fix more precisely the sense and application of the preceding article, the contracting parties declare that, in the case of a rupture between France and England, the reciprocal guaranty declared in the said article shall have its full force and effect the moment such war shall break out; and if such rupture shall not take place, the mutual obligations of the said guaranty shall not commence until the moment of the cessation of the present war between the United States and England shall have ascertained their possessions.

The first question that arises with reference to these articles is whether "the reciprocal guaranty" that by article XII was to be effective from the outbreak of the war between France and Great Britain extended to the *possessions* of the United States at that moment. The French government, after its change of position with reference to the pretensions of the United States in the West, contended that this guaranty extended only to the *sovereignty and independence* of the United States and that, with reference to the *possessions* and *conquests* of the United States,

His Most Christian Majesty's guaranty was not to come into effect till these had been determined by the final treaty of peace. As to *conquests* there can of course be no doubt of the correctness of this view, for the reason that the subject-matter of the guaranty would come into existence, if at all, *only* with the treaty of peace. The *possessions* of the United States, on the other hand, would at any particular moment, what there were of them, be part and parcel of the United States—*would, geographically speaking, comprise the United States.* It was therefore not unreasonable, to say the least, for the American advocates to contend that the guaranty extended by the treaty to the sovereignty and independence of the United States, and admitted by France to be effective from the outbreak of war between France and Great Britain, extended also, from the necessity of things, to the *possessions* of the United States. Furthermore, the guaranty in question is spoken of as *reciprocal.* But unless it extended to the *possessions* of the two powers it was not reciprocal, since it was only certain *possessions* of France that the United States guaranteed by any view of the treaty.

And such direct testimony as we have confirms this view of the matter. Thus, when the American envoys saw that they could not get an unconditional alliance and proposed, as a compromise, that the guaranty in the treaty of the indepen-

dence and liberty of the United States should go
into effect at once, Gérard, speaking in the name
of the Foreign Office, repelled the suggestion by
saying that the independence, liberty, and possessions of the United States must all stand on the
same footing in this regard; that as to all alike
the guaranty was contingent upon the outbreak
of war.[15a] And the conclusion to be drawn from
Vergennes' vehement protest against Florida
Blanca's action in proposing the *uti possidetis* for
the United States in April, 1779, is the same.
This, the French secretary declared, menaced
France's obligations to the United States at an
essential point, which however was the case only
on the assumption that France was already the
guarantor of the territorial integrity of the
United States.[16]

Yet suppose we admit, for the sake of the argument, that France did guarantee the *possessions* of the United States "against all other
powers" only from the close of the war, to what
extent are the engagements incurred by her in
the Treaty of Alliance relaxed? Undoubtedly
to the extent of relieving her from the necessity
of continuing the war with Great Britain for such
possessions, as distinguished from the *sovereignty
and independence* of the *United States.* On the
other hand, the concession does not relieve by one

[15a] Arthur Lee's "Journal," Lee's *Lee,* I. 388. For Gérard's later
view, see *Journals of the Continental Congress,* XXIII. 518-9.

[16] See Doniol, III. 802.

whit the incongruity of active championship by France of the right of Spain, as part of the price of bringing that power into the war and keeping her there, *to seize the possessions of the United States*. In short, the question of the possibility of France's satisfying Spain along the Mississippi harmoniously with her engagements with the United States resolves itself into the question whether the Treaty of Alliance recognized the United States as holding territorial possessions in the Mississippi country, possessions from which, as it subsequently developed, Spain desired to exclude them.

The fifth article of the Treaty of Alliance reads as follows:

If the United States shall think it fit to attempt the reduction of the British power remaining in the *northern parts* of America or the islands of Bermudas those countries or islands, in the case of success, shall be confederated with or dependent upon the said United States.

Here, as in article XI of the Articles of Confederation itself, was a provision looking to the possible accession of Canada to the Americans, or to its conquest, and to one or the other of the even remoter islands of the Bermudas, but entire silence with reference to the region of vastly greater importance to the United States lying to the westward of the Mountains.[17] The implica-

[17] This argument is from the Instructions of Oct. 17, 1780, to Jay, *Journals of the Continental Congress*, XVIII. 941-2. It is as-

tion could not possibly have escaped those who negotiated the Treaty of Alliance on the part of France, and especially since it had earlier been brought under their direct observation again and again. Thus in the outline of a treaty accompanying the instructions drawn up by Congress for "the American plenipotentiary destined for France," of September 17th, 1776, there appears a clear distinction between the portion of the continent thought to be involved by the Revolution and such outlying British dominions as Canada and the Floridas.[18] Again, in the project of a treaty which Deane drew up for the French government this distinction gives way to a specific guaranty to the United States of the "possession of all that part of the continent of North America which by the last treaty of peace was ceded and *confirmed* to the crown of Great Britain."[19] Somewhat later Deane also ap-

sumed throughout this document, which was largely the work of Madison, that the French guaranty of American possessions became operative with the Treaty of Alliance itself, that is, upon the outbreak of war between France and England.

[18] See art. IX of the Plan, *Journals of the Continental Congress,* V. 770.

[19] Wharton, II. 215-6, and footnote. And of like implication are the following items. On the occasion of General Gates' celebration of the Fourth of July at White Plains in 1778, the following toast was offered: "May our brethren in Canada, Florida, and Nova Scotia speedily enjoy the blessings of free states." *Connecticut Courant,* July 14, 1778. *The Pennsylvania Packet* of April 6, 1779, contains a letter from an American gentleman in France, dated Dec. 8, 1778, in which the writer, after reporting

proached the French government with a scheme
for obtaining money for the United States in
France on the basis of security furnished by western lands.[20]

a rumor that Great Britain had offered American independence
through the Spanish ambassador, adds the comment: "We cannot learn that these offers contain anything agreeable respecting
Canada, Nova Scotia, or the Fishery." Read in the light of the
great concern manifested in Congress for the fate of the region
between the Alleghenies and the Mississippi, such items are very
instructive.

[20] Deane proposed his scheme to Congress in his letter of Dec.
1, 1776, Wharton, II. 203-5. "The good and wise part" of Europe, he wrote, "the lovers of liberty and human happiness, look
forward to the establishment of American freedom and independence as an event which will secure to them and their descendants an asylum from the effect and violence of despotic power,
daily gaining ground in every part of Europe. From those and
other considerations . . . emigrations from Europe will be pro-
digious immediately on the establishment of American indepen-
dency. The consequence of this must be the rise of the lands
already settled, and a demand for new or uncultivated land; on
this demand I conceive a certain fund may now be fixed. You
may smile, and recollect the sale of the bear-skin in the fable,
but, at the same time, must be sensible that your wants are real,
and if others can be induced to relieve them, it is indifferent to
you whether they have a consideration in hand or in prospect."
Deane, it must be remembered, came from Connecticut. His
perfected scheme is embodied in his proposals, communicated to
Gérard, Mar. 18, 1777: "First, There shall be laid out in the most
fertile part of the country, purchased or to be purchased of the
natives on the banks of the Mississippi or Ohio, a tract of land
equal to three hundred miles square, which shall be appropriated
as a security for the hiring of money to the United States of
North America. Second, each subscriber or lender of money shall
have secured to him as many acres of that land as he shall sub-
scribe livres, no subscription to be received under 1,000 or 1,200
livres," etc. SMSS., No. 661.

Certainly France was adequately informed of the pretensions of the United States respecting the West. Yet not only is there no record of her having demurred to these claims, but, on the contrary, the evidence clearly proves that both Bourbon governments at first recognized them as valid, as least so far as the territory between the Ohio, the Mississippi, the Alleghenies, and the somewhat variable northern boundary of the Floridas is concerned. So when, in the course of his interview with the American envoys on December 12th, 1777, Vergennes raised the point that Virginia's charter claims, by extending to the South Sea, tended to "trench on Spain's claims to California," and the Americans pointed to the fact that by the Treaty of 1763 a western limit had been set to the Colonies at the Mississippi and suggested that this line be drawn from the source of that river, "this," says Lee in his *Journal,* "was admitted as adjusting the matter properly."[20a] Again, what could have been more explicit than Florida Blanca's assertion in March, 1778, that the Mississippi comprised "a boundary sufficiently definite and visible" between the possessions of Spain and those of the United States?[21] Indeed, it was exactly because he

[20a] Lee's *Lee,* I. 361.

[21] Montmorin to Vergennes, Apr. 10, 1778, Doniol, III. 22. And in the same connection note the implication of certain passages in Aranda's despatches to Florida Blanca of Feb. 23 and Mar. 23, 1778. "I incline," he writes in the former, "to the opinion

recognized this to be the case that the Spanish minister feared the United States to the degree that he did: the prescriptive rights of the United States, sanctioned as they were by France, made the situation irremediable. Vergennes, on the other hand, it will be recalled, was at great pains to allay these fears, but even so, he did not assert that the Americans were intruders in the region between the Mountains and the Spanish domin-

that the great question with the [American] commissioners will be as to retaining Canada and Florida, and that the Congress will make resistance, as it will not want the English for neighbors, but will wish to remain complete and absolute in all that part of North America." Sparks MSS., CII. In the latter occurs the following passage: "Still less will he [the king of Spain] displease the colonies after the signs of protection that he has given them, and being a new power which must come to be a formidable one and upon which he is to border alone and which would never pardon such a turning of the back," etc. The important point is that Aranda here recognizes the United States to be at that date a power bordering on Spanish dominions. Note also the following words from his despatch of Aug. 4 of the same year: "It seems to me that the intention of this Court cannot be to maintain that the new United States should charge themselves with the rest of the Northern Provinces, but that they should be limited to the thirteen confederated from the beginning." Thus the court of London may "avoid the disgrace of losing the whole of the continent of America." The contrast, it will be observed, is between the thirteen confederated Colonies and the northern ones. Another interesting document in the same connection is Franklin's letter of Dec. 12, 1775, to Don Gabriel of Bourbon: ". . . I think I see a powerful dominion growing up here, whose interest it will be to form a close and firm alliance with Spain (their territories bordering)." *Complete Works of Benjamin Franklin*, V. 548. Don Gabriel, therefore, was informed of America's pretensions in the West from the first.

ions On the contrary, he made the very distinction that was common with Americans, between the parts of America in revolt and such outlying regions as the Floridas and Canada; he cited "the vast expanse" of the existing dominion of the United States to prove that it would be ages before America would care for further accessions of territory; and he contrasted the Americans as "peaceable, unambitious *neighbors,*" with the "avaricious, implacable" British.[22] But the Spanish minister, unconvinced by the reasoning of the French secretary, at last came to the decision that it would be necessary for Spain to take the law into her own hands and expel the Americans from the banks of the Mississippi. He did not suggest, however, that the matter was one to be treated of with France, though the conquest of the Floridas, involving American *interests* but not American *rights,* was such a subject. And eventually the Treaty of Aranjuez was signed. Spain's apprehension of the United States had by this time reached its climax, as had also the anxiety of France to bring Spain into the war. Yet on the question of the western limits of the United States the treaty maintained complete silence.

[22] Doniol, II. 785; III. 51, 561. The argument, however, from the distinction made between colonies in revolt, on the one hand, and Canada and the Floridas, on the other, should not, in the case of Vergennes, be pressed too rigorously, since it does not clearly appear whether he regarded Canada as including Quebec as organized under the Act of 1774, though his recognition of Virginia's charter claims would tend to indicate that he did not.

CHAPTER XI

The views finally adopted by the Spanish government with reference to the Mississippi question apparently originated on this side of the Atlantic in the fertile brain of an Havana merchant, one Juan de Miralles, who having been forced by mishap to put into Charleston early in 1778 in the course of a voyage to Cadiz, later received a commission from the captain-general of Cuba to act as a sort of observer of affairs in the United States for His Catholic Majesty.[1]

[1] According to his letter of Feb. 13, 1778, to Galvez, Miralles had set out from Havana for Cadiz the previous Dec. 31, but had been forced by a leakage of the vessel bearing him to put into Charleston, Jan. 9. He had remained there since the latter date because of an interdict upon the departure of vessels from the harbor, due to the presence outside of a British blockading squadron, which had shown itself very unscrupulous in seizing neutral vessels. He intended to sojourn at Charleston till a favorable opportunity offered itself to continue his journey or to return to Havana. Meantime, he asked letters to Washington, Laurens, *et al.* His purpose in visiting Cadiz was to secure the monopoly of carrying negroes to Havana, the right of the existing monopolists being about to lapse. He would like to institute such a commerce from the Southern American states. Would Galvez urge his claims upon the king? As we have already seen, Florida Blanca had announced in September, 1778, that Spain then had,

"A typical Spaniard, infinitely zealous and well-informed in the interests of his court in this part of the world," Miralles came to Philadelphia with the idea that France should conquer Canada and that Spain should conquer "all that the English had acquired by the Treaty of 1763 in Florida and on the Mississippi"; but especially did he "give himself over to all the speculations which the possession of the Floridas and the exclusive navigation of the Mississippi could suggest." And the basis of these speculations was the conviction that sooner or later, the Americans were bound to become the enemies of Spain; that, indeed, this contingency was no remote one.[2]

Miralles' first care was to put himself in close relations with M. Gérard, who seems to have regarded his views, so far as they touched the interests of Spain, with entire complacency. Thus in his despatch of July 25, 1778, to Vergennes, heralding Miralles' appearance at Philadelphia, Gérard wrote:

I have persuaded him to report to his court that Congress would never consent from mere generosity to renounce the navigation of the Mississippi [which is]

---

or would presently have an agent in America to observe developments. I infer that the actual business of despatching such an agent was left to Galvez, who, seeing the opportunity offered by Miralles' accidental presence at Charleston, commissioned him to act in this capacity. The letter just paraphrased is to be found in the Sparks MSS., XCVII. Miralles did not appear in Philadelphia till July, 1778.

[2] Gérard to Vergennes, July 25, 1778, Doniol, III. 293-4.

necessary to serve as an outlet for the immense settlements which the Americans are proposing to make along
the Ohio and other rivers tributary to it; that the expedition commenced by Major Willing in those parts was
about to be followed up; that it had been suggested that
Pensacola be offered Spain, while what the English hold
on the left bank of the Mississippi be retained; that it
appeared to me important that His Catholic Majesty
should calculate upon this difficulty in advance; that the
only means of obviating it, as it seemed to me, was not
to put it in the way of the Americans to formulate demands in regard to the matter, that is to say, to dispense with their aid, indeed to forestall it, by seizing
these lands with Spanish forces alone.

"Don Juan," Gérard concluded, "feels that my
observations are correct and has promised me to
render an account of them."[3]

[3] *Loc. cit.* See also Miralles to Galvez, Aug. 20, 1778, Sparks
MSS. Here Miralles speaks of a plan communicated to him by
Patrick Henry, then governor of Virginia for an expedition
against St. Augustine, the ultimate objective of which was to
be the conquest of the provinces of Mobile, Mississippi, Pensacola, and Florida. The original author of the plan, which called
for the assemblage of three thousand men at Savannah, was the
Marquis de Brétigny, with whom and the president of Congress
Miralles discussed it at length. The latter treated the matter
rather lightly: it was good enough to kill time with over a bottle
of wine. None the less, Brétigny laid the plan before Congress
in French and reported that this body had sent it to the inter-
preter. Miralles expresses the opinion that the conquest will be
easy, but fears that American coöperation will give rise to
pretexts "injurious to the dominions of the king. I say," he continues, "the same as to the conquest of Pensacola, Mobile, Mississippi, and the other countries on the Mississippi river," etc.,
"because if the neighbors assist in the conquest they will surely
claim the use and free passage of this river, . . . so as to pass

But presently we find Gérard going far beyond this tone of disinterested criticism and becoming the avowed champion of the cause represented by the Spanish agent. For this there were several reasons: To begin with, diplomacy, unlike the law, recognizes no such category of questions as *res adjudicatae*. Again, as I have already pointed out, it was the most natural thing in the world for a Frenchman to take the position that England's title to the lands along the Mississippi was founded on conquest alone and was, therefore, open to conquest by an enemy. Yet again, Gérard was well aware of the anxiety of his government to meet the views of Spain at all possible

out to the Gulf of Mexico. It cannot but be apparent to the least informed person . . . how prejudicial this would be." Brétigny's plan was reported to Congress adversely by the Board of War, Oct. 31, 1778, *Journals of the Continental Congress,* XII. 1083; but was again brought before that body by a letter from Miralles Nov. 24, 1779, *ib.,* XV. 1301. This time the plan had the backing of the diplomatic La Luzerne and was also aided by the growing seriousness of the military situation in the South. On Dec. 16, accordingly, it was resolved "that General Lincoln . . . be . . . empowered . . . to . . . concert with the Governor of Havana, or any other person or persons properly authorized by His Catholic Majesty, such plan as shall in his opinion be best calculated to insure the reduction of the enemy's force in the state of Georgia . . . and for the conquest of East Florida." North Carolina voted "nay," and Georgia was not present. *Ib.,* 1388-9. More specifically, Congress' expectations were, that Spain would furnish six vessels of the line and five thousand troops, that Georgia would first be recovered, and that then the joint expedition would turn to Florida. The plan fell through when Lincoln was forced to surrender at Charleston.

points and, in fact, was under specific instructions to forward these views in several respects. Finally, Gérard had little understanding of, or sympathy for the American point of view as represented in Congress.[4]

This body, changing in membership and complexion of opinion from day to day, voicing a variety of local interests and personal animosities, deferring strangely, now to the views of popular committees, now to the pretensions of thirteen petty sovereignties, fell quite without the cut and dried categories of the French representative's experience as a diplomat and bureaucrat. Unfortunately, it was this fact precisely that M. Gérard most fatally failed to recognize. Following his controversy with Congress over the subject of a separate peace, it is apparent that Gérard pictured that body to himself as a species of *landtag* or *diet* of the sort that France in the case of her client states on the Continent sought to dominate by division. In the case of the

[4] A characterization of Gérard by Stormont occurs in the latter's despatch of Aug. 21, 1776: "M. Gérard is the most likely person for M. de Vergennes to employ [in dealing with Deane], and he could employ no man who would undertake such a commission with more alacrity. I have known him long. He has parts, address, and no small share of artifice. He was much trusted at Vienna by M. de Chatelêt, and he has the same spirit of intrigue, the same desperate policy, the same jealousy and implacable hatred of Great Britain." SMSS., No. 1350. It was partly this talent for intrigue that involved Gérard in difficulties with Congress.

Swedish Diet, for instance, it had been the "Hats" and the "Caps," the one the party of France," the other of Russia. So in the case of Congress it was "the Patriots," "the Friends of the Alliance," "the Friends of Peace," on the one hand, "the Swelled Heads" (*"Têtes Exaltées"*), "the Anti-Gallicans," "the Anglicans" on the other. That the latter and its leaders, Richard Henry Lee and Samuel Adams, contemplated treason to the alliance at the first opportunity, Gérard had little doubt; and as the same faction stood for the American claims in the West, it followed inevitably that those claims must be spurious.[5]

It is to be noted, however, that Gérard was shrewd enough to begin his proselyting in Spain's behalf with the representative of a state that had only a very moderate interest in the land question, Gouverneur Morris of New York. To Morris he urged the necessity of Congress' reassuring Spain and suggested, to that end, that

[5] Aside from an interesting but quite inadequate article by John Fiske in the *Atlantic Monthly*, LXIV. 220 ffg., the subject of Parties in the Continental Congress has received little attention in proportion to its importance. Some of the documents in the SMSS. are interesting in this connection; see Nos. 487, 729, 733, 737, 1616. There is also much scattered material to be gleaned from the press of the date; see, for instance, the *Pennsylvania Packet* of May 20, 1778, and *Rivington's Gazette* (Loyalist, N. Y. City), of Mar. 8, 1780. Still more valuable are the despatches of Gérard and La Luzerne; see the Index to Doniol, under "Congrès," "Gérard," "La Luzerne."

St. Augustine, Pensacola, and Mobile, and the exclusive navigation of the Mississippi be guaranteed her. The American replied, in characteristic vein, that he appreciated the necessity of setting limits to the Confederacy, and particularly to the South, since he was thoroughly persuaded that the virtues required by a republic were to be bred only in a hardy climate. Indeed, he himself thought that to hand over the navigation of the Mississippi to Spain from the mouth of the Ohio would be accordant with the best interests of the United States, inasmuch as it was the only measure calculated to keep the growing population between the Ohio, the St. Lawrence, and the Mississippi dependent on the republic. At the same time he was aware that many members of Congress regarded this as a privilege which appertained to the United States *of right* and that, furthermore, there were powerful private interests enlisted in maintaining this right.[6]

Forearmed with this not unfriendly warning, Gérard began a couple of months later approaching groups of delegates with vague insinuations bearing more or less remotely on the matter he had at heart. On December 22d he gave a dinner to which Miralles and several Congressmen were invited, in honor of Jay, who had just been

[6] Gérard to Vergennes, Oct. 20, 1778, Doniol, II. 72-3. As to the private interests involved, see Wharton, III. 135.

elected president of Congress. Sitting *"la pipe à la bouche,"* the participants spent several hours canvassing the subject of what sort of principles ought to govern the new republic in relation to other powers. Gérard admonished his hearers that all Europe suspected the American people of having inherited the aggressive and turbulent spirit of their ancestors and deduced the necessity they were under of proving the contrary. Fortunately they had an opportunity to evidence their love of justice by drawing "a permanent line of separation between the Spanish possessions and their own." A formal proposition to Spain, even though it were rejected, could but do them credit in the eyes of the world, by demonstrating their willingness to renounce both for themselves and posterity all ambition for conquest. His hearers acknowledged the wisdom of his remarks but protested that the American Constitution was incompatible with the spirit of conquest, notwithstanding which they felt confident that Congress "would furnish all the additional assurances that lay within its power." Gérard ought at this point, one would think, have brought forward the question of the navigation of the Mississippi. In point of fact, he kept discreetly silent on that topic. "It is," he wrote Vergennes, "a matter to be handled with secrecy and dexterity," for there existed in Congress, he had found, "the materials of a powerful party" opposed to Spain's interests.[7]

However, Gérard did not long continue in this balancing posture. As usual, Congress was at this date in great financial straits. The idea accordingly suggested itself to the French and Spanish representatives that that body might be induced to sell Spain its "recent conquests in Louisiana and the Illinois country"; and in a series of conferences held at Miralles' and Gérard's dwellings, this suggestion was broached to Jay and certain of his associates. How far negotiations actually proceeded on this basis cannot,

[7] Circourt, *Histoire de l'Alliance,* etc., III. 260-3. An earlier conference of similar purport is more briefly reported in Gérard's despatch of Dec. 12, Doniol, IV. 64-5. These conferences were followed by one with Washington, which is recounted in the despatch of Dec. 30: J'ai observé que l'Angleterre auroit vraisemblablement la plus grande répugnance à céder aux Etats-Unis des territoires qui ne font point partie intégrante des Colonies . . . que les Etats, n'ayant à cet égard qu'un simple droit de conquête, ne doivent naturellement pas s'attendre que leurs alliés faissent la guerre un jour de plus pour leur procurer un aggrandissement étranger aux principes fondamentaux du système de notre union, acquisition désagréée et pleine d'inconviens pour l'Espagne. On a paru sentir vivement la force de cette réflexion, et j'espère que cela contribuera à déterminer les offres à faire à cette Couronne. M. Washington m'ayant demandé quelle compensation le roy demanderoit si ses forces concourraient à la conquête du Canada, ma réponse a été que je l'ignorois, mais que j'étois convaincu qu'elle seroit analogue à lettre et à l'esprit du traité d'alliance." Apparently, while Gérard, in speaking of territory that "formed no integral part of the colonies" had the Mississippi country in mind, Washington thought he was referring to Canada. *Ib.,* 38.

unfortunately, be determined, as the published *Journals of Congress* are silent on the subject, but according to a letter of Miralles, written late in January, Congress had appointed a committee of one member from each state to consider his proposals, and he had been informed by a member that favorable action was all but imminent. Indeed, according to a report of later date, Miralles had named the enormous sum of two hundred million *livres* as the amount that Spain would be willing to pay for the territory she desired, an offer which, had it been made definite, should have been quite irresistible.[8]

Be that as it may, Gérard now began taking the frankest possible tone in discussing the conflict of interests between Spain and the United States in the West. "I stated," says he, reporting a conference that occurred late in January with a committee of Congress,

that the United States had no sort of right to the possessions of the English monarch which would not appertain equally to the king of Spain whenever he should become engaged in war with England; that their right was restricted to the territory which they possessed as English colonies; that in admitting the demand of isolated and scattered establishments, they contradicted the principles of justice and equity which had directed the Revolution . . . ; that . . . the king

[8] For the matter of this paragraph, see Miralles to Galvez, Dec. 28, 1778, and Jan. 22 and 29, 1779; also Rendon to Galvez, May 10, 1780, Sparks MSS., XCVII.

would never prolong the war a single day to procure for them the possessions they coveted; that such benefits were absolutely foreign to the principles of the alliance and especially to the policy of the United States toward Spain, as well as the interests of that power; that good feeling would never be established with Spain so long as she had so great reason for distrust.[9]

In a word, Gérard conveyed the idea that, if his government had ever accepted American pretensions in the West, it did so no longer. In this, however, he was altogether, and probably deliberately, misleading. For it is quite evident that the Foreign Office followed in the wake of its plenipotentiary's opinions in this matter rather than *vice versâ;* and at this date, the Office was still unaware that these had changed.

Early in February Vergennes' despatch of the previous October arrived at Philadelphia, announcing that France had accepted Spain's offer of mediation and urging that Congress proceed at once to formulate the conditions upon which it would consent to peace. The document gives every evidence that the secretary still regarded the United States as the rightful proprietors of the region west of the Alleghenies. Thus speaking of the disposition to be made in the treaty of peace of Canada, Nova Scotia, the Floridas, and the Newfoundland fisheries, it says:

[9] Gérard to Vergennes, Jan. 28, 1779, Circourt, *op. cit.,* III. 264-6.

It would be of advantage, Monsieur, that Congress' ultimatum should include, first, the renunciation of Canada and Nova Scotia, or at least of Canada and the fisheries along the coasts of Newfoundland; secondly, the abandonment in favor of Spain of the Floridas, or of such parts of these colonies as shall meet the favorable acceptance of Spain.

In other words, the distinction between the British colonies in revolt and such outlying regions as the Floridas and Canada still underlies the secretary's thinking about the territorial question; and, as we have already seen, the quite inevitable deduction from this distinction is recognition of the extension of the United States, at least between the Ohio river and the somewhat indefinite northern boundary of West Florida, to the Mississippi.

And of like implication are the secretary's words on the question of the navigation of the Mississippi:

I do not know [he wrote] and I am unable to previse the intentions of the court of Madrid on this subject. But I judge from the situation of places that the Americans will insist upon the liberty of navigating the Mississippi for the settlements which they propose to establish along the Ohio, and I assure you that it would appear astonishing to me should anyone attempt to refuse them this demand. However, there may be some considerations of a local nature that I am ignorant of on the other side of the question, considerations meriting attention. You are in position to obtain the requisite information whether from the Americans themselves or from M. Miralles; and if they appear to be of such a character as to justify the refusal of Spain, you ought to prepare the Americans for it with prudence and management. But in the contrary case, you ought to prevail upon the Spanish agent, not only to avoid charging his court with prepossessions on the subject, but also to lay the matter before it in such fashion that it will find no difficulty in according the Americans the consent which they will not fail to demand of it.[10]

Two weeks later, Gérard addressed Congress as a body on the subject of peace terms. Speaking of the necessity of meeting "the convenience of Spain," he was challenged to explain what he meant:

I answered [he writes] that His Catholic Majesty is too great and generous to desire an acquisition of territory . . . , that it was the security of his frontier and the prevention of trouble with his neighbors that gave him his only concern . . . , that the possession of Pensacola and the exclusive navigation of the Mississippi could alone fulfil this object.[11]

At this date Congress was still hopeful of a recognition from His Catholic Majesty, a hope which Miralles did not scruple to foster by disseminating misleading rumors.[12]   In general

[10] Doniol, III. 569-70.

[11] Gérard to Vergennes, Feb. 17, 1779, Doniol, IV. 110-4.

[12] See *ib.*, III. 294.   The earliest word to reach America of the alliance represented Spain as party to it, SMSS., 821.   The *Continental Journal and Weekly Advertiser* (Boston) of June 18, 1778, contained the following item from a London correspondent: "We can now assure the public that on Saturday a rescript was delivered from the court of Spain recognizing the independence of America."

terms, therefore, Congress was quite willing to declare its intention of meeting Spain's desires. Nevertheless, it was speedily made clear to Gérard by delegates from Virginia and North Carolina, that the navigation of the Mississippi was not a matter admitting of unlimited concession. The West, said they, was filled up with adventurers, fugitives from justice, bandits; this was not by the desire of the states, but it was a fact; the way to civilize these people was to tie them up with industry and property, for which access to the sea by way of the Mississippi was essential to them; that Spain should continue to hold the key to that river, and even to strengthen her control by the acquisition of the Floridas was all right; but at least she must accord the West a port of entry at its mouth and, preferably, a Mediterranean port as well; such a policy would be a boon to Spain's own commerce.[13] Gérard, though obviously impressed by these representations, hastened to disavow any special knowledge of Spain's commercial system; and meantime the matter of concession to Spain was becoming involved with other issues. With the general question of peace terms before it, Congress proceeded to develop principles meant to obtain for the United States as much as possible in all directions, the principle, for example, that the United States was entitled to independence plus all that

[13] Gérard to Vergennes, Feb. 18, *ib.*, IV. 114-5.

had incontestably belonged to the British provinces at the moment of the outbreak of the Revolution; that the very notion of independence
implied the possession of Nova Scotia; and so
on.[14] Noting the trend of opinion, the plenipotentiary brought forward the suggestion that the
fixation of boundaries be deferred till the negotiation of peace,—a suggestion designed to give the
mediating power a chance to make its voice heard.
The idea, he regretfully admits, found no
partisans.[15]

In fact, Gérard was soon to discover that his
troubles had only begun. From his first reception of the news of mediation he had urged that
Congress should hasten its work. In the middle
of March, however, that body began a four
months' wrangle over the question whether the
United States should refuse any peace by which
Great Britain did not accord them the privilege
they had enjoyed as her provinces of participat-
ing in the Newfoundland fisheries. The interest
back of this proposition was a local one, but vital
to the locality concerned.[16] It was also ably

[14] The father of this species of dialectic was Samuel Adams, *ib.*,
83, footnote 1, and 93, footnote 1.

[15] *Ib.*, 92.

[16] For some contemporary newspaper discussion of the propriety
of making the right to fish off the Grand Banks a *sine qua non* of
peace and of delaying Congress' decision in the matter of peace
terms for the benefit of New England, see the *Pennsylvania
Evening Post* of early July, 1779, and the *Pennsylvania Gazette*
of June 23. Of especial interest in this connection is a manu-

represented and soon had a powerful party at its
behest. And not only was the French government's program of facilitating peace put in jeopardy by the proposal to make the fisheries a *sine
qua non* condition, but the privilege sought could
by no stretch of the terms of the Treaty of Alliance be brought within its purview. Gérard's
blood was aroused as it had not been before, and
this time at least, it is impossible not to accord
him a measure of sympathy. "I told them," he
records in his report of May 14th, "that I was
convinced that England would grant them the
fisheries by the same title as that by which they
had previously held them, to wit, as subjects of
the British crown, but that they had no need of
the aid of France for that arrangement."[17]   At
this date he thought he had a considerable ma-

script in the office of the secretary of state of North Carolina,
unsigned and undated; but in the hand of Thomas Burke, a North
Carolina member of the Continental Congress at this period.
The document, for a transcript of which I am endebted to Mr.
Waldo T. Leland of Washington, comprises an account of the
proceedings in Congress from March to July, 1779, relative to
peace terms.   Burke expresses sympathy for New England's
interest in the fisheries but condemns the New England leaders
for the lengths to which they pushed their claims.   "Their
claims," he writes, "extended so far as to interfere with the
rights which must by the Law of Nations belong to Britain after
the war . . . and such rights as Britain is always jealous of in
so high a degree that she would make war at any time to prevent
encroachments on them."   It is to be noted that Burke does not
regard the territorial question as having caused delay.

[17] Doniol, IV. 138.

jority of the delegates with him but a month later he had to confess that "the Party of Peace" was in a serious predicament, due largely, he charges, to the hostile influence of Thomas Jefferson.[18] The crisis came the middle of July, when Jay and "two other well-intentioned delegates," "torn and battered by the fray" and foreseeing civil war if New England was longer opposed, advised the French representative that the game was up. In the interview that followed Gérard by turns pleaded with, threatened, and cajoled his interlocutors: France was a great power and would remain one even if America deserted the alliance, but that America, taking counsel of her sense of shame, would never do. The prospect, however dismaying, would never force the king "to submit his neck to the yoke they would fain impose upon him."

I added that some people appeared to entertain the wish of breaking down the relations of France with Spain, but that I believed myself able to predict that, if the Americans had the audacity to reduce His Majesty to the necessity of choosing between the two, his decision would not be in favor of the United States; and I saw with astonishment and grief that the guardians of America's welfare saw in public affairs only their own factional and local interests, as if the whole world would bow down before their capricious and changeable resolutions, confined within the circle of their own advantage, . . . that certainly the king would not con-

[18] *Ib.*, 135 ffg., 153-5, 165-7, 174-5, etc.

sent to consume the rest of his realm through a succession of years in order to procure a small increase of fortune for a few New England shipowners.[19]

These vigorous representations met with a degree of success. For in the instructions finally voted by Congress on August 14th the claim to a share in the Newfoundland fisheries was, so far as the anticipated treaty of peace was concerned, left to the chances of negotiation and its recognition made a *sine qua non* condition only of the commercial treaty with England which it was expected would follow the conclusion of hostilities.[20] But in doing this much, Gérard had done his utmost. The making a commercial treaty with England dependent upon American participation in the fisheries was to the prejudice of the tobacco states, whose further interests in the West, accordingly, Congress was less disposed than ever to sacrifice. By the same instructions of August 14th, the western boundary of the United States northward of 31° north latitude was asserted to be the Mississippi, and the recognition by Great Britain of this boundary was made an ultimatum.[21] A month later further

[19] Gérard to Vergennes, July 14, *ib.*, 177-81; see also, same to same, July 18, *ib.*, 219-23, where the plenipotentiary vigorously attacks the selfishness of individual states.

[20] *Journals of the Continental Congress*, XIV. 960-1. However, a treaty of commerce could have been entered into by the "unanimous consent" of the states, without Great Britains' having met the *sine quâ non*.

[21] *Ib.*, 958-9.

resolutions were adopted proffering the assent of the United States to His Catholic Majesty's conquest of the Floridas, on condition that he accede to the treaties between the United States and France, and "provided always, that the United States shall enjoy the free navigation of the river Mississippi into and from the sea." Also, the American negotiator was "particularly to endeavor to obtain" for Americans, their vessels and merchandise, a free port or ports south of the thirty-first parallel.[22]

On October 4th, John Adams, a reliable champion of New England's interests, was appointed the representative of the United States for the purpose of negotiating peace and John Jay, whose attitude on the boundary question was at this date somewhat ambiguous, American representative at Madrid.[23] Meantime, Gérard, broken in health and awaiting the arrival of his

[22] *Journals*, XV. 1084, under date of Sept. 17. On Oct. 13, Witherspoon of New Jersey, seconded by Governeur Morris of New York, moved that "the claim of a free navigation of the Mississippi" be receded from if the obtaining of it "be found an insuperable bar to the proposed treaties of amity and commerce between these states and His Catholic Majesty," *ib.*, 1168. The motion was voted down. Its ultimate triumph is discussed *infra*.

[23] *Ib.*, 1142-3. The result was arrived at, after a long contest, by a combination of Jay's and Adams' friends. See *ib.*, 1107 and 1113. It should be noted that Adams' known bias supplied the deficiency of his instructions with reference to the fisheries, while Jay's instructions on the Mississippi question made his personal opinion a matter of indifference.

successor with impatience, had become thoroughly disgusted with Congress. "The only way to save America from her madness and despite herself," he wrote Vergennes, "would be for the king to take advantage of the delay and conclude a peace along the general lines of the alliance."[24] The appointment of Jay afforded him a measure of consolation at the moment of his withdrawal from America, but even that was far from concealing his practical defeat.[25]

[24] Despatch of July 31, Doniol, IV. 201.
[25] See *ib.*, 211. For the exchange of compliments between Gérard and Congress that attended the former's leave-taking, see *Journals*, XV. 1072-4, 1085.

CHAPTER XII

THE MISSION OF LA LUZERNE

Compared with that of his predecessor, the mission of Louis XVI's second plenipotentiary to his republican allies was a pronounced success. In great part no doubt the circumstances of the war, as we shall see presently, made the Chevalier de La Luzerne's triumph inevitable, but this fact should not obscure to us that gentleman's own personal deserts in the least. Affable of address, good-natured, sensible, direct, bent on discovering and reporting the *facts* rather than a confirmation of his own *views* about things, experienced in meeting men on their own level, turning a discerning eye upon vulnerable points of character, and with a wholesome endowment of the spirit of *laissez aller,* La Luzerne acquired a personal ascendancy over Congress in matters touching the common cause of France and the United States that had never fallen to the lot of the acrid and pedantic Gérard, even in the honeymoon days of the alliance. His methods, it must be admitted, were not always unexceptionable, for if we are to believe his own accounts, he sought on occasion to "accelerate public opinion" as expressed in Congress by well-placed *douceurs,* whereas Gérard seems to have done nothing more reprehensible than to subsidize pamphleteers and writers for the papers. On the whole, however, the Congresses that the later envoy had to deal with were of higher average character than some that had come earlier; and his greatest triumph, the voting of the Peace Instructions of June 15th, 1781, was brought about with the assent and assistance of men who would have scored bribes.[1]

[1] For a characterization by the Englishman Wraxall, see Wharton, I. §84 (p. 425). "The Count de La Luzerne," wrote Gouverneur Morris, "is an indolent, pleasant companion, a man of honor and obstinate as you please, but he has somewhat of the creed of General Gates, that the world does a great part of its own business without the aid of those who are at the base of affairs," *ib*. For testimony to La Luzerne's services to the military establishment, see La Fayette to Vergennes, May 20, July 23, Oct. 4, 1780, and Feb. 1, 1781, SMSS., Nos. 1625, 1626, 1627, and 1633. La Fayette notes that La Luzerne pays no attention to the quarrels of private individuals and that he is held in the greatest esteem both in and out of Congress. Another item to the same effect is to be found in *Rivington's Royal Gazette* of May 3, 1780. In a letter of the previous month from a gentleman in Maryland to a correspondent in St. Eustatia, complaint is made that France has "gained an absolute ascendancy over the councils and government of the country." "M. Gérard . . . laid the foundation of French influence. M. La Luzerne . . . has steadily pursued the same steps." He advised Congress to pass the act of Mar. 18, 1780, redeeming the Continental currency at the ratio of 40 to 1. He "commands the majority of that body as much as the English ministry do that of the British Parliament. He has told them that if they mean to govern this continent, they must keep the people poor. . . . This, says he, is our maxim in France. . . . Poor men

At the outset, however, La Luzerne was forced to treat the situation before him more or less from the point of view of others, since his first instructions, bearing the dates July 18th and September 25th, 1779, were prepared by the French Foreign Office exclusively in the light of the information that had come from Gérard. We are not surprised, then, to find these despatches setting forth the following ideas: That there existed in Congress a party headed by the Lees and Adamses which, if it had not "already sold out to England," at any rate sought to establish principles diametrically opposed to the alliance; that this party stood for a separate negotiation with England to be followed by an alliance with that power, for the prolongation of the war for objectives outside the scope of the alliance, and for opposition to the interests of His Catholic Majesty; that since Spain was now a party to the war and thus a defender, at least indirectly, of American independence, it was the duty of Congress to satisfy that power in the matter of a fixed western boundary for the United States, the navigation of the Mississippi, and the con-

make the most obedient subjects and the best soldiers." For instances of La Luzerne's intervention with Congress in behalf of greater military efficiency, see Wharton, III. 683-5 and 803-5. Though he did not mingle in the quarrels of individuals and factions, he did combat openly Arthur Lee's candidacy for the secretaryship of Foreign Affairs, in 1781, and with success, securing the selection of Robert R. Livingston. See Doniol, IV. 597.

quest of the Floridas; that the United States had
no title to the lands adjoining the Mississippi,
but that that region was still English and therefore subject to conquest by Spain, and that Spain
ought to conquer it with a view to procuring
"clear, exact, precise, and unchangeable" limits
to the pretensions of the United States and especially "to forestalling the hopes of conquest to
which the provinces of the South might give
themselves over"; that the Americans probably
never had any right to navigate the Mississippi,
since "the boundaries of the British provinces
did not extend to that river" and it would be
absurd for them to claim the right on the score
of England's title; that the Floridas did not appertain to the United States under any title, but
that Spain had the greatest interest in reposses-
sing herself of this colony, which was so necessary
to insure her commerce on the Gulf of Mexico
from outside disturbance; that the guaranty
pledged by France to the United States by article
XI of the Treaty of Alliance was definitive only
as to their sovereignty and independence and
would extend to their possessions only from the
close of the war; that the French government
was confirmed in its espousal of Spain's interests
in North America by the consideration that it
was itself without interest in seeing that continent "enjoy the rôle of a power or in seeing her
in a position to give disquiet to her neighbors";

that, in other words, "the only purpose of our views with reference to the United States is that they shall be independent and peaceable."[2]

La Luzerne received the despatch of July 18th on January 20th, 1780, seven months after it was penned, and a few days later communicated its purport to Congress. At one point, however, he deviated conspicuously, if not from the letter, at least the spirit of his instructions. For while Vergennes' obvious intention had been that the whole influence of France should be brought to bear upon Congress in the interest of Spain, La Luzerne had been long enough on the ground to have discovered that this would never do. For the tone of advocating Spain's views he accordingly substituted that of impartially reporting them, with the result of implying that his own government's concern was limited to having brought to an end an unfortunate difference of opinion between its allies. But his discretion availed him little. For one thing, the very fact that Spain was now in the war for her own objects prejudiced his efforts; for it was well argued that the principal reason for concession to Spain

[2] The most material portions of these documents are given in Doniol, IV. 224-5 and 357-61. They are given complete in Circourt, *op. cit.,* III. 266-84. *Cf. Journals of the Continental Congress,* XXIII. 518-9, where is quoted an argument of Gérard's, dated May 22, 1779, on the guaranty. This, says the envoy, "ne commercera qu'à l'époque à laquelle les possessions des Etats-Unis auront été constatées par la cessation de la guerre."

had been all along to make her a party to the war, whether as an ally of the United States or not, and that this reason was now at an end. Moreover, as it chanced, La Luzerne was also under the necessity at this juncture of disclosing to Congress the final terms on which Spain had offered mediation to Great Britain and Vergennes' objections thereto. Such candor, on the part of our ally, as well his opposition to the principle of the *status quo,* was of course most reassuring, but the effects of the communication upon Congress' attitude toward His Catholic Majesty was naturally bad. When therefore, La Luzerne reported, it was learned that the Spanish monarch claimed the right to conquer the lands to the east of the Mississippi, he found himself confronted with "reasons already very powerful" to which were now added "unfavorable dispositions," and his endeavors to rebut the American claims, he frankly owned, "made little impression." This was early in February. A month later the Philadelphia *Gazette* published an account by Miralles of recent Spanish successes along the Mississippi. The effect of this disclosure was, La Luzerne wrote his government, great public excitement and a universal disposition to assert the American title to this territory. Thus it was pointed out that several states had sold and were still selling lands in the regions involved; that adventurers from the states were planting the banners of their provinces there; that George Rogers Clark had, in behalf of his state Virginia, been waging war against the British posts in the Northwest for nearly two years. In his perplexity La Luzerne turned to Miralles, who astonished him by disclosing the fact for the first time that he possessed neither any direct authority from Madrid nor yet any certain knowledge of its intentions. Nevertheless, the arrival at this moment of the despatch of September 25th forced the French representative to renew his efforts in Spain's behalf, which he did with the usual measure both of discretion and effect. Even delegates whose friendship to the alliance could not be questioned expressed regret that Spain should thus seek to sow seeds of discord between herself and the United States. Some months later La Luzerne reported the following words of a Virginia delegate, with reference both to the land question and the question of the navigation of the Mississippi: "We should be endeavoring to deceive Spain if, in treating with her, we obligated ourselves to make a renunciation that the nature of things renders impossible." In the same report, La Luzerne also noted that the delegates from the Northern states, though without direct interest in the matter, generally sustained the pretensions of the South.[3]

[3] For this paragraph, see Doniol, IV. 331-7 paraphrasing reports from La Luzerne between the dates Jan. 25 and Aug. 25,

La Luzerne's candid, if somewhat discursive, reports furnished his government for the first time with anything like a true picture of Ameri-

1780. Some further items of the same purport are given in P. C. Phillips, *The West in the Diplomacy of the American Revolution*, pp. 150-84, *passim*. On Aug. 22, the Virginia delegates laid before Congress instructions from the legislature of their state reasserting Virginia's charter claims and the American right to navigate the Mississippi, *Journals*, XVII. 755; *Papers of the Continental Congress*, No. 71, I. fol. 391. This action on the part of Virginia led Congress, on Oct. 4, to instruct Jay to adhere to his former instructions on the navigation question, and on Oct. 17, to accept the before cited letter of Oct. 17, prepared by Madison to urge the American claims in the West at length, *Journals*, XVIII. 900-2 and 935-47. In the latter document attention is paid to the Spanish claim of a right by conquest to some of the western country. It is answered: "1. That these possessions are few in number and confined to small spots. 2. That a right founded on conquest . . . cannot comprehend the circumjacent territory. 3. That if a right to the said territory depended on the conquests of the British posts within, the United States have already a more extensive claim to it than Spain can acquire, having by an important success of their arms obtained possession of all the most important posts and settlements on the Illinois and Wabash, rescued the inhabitants from British domination, and established civil government in its proper form over them. They have, moreover, established a post on a strong and commanding situation near the mouth of the Ohio; whereas Spain has a claim by conquest to no post above the northern bounds of West Florida except that of the Natchez, nor are there any other British posts below the mouth of the Ohio for their arms to be employed against. 4. That whatever extent ought to be ascribed to the right of conquest, it must be admitted to have limitations which in the present case exclude the pretensions of His Catholic Majesty. If the occupation by the king of Great Britain of posts within the limits of the United States, as defined by charters derived from the said king when constitutionally authorized to grant them, makes them lawful objects

can opinion on the Mississippi question. Furthermore, they arrived at Versailles at a time calculated to impart to their message considerable poignancy.

Throughout the greater part of 1780 and into the year following, His Catholic Majesty, practically withdrawn from the war, was engaged in peace negotiations with an English emissary. That Spain intended actually to abandon her alliance with France, Vergennes professed not to believe, but he very justifiably feared that she again sought to impose the *status quo* on the United States.[4] This, however, he wrote Mont-

of conquest to any power than the United States, it follows that every other part of the United States that now is, or may hereafter fall into the hands of the enemy, is equally an object of conquest. Not only New York, Long Island, and the other islands in its vicinity, but almost the entire states of South Carolina and Georgia might by the interposition of a foreign power at war with their enemy, be forever severed from the American confederacy and subjected to a foreign yoke." Madison was greatly assisted in this argument, as indeed were the American advocates generally, by the fact that at this period the today familiar rule of "effective occupation" had no place in International Law. See also the *New York Gazette* of July 15, 1780, where the writer calls for the early "conquest of the continent." Evidently, popular expectations in this matter still ran high.

[4] Vergennes to Montmorin, Mar. 31, Apr. 21, June 12, June 30, July 6, and Sept. 28, Doniol, IV. 450-1, 453, 467-84. It is not impossible that Vergennes took too charitable a view of the Spanish government's proceedings at this time. According to a recent account of Cumberland's mission, based on English sources, Florida Blanca offered, in return for Gibraltar, to withdraw from the war and "to pay besides in ships, treasure, and territory." On the British side, according to the same account, "four Cabinet coun-

morin, would be to sacrifice the honor of France, the substantial purpose of the war, and in the long run Spain's own interest. The English and Americans, left in juxtaposition, would reunite their forces. Incited by the English, the Americans would penetrate to the heart of Mexico, whose people they would encourage "to aspire to a sweeter government." Then indeed would Spain have cause to fear the example of American independence.[5] These arguments made as little impression upon the Spanish monarch and his minister as they had two years before. As late as the end of October, with New York City, the Carolinas, and Georgia now under British control, Florida Blanca openly defended the *status quo* for the United States.[6]

cils met on the business" and finally formulated the English terms, which however were still more exorbitant. M. A. M. Marks, *England and America, 1763-1783* (London, 1907, 2 vols.), II. 1196-7.

[5] Doniol, IV. 450-1, 453, and 480.

[6] *Ib.* 409. Vergennes comments on Florida Blanca's attitude in his despatch to Montmorin of Jan. 22, 1781, thus: "M. le Cte. de Floride Blanche croit, M., que nous serions fort heureux si nous parvenions à obtenir le *statu quo,* pour l'Amérique sep'le. Ce ministre n'a donc pas jetté les yeux sur la carte de cette partie du monde pour voir ce que ce seroit qu'un pareil *statu quo* dans le moment actuel; ou bien il désespère entièrement de notre cause, ou enfin il nous croit assez légers pour abandonner les Américains sans la nécessité la plus urgente. La vérité est, M., que si le Roi stipuloit l' *uti possidetis* à l'égard des Etats-Unis, il les mettoit entièrement à la merci des Anglois; il porteroit d'ailleurs atteinte à sa réputation; il autoriseroit les Américains à la défection, vers laquelle la cour de Londres dirige essentiellement toute sa politique." *Ib.* 510. The *statu quo,* in short, would represent the

But of even more importance than the selfishness of Spain's course in determining Vergennes' attitude at this time on the Mississippi question was the appearance of John Adams at Paris early in February, 1780. In the long run, this visit of Adams to the French capital resulted somewhat equivocally for American interests, since it furnished Vergennes a reasonable pretext to demand the Congressional Instructions of June 15th, 1781. Immediately, however, the impression of obstinacy and independence given by Adams, taken in connection with Spain's contemporary proceedings, led the French government to ratify the policy of *laissez faire* that had already been put into effect by La Luzerne with reference to the matters at issue between France's allies.

Adams had hardly arrived in Paris than he startled Vergennes with the suggestion that he considered it his right and duty, though a general peace was no longer in prospect, to communicate to the British government his powers to conclude with it both a treaty of peace and a treaty of commerce.[7] Vergennes, who connected Adams with that faction in Congress which, according to Gérard, had been bent on a separate peace with England, at once had visions of an

entire defeat of the purpose of the alliance. At this very date this was just what, Vergennes feared, impended. See following chapter.

[7] Adams to Vergennes, Feb. 12, 1780, Wharton, III. 492-3.

outcome to France's efforts in behalf of America
that would have been ironical in the extreme.[7a]

To be solicitous about a treaty of commerce before
peace is established [he wrote Adams] is like being busy
about furnishing a house before the foundation is laid.
In the situation in which America stands at present with
regard to England, to announce to that power that they
have forgotten her system of tyranny, her cruelties,
and her past perfidy, is discovering too great a degree
of weakness, or at least too much good nature, and
inviting her to believe that the Americans have an
irresistible predilection for her. . . . To propose a
treaty of commerce, which must be founded on confidence and a union equivalent to an alliance, at a time
when the war is raging in all its fury . . . , what is it
but to give credit to the opinion which all Europe enter-
tains, . . . that the United States incline toward a
defection, and that they will be faithful to their engagements with France only till such time as Great
Britain shall furnish them a pretext for breaking
them?[8]

But Adams, quite obsessed with the idea that
the time was ripe for an appeal to English public
opinion in behalf of peace and the recognition of
American independence, refused to be convinced
by the French secretary's logic, though he eventually deferred to the latter's urgent request to
postpone action on his opinion till further in-

[7a] See especially Vergennes to La Luzerne, June 3, Doniol, IV.
414.

[8] "Observations on Mr. J. Adams' Letter of July 17, 1780,"
Wharton, IV. 3-6.

structions from Congress.[9] But this was only
after repeated argument on the subject, and
meantime other irritating issues had arisen between the two men.

Thus in June the question came up of the
justice of the "40 to 1" Act of March 18th, to
foreign holders of Continental currency. Approached on the subject, Adams prepared what
was an able defense of Congress' action,[10] but to
it added in conversation with agents of the Foreign Office, some rather unnecessary frills:

The course Congress had taken was wise, indeed very
wise, just, very just; and those who complained of it
were either English emissaries or spies . . . [More-
over] the French had less reason for complaint than any
body else . . . since were it not for America, to whom
France should understand she was under the greatest
obligation, England would be too powerful for the
House of Bourbon, and Russia, Denmark, Sweden,

[9] Adams to Vergennes, July 26, *ib.*, 7-11. Congress disapproved
of Adams' efforts to communicate his powers to the British government. "Congress consider your correspondence with the Count
de Vergennes on the subject of communicating your plenipotentiary powers to the ministry of Great Britain as flowing from
your zeal and assiduity in the service of your country; but I am
directed to inform you that the opinion given you by that minister relative to the time and circumstances proper for communicating your powers and entering upon the execution of them is
well founded. Congress have no expectations from the influence
which the people of England may have on the British counsels. . . ." Huntington, President of Congress, to Adams, Jan.
10, 1781, Wharton, IV. 229.

[10] Adams to Vergennes, June 22, *ib.*, III. 809-16.

Portugal, and Holland would never be confederated against that power.[11]

A month later Adams wrote Vergennes, *àpropos* the despatch of Ternay and Rochambeau's expedition, to urge that a French fleet be maintained somewhere along the American coast over winter, emphasizing especially the value to be derived from thus keeping the British line of supplies and communications constantly menaced. Certainly this was a sensible idea enough. Unfortunately, in pressing it upon the French government not only was Adams invading the province of Franklin, but he brought to his self-assumed task the most egregious lack of tact. "Let the whole system of France be considered," he wrote, quoting from a current English circular,

from the beginning down to the late retreat from Savannah, and I think it is impossible to put any other

[11] Doniol, IV. 416 fn. This was on June 17, but more than a month earlier Adams had written to Genêt to much the same effect: "To suppose that France is sick of the part she has taken is to suppose her sick of that conduct which has procured her more respect and consideration in Europe than any step she ever took. It is to suppose her sick of that system which enabled her to negotiate the peace between Russia and the Ottoman Porte, as well as the Peace of Teschen; that system which has enabled her to unite in sentiment and affection all the maritime powers— even the United Provinces—in her favor and against England. It is to suppose her sick of that system which has broken off from her rival and natural enemy the most solid part of her strength; a strength that had become so terrible to France and would have been so fatal to her." Adams to Genêt, May 9, 1780, Wharton, III. 667.

construction upon it but this, viz., that it has always been the deliberate intention and object of France, for purposes of her own, to encourge the continuation of the war in America in hopes of exhausting the strength and resources of this country [England] and of depressing the rising power of America.

True, he himself disavowed harboring any such belief, but he strongly implied that, in view of the desultory fashion in which France had thus far waged war, it was by no means an unreasonable belief, and also, that it was one which was likely in time to gain a strong foothold in the United States.[12]

Vergennes' response is dated a week later. It announced that there was "every reason to believe that they [Ternay and Rochambeau] will take their station during next winter in North America," and continued: "You will perceive, sir, by this detail, that the king is far from abandoning the cause of America and that His Majesty without having been solicited by Congress, has taken effectual measures to support the cause of America."[13] Adams' spontaneous reaction to this intelligence was most enthusiastic. "I assure Your Excellency," he wrote the day following, "that scarcely any news I ever heard gave me more satisfaction."[14] But this was due to the fact that he had not given proper attention to the state-

[12] *Ib.*, 484-55.
[13] *Ib.*, 870-1.
[14] *Ib.*, 872.

ment in Vergennes' letter that His Majesty's action had not been solicited by Congress. In his letter of July 27th to the secretary he proves at length that Congress had asked for just such aid as was at last being furnished, as early as 1776, and had repeated the request several times since.[15] This was the straw that broke the camel's back. Up to this time Vergennes seems to have kept his temper with the New Englander fairly well, but on July 29th he wrote him that henceforth His Majesty's government would confine its dealing in matters affecting the two allies to Dr. Franklin.[16] A few days afterward Adams withdrew to Holland.[17]

But some time before this upshot of the matter, Vergennes had come to the conclusion that the standing of the alliance with the American Congress, whose chosen representative Adams evidently was, was too delicate to be further jeopardized by France's appearing in the thankless rôle of champion for Spanish interests where these conflicted with interests of the United States. In his despatch of June 3rd, 1780, to La Luzerne the French secretary reiterated his personal belief that Spain had the right to seize the lands to the east of the Mississippi if she could,

[15] *Ib.*, IV. 12-4.
[16] *Ib.*, 16-7.
[17] Here, too, his conduct was quite displeasing to Vergennes, *loc. cit.*, 562-3; V. 48.

that whatever might be the terms of the charters of the Southern states, the English were still the proprietors of these lands, and that there was, therefore, nothing to oblige Spain to hand over to the Americans such of them as she should conquer. But, he continued, that was not a matter for France to decide, wherefore La Luzerne should utter no opinion on the subject but should leave the whole question with Miralles. The French envoy should limit himself to advising influential members of Congress "not to use the language of right to the court of Madrid, but rather to appeal to its magnanimity." Finally, he added that he had confidential word to the effect that the Spanish government was strongly disposed to surrender to the Americans the east bank of the Mississippi above the Floridas and to accord them "some sort of navigation of the river."[18] And his despatch of August 7th was along sugstantially the same lines. The pretensions of Spain, said the minister, "are very delicate to treat of; our intervention has not been asked for, and silence will be without disadvantage." La Luzerne should therefore merely avail himself of such occasions as chanced to offer "to bring Congress to have confidence in the Catholic

[18] Doniol, IV. 427-8. In a despatch to Montmorin, dated June 12, Vergennes reiterates his interpretation of the guaranty clauses of the Treaty of Alliance: "La garantie des domaines des Etats-Unis est éventuelle, son étendue ne sera déterminé que par la future pacification," ib., 459-60, footnote.

king and to decide the question of the lands along the Mississippi without prejudice."[19]

Notwithstanding these despatches, in October, 1780, while La Luzerne was absent at Hartford attending a conference between the American and the French commanders on the military situation, his youthful secretary Marbois, at the instance of Rendon, the successor of Miralles, who was now dead, presented Congress an extended memoir showing, "with the greatest energy," "the absence of any foundation" for the American pretensions in the West and "giving them to understand that they need not expect the king of Spain to assent to them."[20] The following February 15th Congress did, in fact, decide upon a measure of concession to Spain, when it instructed Jay to recede from the demand for the right to navigate the Mississippi below 31° north latitude and a free port there, "provided such cession shall be unalterably insisted upon by Spain."[21] But the

[19] *Ib.*, 429.

[20] Rendon to Galvez, Oct. 20, 1780, Sparks MSS., XCVII; Doniol, IV. 593-4. Marbois was assisted in the preparation of this letter by Jenifer of Maryland, one of the leaders of the "landless" state faction, P. C. Phillips, *op. cit.*, 182-3. Jenifer, then president of the Maryland senate, had stated his views at length to Gérard, early in July, 1779, Doniol, IV. 168-70.

[21] *Journals*, XIX. 152-4; Wharton, IV. 267-9. This resolution was in immediate consequence of instructions received by the delegates of Virginia, authorizing them to assent to the terms indicated in the interest of a "speedy conclusion of an alliance with Spain," *Journals, loc. cit.* 151. The motive underlying this resolution was distrust of the negotiations then going on in Spain.

decision was due not to Marbois' representation of Spain's rights, which indeed was answered on the spot, but to the state of the war, and the question of the lands along the river was not affected by it. Four days later—but four months after Marbois' intervention—Vergennes again wrote La Luzerne touching the Mississippi question. The envoy was urged to follow his former instructions and to leave it to Congress to discuss its pretensions directly with Madrid through its own plenipotentiary. It seems not unlikely that the despatch was elicited by intelligence of young Marbois' officiousness.[22]

In brief, then, while the claim of the United States before 1783 to a western boundary along the Mississippi was by no means an invulnerable one, its validity seems originally to have been taken for granted by Vergennes, as was also that of the even less well-grounded claim to a right to

It was feared that Spain might be detached from the war and that this might lead to peace on the basis of the *uti possidetis*. See *Writings of James Madison,* I. 101ff.; IX. 86-9. On August 10, a second resolution was offered to empower Jay "to make such further cessions of the right of these United States to the navigation of the river Mississippi as he may think proper," etc. It was voted down unanimously, *Journals,* XX. 853-4. The feeling in Congress at this latter date was anything but cordial toward Spain on account of the action of the Spanish commander in allowing the British garrison at Pensacola, on the surrender of that post to the Spanish forces, to retire to New York. See the order adopted this same date, *loc. cit.,* 854.

[22] Doniol, IV. 593-4.

navigate the lower course of the river to and
from the sea. Also, both the language and history of article XII of the Treaty of Alliance
rendered plausible the American contention that,
from the moment the treaty became operative,
His Most Christian Majesty became guarantor
of the territorial integrity of the United States.
In his instructions to La Luzerne, however, of
July and September, 1779, Vergennes not only
rejected this interpretation of article XII, but
assumed outright championship of the theory that
the left bank of the Mississippi, northward of
the Spanish boundary, was still English and that,
therefore, Spain, being then at war with England,
had the right to conquer it. In bringing about
this change of attitude the material factors were,
first, Vergennes' desire to remove the principal
obstacle to Spain's hearty participation in the
war, namely, fear of the Americans, and secondly,
the misinformation that had come from Gérard
as to the intentions of the so-called Anti-Gallican
party in Congress and the extent to which the
Mississippi boundary was desired by all factions;
but there is no item of evidence showing an ulterior idea in the mind of the secretary that France
herself would wish some day to recover Louisiana. When presently he came to understand the
real trend of American opinion in this matter
and the probable risk involved in attempting to
traverse it, Vergennes returned to his original

position, that it was for Spain and the United States to settle by themselves the questions in issue between them. This was conspicuously the position of the French government and its representative at Philadelphia when Congress voted the Instructions of June 15th, 1781,—a fact to be remembered in adjudging Congress' willingness at that time to entrust American interests so completely to the keeping of France. Whether, once vested with this power, France still adhered to her attitude of aloofness, which after all rested upon considerations of policy and not of right, is reserved for later consideration.

CHAPTER XIII

THE CRISIS OF THE REVOLUTION

On September 27th, 1780, Vergennes addressed the king the following letter:

Sire, your Majesty learned yesterday the details which the Count de Maurepas had to communicate with regard to the financial situation. They are truly alarming and seem to leave no other recourse than peace and a very speedy peace. Spain feels the same press of necessity that France does and her inclination is very evident. Does Your Majesty desire to instruct his ambassador at Madrid to encourage and promote this inclination? I have not the least fear, Sire, that the Count de Montmorin would not acquit himself of such a commission, extremely difficult and delicate though it would be, with equal prudence and celerity. But once the avowal were made to Spain that we have need of peace and that we rely upon her to obtain it for us, there is no one, Sire, who could answer for the consequences or assure Your Majesty that the interest of his reputation and his glory would not be compromised. I speak only of that, Sire, since all other things are in comparison as nothing. I entreat Your Majesty to take the matter into consideration and to consult the Count de Maurepas. If the outcome of your deliberations favors an effort for peace through Spain, I very humbly beseech Your Majesty to transmit me the order in writing. The circumstances which constitute the necessity of unhappy courses are soon forgotten, while the evil effects which ensue become but the more evident with the passage of time.[1]

It requires no inordinate effort to perceive in this document the record of a critical moment in the history of the alliance and of the Revolution itself. Fortunately for the cause of American independence Vergennes' prompt and astute intervention with the king saved the day. Early in October the secretary forced the retirement of the incapable Sartines from the Marine in favor of Castries and early in January he effected a similar reorganization of the Department of War under the talented Ségur.[2] Meantime, as these changes indicate, the royal assent had been obtained to a new campaign, though that it would probably be the final one of the war Vergennes at once recognized, not only because of the condition of the royal exchequer but also because of the situation on the Continent. With the powers announcing in rapid succession their adherence to the League of Neutrals and with Holland breaking openly with England, the European horizon wore a smiling countenance for France at

[1] Doniol, IV 488.

[2] *Ib.,* 488-90. Says M. Doniol of Vergennes' triumph: "Si, cependant, les petitesses des hommes trouvent encore à s'agiter quand de grandes préoccupations dominent, ce ne sont ces petitesses qui commandent. Il s'agissait du sort de la France en Europe; tout se subordonna à ce grand intérêt, conséquemment fut remis aux mains de M. de Vergennes," *ib.,* 490.

the opening of 1781. Diplomatic combinations, however, are extremely kaleidoscopic affairs; besides which the recent death of the empress, by releasing the yet untested proclivities of Joseph II from a control that had usually been friendly to France, was a special factor of uncertainty.[3] Then, early in 1781 came a formal offer from Joseph and the czarina of joint mediation between France and her allies, and Great Britain. Inasmuch as the offer represented the young emperor's initial venture in the field of Continental politics, Vergennes at once decided that it was to be treated with consideration. Moreover, he could but reflect that, if worse came to worst, so honorable a way to peace might prove very welcome.[4]

An open road to peace at the end, if it were

[3] See Vergennes to Montmorin, Feb. 14, 1781, *ib.*, 544-5. "Il seroit souverainement malheureux que cette campagne si se passât comme la précédente sans rien produire d'effectif. Tout nous invite à songér à finir cette guerre; les moiens de la soutenir s'épuissent tous les jours, et la disposition de l'Europe qui jusqu'ici nous a été si favorable peut changér d'un moment à l'autre. Les Anglois ont de grands moiens pour tentér l'ambition de l'empereur et pour le satisfaire; l'offre que ce prince vient de nous faire de sa médiation peut nous faire concevoir l'espérance qu'il ne se rendra pas si aisement à leur séductions quand bien même nous n'aurions pas d'autres motifs de comptér sur sa persévérance dans l'alliance mais il n'est pas sans exemple que la vertu la plus ferme soit ébranlée. Pour parér à tous les inconvéniens impossibles à prévoir, nous ne devons nous occupér qu'à finir cette guerre; nous n'y parviendrons pas sans frapér un grand coup," *ib.*

[4] Vergennes to Montmorin, Jan. 22, 1781, *ib.*, 524-8.

humanly possible, of a successful campaign—
such, in brief, was Vergennes' program for 1781.
One question remained, that of the military objective of the coming campaign, and on this
there were three contending views. A party at
court, composed of the adherents of Choiseul and
Chatelêt sought to discredit Vergennes' policy by
clamoring for a war of aggrandizement, to be
waged especially in the West Indies.[5] Spain, on
the other hand, at last disillusioned of the idea
of getting anything valuable except by fighting
for it, was now demanding that she be assisted to
conquer Gibraltar and Jamaica.[6] Lastly, from
America came the reiterated suggestion that,
since American independence was the main objective of the war, North America was its natural
and most advantageous theatre.

The despatch of Rochambeau and Ternay to
America early in 1780 has already been noted.
For this determination on the part of the French
government to add military assistance to naval
and financial and for its acceptance of the for-
mula of "a constant naval superiority in American waters," which Ternay's squadron was

[5] *Last Journals of Horace Walpole,* II. 438-9. See also, for
later efforts on the part of this same faction to discredit Vergennes' policy, Doniol, V. 186-7 and footnotes, and *Revue d'Histoire diplomatique,* VII. 550-1.

[6] France's refusal to coöperate with Spain in an attack upon
Jamaica had been one of Spain's grievances in 1780, Doniol, IV.
496.

designed to realize, the United States were principally indebted to La Fayette, who had spent all
the first half of the year 1779 in France pleading
America's cause to Maurepas and Vergennes.[7]
Unfortunately, two-fifths of the army of ten
thousand that had been intended for Rochambeau's command was blockaded at Brest by a
British squadron before it got away, while the
naval portion of the expedition was rendered useless at Newport in the same manner shortly after
its arrival. And the total result at the end of the
first year of the expedition was that it had disappointed all the expectations it had aroused,—
had, in truth, created the impression on American
minds of a promise made and not fulfilled.[8]

But a much more important consideration with
those who at the end of 1780 besought France to
lend the United States more extensive and direct
aid was the state of the war in America at this
period. Despite the alliance, American independence had never been so near collapse. The
British army now held New York, the Carolinas,
and Georgia, while the British fleet ravaged the
coast. Congress was bankrupt and forced constantly to resort to the most wretched expedients
to obtain money or to dispense with its employ-

[7] Charlemagne Tower, *The Marquis de La Fayette in the American Revolution* (Philadelphia, 1901, 2 vols.), II. ch. XVIII; Doniol,
IV. ch. V.

[8] Tower, *op cit.,* II. 125, 132, 157.

ment.   The Continental Army, without pay,
food, or clothing and enlisted for short terms, was
ever on the verge of dissolution.   And the political situation was no better.   With public spirit at
the lowest ebb, the war had become throughout a
great part of the country the desperate venture of
a minority, sometimes a small minority.   The
Articles of Confederation were still in abeyance,
the states were indifferent to their duties, the
authority of Congress was flouted daily.   To this
situation the treason of Arnold was the natural
climax.[9]

The outstanding features of American conditions in the autumn of 1780 were already before
Vergennes from the correspondence of La Luzerne.   Indeed, it may be said that almost from
the moment of the signing of the American treaties the secretary had undergone a progressive
disillusionment in the military prowess and political competence of France's republican allies:
"the inertia of democratic institutions," which
had furnished him an argument in his efforts to
reconcile Spain with the idea of American independence, he had soon found to be no mere

[9] On this topic there is a superabundance of material. See Doniol,
IV. ch. VII; Tower, op. cit. II. chs. XX-XXII; Lecky's American
Revolution (Woodburn, ed., New York, 1908), ch. III; Writings
of Washington (W. C. Ford, ed., 14 vols.), VIII and IX, passim;
SMSS., Nos. 733, 737, 747, 1624-32; Wharton, IV. 256 and V.
151, etc.

truism.[10] Yet it is an interesting fact that to those
Frenchmen who had come into personal touch

[10] "I avow I have but feeble confidence in the energy of the United
States," Vergennes to Montmorin, Nov. 27, 1778, Doniol, III. 581.
A very censorious critic of the Americans was Kalb, whose letters
to Broglie were probably seen by Vergennes, as they are to be
found in the archives of the Department of Foreign Affairs. See
e.g., Doniol, IV. 19 fn. Kalb charges the American character with
braggadocio, dissipation, corruption, irresolution, lack of patriot-
ism, Anglomania, SMSS., Nos. 821, 838, 845, 1971, 1987. For a
partial confirmation of some of these strictures by a more lenient
critic, see La Fayette to Vergennes, *ib.,* No. 1609. See also a
letter from the "Hon. J. Trevor to Mr. Secretary Fox," dated
Ratisbon, Apr. 16, 1782. The writer gives an account of a conversation with the son of one of the Elector Palatine's ministers
at the Diet, who had served as aide-de-camp to Rochambeau, and
who had come away from America greatly disappointed with
France's allies. *Fifth Report (1876) of the Historical Manuscripts Commission,* the Lansdowne Papers, p. 253. Nor were the
French the only ones who were disappointed. "The generosity of
our allies," wrote Washington in Aug., 1780, in a letter to the
President of Congress, "has a claim to our gratitude, but it is
neither for the honor of America nor for the interest of the common cause to leave the work entirely to them," *Writings* (Ford,
ed.) VIII. 390. "Had America," began *Crisis No. IX,* written
on the occasion of the surrender of Charleston, "pursued her
advantage with half the spirit she resisted her misfortunes, she
would before now have been a conquering and a peaceful people;
but lulled in the lap of soft tranquillity she rested on her hopes,
and adversity has only convulsed her into action." Vergennes, in
coming to depreciate the military capacity and public spirit of the
Americans as a whole and to emphasize the necessity of controlling Congress, showed a true appreciation of the character of
the Revolution in its last days. Indeed, even the victory at Yorktown did little to break up the popular inertia that tied the hands
of Congress. See La Luzerne's elaborate and very informing
report on the situation at the end of 1781, *Revue d'Histoire diplomatique,* V. 421-36.

with the American cause, that cause had never appeared in more appealing light than at this moment of its greatest prostration. The explanation, I think, is to be found in the personal ascendancy of Washington, whose intrepidity and fortitude naturally stood forth all the more strikingly as the other mainstays of the Revolution fell away.[11]

At almost the very moment that Vergennes was intervening to prevent France's withdrawal from the war, a conference, consisting of Washington, the French commanders, the French envoy, and one or two others, was assembling at Hartford, Connecticut, to consider plans for the coming campaign in North America. It had already been determined that the objective of the campaign ought to be the capture of New York City. It was now further resolved that, in order to render this objective feasible, the French commanders should ask their government to send to America enough men to raise Rochambeau's force to 15,000, enough money to enable Congress to maintain a like force, and a sufficient fleet to command the American waters. The conference's decisions were conveyed to France by Rochambeau's son on a vessel detailed for the

[11] For the change in Kalb's opinion of Washington from unfavorable to favorable, *cf.* his letters of Oct. and Dec., 1777, to Broglie, SMSS. Nos. 755 and 761. For some tributes by La Fayette, see *ib.*, 1625, 1627, 1632.

purpose by Ternay, late in October. In the middle of February, young Laurens sailed for France with a similar commission from Congress. He bore with him the friendly injunction of Rochambeau "to open his heart as to the state of this unhappy land, if it be not promptly and powerfully succored."[12]

The response of the French government to these demands was certainly not illiberal either in proportion to America's deserts or its own means. Measured, however, by the demands themselves it was meagre enough. The request that was met most generously was the financial one. Congress had asked for a loan of twenty-five millions *livres*. In return Louis gave outright six millions *livres,* to be spent in France under the direction of Franklin, and later consented to underwrite a loan of ten millions, to be obtained in Holland. The request of the Hartford Conference for more troops, on the other hand, was denied almost *in toto,* and even the contingent of Rochambeau's force that had been blockaded at Brest was kept back. As to naval aid, Vergennes expressed himself as follows:

[12] For the above, see Doniol, IV. ch. VII, and Tower, *La Fayette,* II. 159-63, 195-200, 270. La Luzerne suspected that the sending of Laurens to France might represent an intention to supersede Franklin, Doniol, IV. 390-1 and fn. Laurens' conduct in France, characterized as it was by youthful zeal and ignorance of diplomatic forms, was irritating to the French minister, but it seems clear that he should be credited with the king's endorsement of the Dutch loan, *ib.,* 558-62; Wharton, IV. 317-55; *passim,* and 685-8.

The Count de Grasse, who commands our fleet in the Antilles, has been ordered to conduct, sometime toward the approach of next winter, a part of his fleet to the coast of North America, or to detach a portion of it to sweep the coast and to coöperate in any undertaking which may be projected by the French and American generals, or to form a part of it if they are unable to coöperate. The number of ships to be sent to the North will depend upon the need which the Spanish have of our assistance. . . . If they have made preparations for some great enterprise, we shall have to lend them a hand; for if a serious blow is struck at the common enemy and it is successful, the advantage will be equally great for all the allies. The important point is to weaken the enemy, to crush him if possible; the locality is of little importance.

In short, the rendition of naval aid to the United States was subordinated to the project of assisting Spain in the West Indies, and, it may be added, before Gibraltar.[13]

Why was Spain thus preferred to the United States? The question is easily answered. If France was under obligation to secure American independence before she could honorably make peace, not less was she under obligation, now that Spain was ready once more to take an active part

[13] Doniol, IV. ch. XI; Tower, *op. cit.*, II. ch. XXIV. In the interest of accuracy, it should be noted that the government's decision not to send more troops to America was receded from at the time of Grasse's sailing for the West Indies to the extent of sending with him a reinforcement of six hundred and sixty men for Rochambeau's force. On Apr. 5, Grasse detached the *Sagittaire* from his fleet to carry this force to Newport, where it arrived on June 10th. Tower, pp. 283, 392-3.

in the war, to obtain something valuable for that power too. But more than that, the Spanish marine was now in better fighting trim than it had been at any earlier period of the war. As between an ally able to contribute something to the common cause and one needing constant bolstering, good sense dictated that the real work of the campaign should be undertaken in coöperation with the former. On the other hand, this does not mean that Vergennes' effort to minimize the importance of the matter of locality is necessarily sound. Were England to be really *crushed,* then, of course, the way would lie open for France to satisfy both her allies to the completest extent, but of this there was, after all, little likelihood. Such being the case, however, it was altogether probable that, at the close of hostilities, England would be more strongly lodged in certain *localities* than in others; and this fact might very conceivably work to the detriment of one ally as against the other. In point of fact, at the very moment he wrote the above quoted words, Vergennes already had in mind the possibility of France's acquiescing in a very substantial curtailment, from the American point of view certainly, of American independence, if an otherwise available opportunity for peace should offer itself.

Vergennes communicated to La Luzerne his government's decision with reference to the demands of Congress and the Hartford Conference in a despatch dated March 9th. In the same despatch and two later ones, dated respectively April 19th and June 30th, he further instructed the envoy as to the course of action that France expected on the part of Congress touching the diplomatic interests of the alliance:[14] Congress was to be frankly informed that, in view of threatened developments on the Continent, peace might at any time become of the utmost importance to France, and was, therefore, to be urged to accept the proposed mediation without delay. By the same token, it also behooved Congress to endeavor to win the good will of the mediating powers by the moderation of its pretensions, "save in the matter of independence, which admitted of no modification."[15] The American envoy at the mediation, on whose right to enter it on a proper footing France would unremittingly insist, would be John Adams. On account of Adams' unfortunate personal qualities which would "give rise to a thousand unfortunate episodes calculated to exasperate his fellow negotiators," Congress ought to empower His Majesty's ministers to interpose to curb him

[14] Doniol, IV. 553-6, 588-91, 601-3; *Journals of the Continental Congress,* XX. 562-9, 669-74, XXI. 986-93. The extracts in Doniol are incomplete, but it is possible to supplement them from La Luzerne's reports to Congress.

[15] Doniol, IV. 555.

whenever necessary.[16] Finally, Congress ought to be brought, albeit by the most delicate means, to realize the possibility that, in view of England's settled opposition to an outright recognition of independence and of the existing state of the war, the mediating powers might propose a truce based on the *status quo*.[17] That the United

[16] *Ib.*, 551 fn., 589.

[17] *Ib.*, 552-3, 601-3; *Journals*, XX. 672. The first hint that France might consent to the *status quo* for the United States is contained in Vergennes' despatch of Sept. 25, 1780, to La Luzerne, written at the moment when, as we have seen, the continuance of the war was in the balance. "Au surplus, M.," Vergennes wrote on this occasion, "je présume que le véritable objet des inquiétudes que l'on vous a marquées c'est le *statu quo;* il seroit effectivement on ne peut pas plus fâcheux pour l'Amérique dans l'état actüel des choses, et nous sommes bien déterminés à ne le point stipuler pour les Américains; ce sera à eux à juger, lorsqu'il sera question de cet objet,' de la persévérance ou des sacrifices que les conjonctures exigeront de leur part. Au reste, M., je désire que vous vous absteniez de traiter cette matière délicate dans ce moment cy . . . ." Doniol, IV. 536 fn. France, then, would not *stipulate* the *status quo,* but would leave the question of its acceptability to Congress. However, Vergennes was very fearful that Spain, still in negotiation with Cumberland, would stipulate it, as she had in 1778. In his despatch of Nov. 27, 1780, he roundly denounced Florida Blanca's policy as grounded in passion, prejudice and selfishness, *ib.*, 506-8. In his despatch of Jan. 22, 1781, he declared that if the king of Spain should stipulate the *status quo* in regard to the United States he would put them at the mercy of England and would give the Americans good reason to abandon the alliance. "Spain," said he, "will put her interests before everything else . . . and she looks upon independence with regret," *ib.*, 510-11. Vergennes' later attitude on this question was formulated in a memoir in the hand of Rayneval, his secretary, on which is based in part his despatch of Mar. 9. This memoir comprises the following points: "1. It is for the

States were profoundly interested in maintaining
the integrity of their union was, of course, altogether indisputable.   Indeed, the king himself
was of the same way of thinking, both because of
his plighted word and also because of his own
interests, wherefore he would alter his present

king of England, author of the war, to make some sacrifices for
peace. 2. The first of the sacrifices to be made is independence
for North America. 3. This independence may be assured either
by a definitive treaty or a truce. 4. The king of England, which-
ever method is adopted, will be able to treat directly with the
Americans, through the intervention of the mediating powers. 5.
The truce will run for 20, 25, or 30 years, etc. The United States
will be treated as independent in fact, and no restriction shall
be imposed upon them in the exercise of the rights of sovereignty.
6. It would be desirable to avoid the *status quo* if possible; but
in case that could not be, it will be advantageous to limit it to
South Carolina and Georgia and to stipulate for the evacuation
of New York. 7. The proposition of the truce cannot be made by
the king to Congress, if it should be united with the *status quo,*
but if the two propositions are isolated, His Majesty will engage to procure Congress' sanction of the truce, if he has the
secret assurance that New York will be accepted [excepted?].
8. In case of a truce the king will propose to the Americans, if it
is necessary to do so, a new convention the object of which will
be to guarantee the Americans against attack by England after
the expiration of the truce."   In a word, while the king would
leave the unpleasant business of proposing the *status quo* to the
mediating powers, he would accept it and bring Congress to do
so, if it were confined to South Carolina and Georgia.   There was
a rumor in Boston that the *status quo* had been accepted for the
United States, to apply to Georgia, South Carolina, and Maine,
as early as April, 1780, *Continental Journal and Weekly Advertiser,* April 13, 1780.   It may be that the uneasiness to which
Vergennes refers in his despatch of Sept. 25 (*supra*), was caused
by this rumor.

resolution only when he saw "the absolute impossibility of obtaining peace without such a sacrifice." None the less, the sacrifice was one that lay "in the order of possibilities"; and, if it should become necessary, it would have to be accepted with resignation. "The greater part of the Belgian provinces had thrown off the Spanish yoke originally, but only seven had finally maintained their independence"; and "it frequently happens that circumstances give the law to the most powerful sovereigns, forcing them to modify plans the best conceived."[18]

In short, Vergennes plainly indicated, that if an otherwise available peace offered itself, he would not resist the *status quo* for the United States indefinitely, though he had declaimed against it so bitterly a few months before; and further, that while to Congress would be reserved the formal decision in the matter, it would be expected ultimately to take the same position with as good grace as possible, and so save the king's face.

The passages above paraphrased, however,

---

[18] Doniol, IV. 601-3. Vergennes continues: "Mais vous aurez la plus grande attention de ne parler que comme de vous-même et de ne point laisser apercevoir que vous y êtes autorisé, parceque dans ce dernier cas les Américains supposeroient que le Roi a d'avance pris le parti de les abandonner et ils croient tout perdu; Sa M'té est résolue de ne leur proposer aucun sacrifice, elle croit devoir laisser ce soin fâcheux aux deux cours médiatrices, si jamais il devient nécessaire," *ib.*, 603.

touching the *status quo,* are from the despatch
of June 30th and were never brought to Congress' attention. The conference which La Luzerne held with a committee of Congress on May
28th,[19] and which led to the voting of the famous
Instructions of June 15th, was based upon the
despatch of March 9th, in which, while the possibility of the *status quo* is suggested, the French
government's attitude toward such a proposition
is left somewhat vague. Even so, La Luzerne
evidently thought it more in accord with the
"delicacy" required by the situation not to bring
forward this part of the despatch of March 9th
till after Congress had defined the terms on which
it would make peace, nor did he do so till June
18th.[20] At the earlier conference the envoy's discourse was all of mediation, moderation, Mr.
Adams' deficiencies, and the necessity of confidence in France. "If," said he, "Congress put
any confidence in the king's friendship and
benevolence; if they were persuaded of his firm
resolution constantly to support the cause of the
United States," they would order their plenipotentiary "to manifest a perfect and open confidence in the French ministers" and "to take no
steps without the approbation of His Majesty."
In other words, he invited Congress to surrender
to France the diplomatic autonomy of the United

[19] *Journals of the Continental Congress,* XX. 562-9.
[20] *Ib.,* 672.

States during the approaching peace negotiations. Far from spurning the invitation, Congress accepted it without stipulating a condition
or registering a scruple.

By the opening paragraph of its Instructions
of June 15th, 1781, Congress accepted mediation
at the hands of Their Imperial Majesties; by the
second, it made independence "by peace or truce"
and the maintenance of the alliance with France
sine qua non conditions of a treaty; by the third
and fourth, it indicated its confidence in His Most
Christian Majesty and his ministers in the following terms:

As to disputed boundaries and other particulars we
refer you to the instructions formerly given to Mr.
Adams, dated August 14, 1779, and October 18, 1780,
from which you will easily perceive the desires and expectations of Congress; but we think it unsafe at this dis-
tance to tie you up by absolute and peremptory
directions upon any other subject than the two essential
articles above mentioned. You are therefore at liberty
to securing the interests of the United States in such
manner as circumstances may direct and as the state of
the belligerent and disposition of the mediating powers
may require.

For these purposes you are to make the most candid
and confidential communications upon all subjects to the
ministers of our generous ally, the king of France; to
undertake nothing in the negotiations for peace or truce
without their knowledge and concurrence, and ultimately
to govern yourselves by their advice and opinion, endeavoring in your whole conduct to make them sensible
how much we rely on His Majesty's influence for effec-

tual support in everything that may be necessary to the present security or future prosperity of the United States of America.[21]

Little wonder that the critics of the instructions declared that "never before had one state put itself at the mercy of another so completely and imprudently"![22] Little wonder that La Luzerne boasted that "the negotiation was placed actually in the hands of the king save on the question of independence and the treaties"![23] Let us see what were the considerations that moved Congress to make so extraordinary a concession.

The instructions were asked for, as we have just seen, as a means of curbing John Adams. But no sooner were they voted than Adams was superseded by a commission consisting of himself, Jay, Franklin, Jefferson, and the elder Laurens.[24] Delegates who had opposed La Lu-

[21] *Ib.,* 651-2. For the complete proceedings, see *ib.,* 605-50.

[22] See La Luzerne to Vergennes, June 23, 1781, Doniol, IV. 623-4. Other objections were, "that when the people became informed of the circumstances, the malicious would not fail to say that Congress had sold out to France; that the plenipotentiaries would fill a sorry rôle at the conferences; that five important persons were being sent abroad to be the passive witnesses of our [France's] conduct; that we [the French] had very confused, even false, ideas touching the fisheries, the boundaries, the confiscations, etc."; that the instructions were an affront to the dignity of the thirteen states, had been adopted with precipitation, and had finally been rendered useless by the action of Congress in supplanting Adams with a commission, *ib.*

[23] Same to same, June 11, *ib.,* 604.

[24] The "ultimately to govern" clause was adopted by Congress on June 11, *Journals,* XX. 626. Immediately thereafter a motion

zerne's demands in the first instance now renewed
their attack, insisting that in addition to being

that had been previously defeated, was reconsidered and carried
to join two persons to Mr. Adams in negotiating the peace, *ib.,*
628. Jay was elected on June 13, *ib.,* 638. Franklin, Laurens, and
Jefferson were added to the commission on June 14, *ib.,* 648. The
reason for a commission of five is suggested by Witherspoon thus:
"They added more members to Mr. Adams and those from different parts of the continent. This removed every suspicion or fear
that the interests of one part would be sacrificed to secure that of
another," *Thomson Papers,* 100 (Debate of Aug. 8, 1782). Madison explains why Franklin and Jay alone were unsatisfactory
thus: "The former being interested as one of the land companies
in territorial claims, which had less chance of being made good in
any other way than by a repossession of the vacant country by the
British crown; the latter belonging to a state interested in such
arrangements as would deprive the United States of the navigation of the Mississippi and turn the western trade through New
York; and neither of them being connected with the Southern
States." *Writings of James Madison,* I. 299 (Debate of Dec. 30,
1782). La Luzerne also thought that Franklin might be influenced through his interest in lands on the left bank of the Ohio
to oppose Virginia's claim in favor of Great Britain, and so advised Vergennes, Report of June 30, 1781, Doniol, IV. 622. The
events of the negotiations of 1782 show that distrust of either
Jay or Franklin was entirely misplaced. Neither Laurens nor
Jefferson participated in the peace negotiations. The former,
while on the way to fulfil a mission to Holland, in Sept., 1780, was
captured by the British and later lodged in the Tower of London
under a commitment for treason. He was still in the Tower when
he was appointed peace commissioner, but was released Dec. 31,
1781, on the expectation that Cornwallis would be exchanged for
him. However, he lingered on in England for another year. His
conduct was made the subject of much contemporary criticism,
which his biographer succeeds in answering, at least in part. D. D.
Wallace, *Life of Henry Laurens* (N. Y., 1915), 354-419. Jefferson, who was governor of Virginia at the time, declined a
place on the commission.

mischievous the resolutions were also superflu-
ous.[25]   The attack failed, however, even to induce
a reconsideration of the question;[26] and if the
testimony of Madison is to be relied upon, the
instructions were finally adopted in the form
given above without dissent.[27]

La Luzerne credited what—and not without
justification—he regarded as a triumph for himself no less than for France, largely to personal
factors.   Early in May, he tells us, he had
"opened his purse" to General Sullivan "the hero
of Newport," a *coup* which had broken the back-
bone of the so-called "New England League" and
secured New Hampshire's vote for the instructions from the outset.[28] Also, as it happened, the
"landless" state party, which was comparatively
indifferent even when not hostile to American
pretensions to a boundary at the Mississippi, had

[25] See note 22, above.

[26] *Journals,* XX. 650.

[27] *Thomson Papers,* 65 (Debate of July 24, 1782).   In meeting
the attacks of members on the instructions, La Luzerne took the
position that, "if we [the French] consulted our own interests
rather than those of our allies, we ought to desire that the American plenipotentiaries had all the powers that certain people wished
to reserve to them."   Also, he professed to be very reluctant to
accept for France a trust that did not represent the deliberate
will of Congress.   "L'effet de ce langage, Monseigneur," he continues, "a été de faire reconsidérer ces resolutions et de les con-
firmer, ainsi que je l'espérois permament.   Le président du Congrès m'a dit qu'elles étoient expediées par *l'Anna.*"   Doniol, IV.
624-5.

[28] *Ib.,* IV. 608 and fn.

at this moment its two most influential spokes-
men in Congress, Witherspoon of New Jersey
and Jenifer of Maryland. On the other hand,
the Adams and Lee families, champions respectively of the New England fishing interest and
the Western land interest, both lacked their usual
member. Certainly, La Luzerne himself could
hardly have chosen a Congress more to his liking.

But while the personal factor may account for
the votes cast by New Hampshire, Maryland, and
New Jersey for the Instructions of June 15th it
does not account for the votes of Pennsylvania,
Virginia, the Carolinas, and Georgia. How, then,
we may ask, did the men from these states, men
like Madison and Jones of Virginia, for instance,
reconcile such a remarkable abdication of power
by Congress to a foreign, albeit allied, government with sound public policy?

La Luzerne's *finesse* in the matter of the
status quo has just been mentioned. Nor was this,
by any means, an isolated circumstance. To the
same general category belongs also the fact that
Congress, being ignorant of the terms on which
Spain had entered the war, was in no position to
previse the complicated tangle of obligations in
which France would find herself if the war turned
out to be only partially successful.[29] There was,

---

[29] In this connection the following passage from a speech made
by Arthur Lee in the course of the Congressional debate of Aug.
8, 1782, in favor of reconsidering the Instructions of June 15, is

in other words, so far as Congress knew, no compelling reason why France should *not* be trusted: on the contrary, there were excellent reasons why she should be. Months before this her envoy had ceased championing Spanish interests where these conflicted with American. More recently, abandoning the no longer applicable views of his court as to the establishment of a balance of power in America, he had given his assent to an invasion of Canada and had followed this up by urging

instructive: "It is not sufficient that the independence of these states is secured. But he doubts whether even that is secured by the instructions. He is afraid of the accompaniment. That we shall be so circumscribed in our boundaries that our independence will be a nugatory independence. France in making a treaty will be governed by her own interest and from her long and close connection with Spain and prefer it to ours. Is it wise, is it proper to give a nation the absolute disposal of our affairs that is under the influence of two interests which she is bound to consult in preference to that of these states? This unlimited confidence will render us despicable in the eyes of France and less attentive to our rights. We have been informed by a minister of France that Spain has large claims on the lands beyond the Mountains. Her conduct shews that she means to support her claim to that country. She wishes to confine us to the lands lying below the heads of the waters falling into the Atlantic. We are told that she thinks she has a right to possess herself of all to the westward. And shall we submit it to France, her old friend and ally, whether her claims shall be confirmed, and we be excluded from the possession of that country?" *Thomson Papers,* 95-6. Lee was the strongest critic of the Instructions of June 15. Yet it will be noted that even he does not suspect that France is under any special obligations to Spain in connection with the then existing war. Also, it will be noted that he does not charge France with having championed Spain's claims to the western country.

renewed efforts in the Northwest.[30] Rising above
all other considerations, however, were these two:
the state of the war and the source from which
peace offered itself. The generality of Americans had long felt in June, 1781, that the fate of
the United States rested almost entirely with
France, whence it followed that Congress could
not do better than to vest France outright with
the trusteeship of American interests. The development at this moment of a prospect of peace
through the mediation of powers that had never
yet recognized American independence naturally
confirmed this logic, and the more so since it was
not known what degree of pressure these powers
were prepared to bring in order to end the war.[31]

[30] Phillips, *The West in the Diplomacy of the American Revolution,* 190-1 and 194, and notes. It was not La Luzerne's idea that
the United States should retain the Western country necessarily
(*vd.* Doniol, IV. 622), but "he recognized that the possession of
the Great Lakes would place the Americans in a much better position to negotiate with Great Britain," Phillips, *loc. cit.*

[31] "In opposing the motion [for reconsideration of the Instructions of June 15], many considerations were suggested, and the
original expediency of submitting the commission for peace to the
counsels of France descanted upon. The reasons assigned for this
expediency were, that at that juncture when the measure took
place the American affairs were in the most deplorable situation, the Southern states being overrun and exhausted by the
enemy . . .; that the old paper currency had failed . . . . In the
midst of these distresses, the mediation of the two Imperial
Courts was announced. The general idea was that the two most
respectable powers of Europe would not interpose without a serious desire of peace and without the energy requisite to effect it.
The hope of peace was, therefore, mingled with an apprehension

Upon the Instructions of June 15th there is impressed a twofold character. On the one hand, they constitute a real tribute to the essential magnanimity of the French design in intervening in the Revolution, to that quality of largeness about Vergennes' project that forbade an abandonment of American independence save in the face of conditions that meant recognizable defeat for France herself. On the other hand, this tribute was no merely sentimental one: it was conditioned by the deliberate calculation that, in view of the actual status of the belligerent parties in America and of the auspices under which peace was to be negotiated—a peace which America needed no less than France,—the United States could not act more prudently than to bestow the most ungrudging and unstinted confidence upon their ally.[32]

It thus becomes pertinent to inquire further,

that considerable concessions might be exacted from America by the mediators as a compensation for the essential one which Great Britain was to submit to. Congress, on a trial, found it impossible, from the diversity of opinions and interests, to define any other claims than those of independence and the alliance. A discretionary power, therefore, was to be delegated with regard to all other claims." Debate of Dec. 30, 1782, *Writings of James Madison*, I. 298-9. Madison, however, rather exaggerates the possibility of a coercive intention on the part of the mediators. *Cf.* La Luzerne's conference with the committee of Congress, of May 28, 1781, *Journals*, XX. 562-9. See also *Thomson Papers*, p. 65.

[32] "At worst," the apologists of the instructions urged, they "could only be considered as a sacrifice of our pride to our interest," *Writings of Madison*, I. 300.

what—British recognition of independence aside —were the expectations that underlay these instructions? The instructions themselves referred the American commissioners back to the instructions of August 14th, 1779, but this reference leaves us still in the dark as to the degree of confidence felt by Congress that the objectives so defined would be achieved. A much more informing document is the report of La Luzerne of June 13th, 1781, which, on the basis of a careful canvass of all varieties of opinion in Congress at this date, arrived at the following conclusions: 'that if the Ohio formed their boundary the Thirteen States would not complain; that, indeed, they would believe themselves under obligations to the king for all that they obtained more than this; that they would not reject the peace if circumstances necessitated some greater concessions; that the peace would be less agreeable in proportion as this line were hewn away from'; 'that if circumstances forced them to adopt as boundaries the mountains which divide the rivers that flow into the Atlantic from those that flow to the west, the peace would be accepted and ratified, but would meet with general criticism and would cool the ardor of French partisans, and it would be difficult to persuade the Americans that their interests had not been sacrificed'; that a treaty whereby any State were cut off from the Confederation could not be ratified; that they would prefer "to continue the war, however difficult it might be, to allowing England a single post in Georgia or in any other part of the Thirteen States"; that if it were necessary to depart from the ultimatum of 1779, it was to be desired that the concession should be made, "not in favor of the English, but that the right of the Indians should be reserved to the intervening lands."[33] The recorded votes on various amendments offered to the instructions while they were under discussion and on the secret instructions which it was at first proposed should accompany them confirm these conclusions to a striking degree.[34]

But as every one knows, the Instructions of June 15th had no influence on the negotiations leading to the Peace of 1783. Directly this was due to the initiative of John Jay, whose course

[33] Doniol, IV. 617-21.

[34] See especially *Journals*, XX. 608-15. The two articles of secret instructions adopted on June 7, ordered the commissioners to use their "utmost endeavors to secure the limits fixed exactly according to the description in your [their] former instructions," and if they failed in that, to make peace "without fixing northern and western limits," *ib.*, 608. The day following, however, Virginia having failed to secure an amendment to the instructions asked for by the committee that would have prevented any cession south of the Ohio, the secret articles were reconsidered and lost, *ib.*, 615. La Luzerne, however, was somewhat suspicious lest some such instructions had been forwarded. "J'ai soupçonné qu'il pouvoit y avoir des instructions qu'ils [the plenipotentiaries] auroient ordre de nous cacher, mais rien n'a encore confirmé ce soupçon, et la confiance me paroît illimitée," La Luzerne to Vergennes, June 13, 1781, Doniol, IV. 619.

will be considered in the following chapter as
furnishing the best pragmatic test of the policy
of the Foreign Office at that juncture. Back of
Jay's decision, however, and making it possible
was the Yorktown campaign, to which, accordingly, a few words must be devoted.

It will be recalled that Vergennes had set the
approach of winter as the time for the Count de
Grasse's visit to American waters. The admiral
himself, however, evidently held quite different
views on this matter, for in a letter to Rochambeau dated March 29th, one week after he had
left Brest, he announced that he would reach
Santo Domingo by the end of June, and continued thus:

It will be toward the 15th of July at the earliest that
I shall be able to reach the coast of North America.
But it is necessary, in view of the short time I shall have
to remain there—for the season will force me to leave
in any event—that every preparation likely to aid in
the success of your projects shall be completed, so that
nothing may delay us an instant in beginning our
operations.[35]

This letter reached Rochambeau at Providence
on June 10th. Already this gallant friend of
America, who had been deeply disappointed by
the king's rejection of the plan of the Hartford
Conference, had conceived the idea that the
Count de Grasse might yet "save the country."

[35] Tower, *op. cit.,* II. 398.

Thus writing the admiral from Newport on May 28th he had urged "the gravity of the crisis in America, especially the Southern states, at this moment," and that, "without the naval superiority which he [the Count de Grasse] can bring," "none of the means within our control can be made available."[36] Then in a postscript, added three days later, he had further proposed that Grasse bring with him from the West Indies a corps of five or six thousand men and twelve hundred thousand *livres* in specie, since this could be obtained at par in the Antilles, while in the United States it was at a premium of from twenty-five to thirty per cent.[37] Now, on June 11th, he wrote Grasse a second time, including duplicates of the earlier letter and postscript and repeating their recommendations with renewed urgency.[38]

Grasse's reply, which was dated at Cape Santo Domingo on the 28th of July, reached Newport on August 12th, and was favorable beyond reasonable expectation. The admiral announced that he would sail for Chesapeake Bay on Au-

---

[36] *Ib.*, 390.

[37] *Ib.*, 391.

[38] *Ib.*, 398-400. Note also these expressions from a letter of June 16: "General Washington has but a handful of men . . . . This country has been driven to bay, and all its resources are giving out at once. The Continental money has been annihilated," *ib.*, 397. These letters are published in full in Donial's fifth volume and the originals are now in the Library of Congress.

gust 13th, as, he continued, this is "the point which appears to me to have been indicated by you, . . . Messrs. Washington, La Luzerne, and Barras, as the one from which the advantage which you propose may be most certainly attained." He would bring with him, he proceeded, three thousand men, from twenty-five to twenty-nine war-vessels, a quantity of siege artillery, and the sum of 1,200,000 *livres* in specie. The one disappointing feature of the reply was the time limit it set for the projected operations. That he was able to come at all to the coast of North America, Grasse indicated, was due to the fact that the Spanish commander, Admiral de Solano, was not yet ready for active operations; but this condition would cease with the approach of the winter months, for which reason the French fleet and the troops it brought with it would have to leave the continent by October 15th.

As the whole expedition [the admiral wrote] has been undertaken at your request and without consulting the ministers of France or of Spain, although I have felt myself authorized to assume certain responsibilities in the interest of the common cause, I should not venture to change the entire arrangement of their projects by transferring so important a body of troops. You will perfectly understand, my dear Count, how necessary it will be to make the best use of this precious time.[39]

Thus the Yorktown campaign was due to the fortunate—not to say, fortuitous—coincidence of

[39] Tower, *op. cit.*, II. 401-4.

three circumstances: Rochambeau's friendly
solicitude for the American cause, Grasse's patriotic willingness to stretch a point in his instructions for the general good, Solano's unreadiness,
so characteristically Spanish, for the enterprise for
which Grasse's expedition had been planned.   In
other words, Cornwallis' surrender owed little or
nothing to the intention of the French government
itself. And by the same token, the results of the
campaign of 1781 were from the point of view of
the French Foreign Office, somewhat disappointing. It had been hoped to hasten peace by striking
a decisive blow the immediate fruits of which were
to go to Spain and furnish her sufficient inducement to quit the war. The decisive blow had been
struck, true enough, but its direct beneficiary was
America. The result—which was confirmed by
Grasse's later defeat in the West Indies—was
twofold: With Gibraltar and Jamaica both still
safely British a new campaign had to be planned
for the behoof of Spain. With the British forces
abandoning all their inland conquests in the
South, the application of the *status quo* to the
United States became impossible.[40]

[40] See in this connection the secretary of Foreign Affairs' communication to Congress on November 23, 1781, of the result of a
recent conference with La Luzerne based on a despatch from
Vergennes dated September 7. As presented by the envoy,
this despatch emphasizes France's championship of American interests, her refusal to accede to the terms of the mediation of
the imperial courts until they should agree to acknowledge the

Nor may the reaction of patriotic American sentiment to the event at Yorktown be altogether ignored. Spontaneous as were popular jubilation at the triumph of the allied forces and gratitude to the French for their assistance, they did not blind Americans at all to the strengthened diplomatic position of the United States. Within a little over a week from Cornwallis' surrender the Massachusetts legislature passed resolutions ordering its delegates in Congress to press for instructions to the American peace commissioners to obtain British recognition of the right of Americans to share in the Newfoundland fisheries.[41] With the introduction of these resolutions into Congress a fortnight later debate began afresh on the merits of the Instructions of June 15th, to be renewed from time to time till the very end of the war.[42] All efforts, however, to procure the outright repeal of these instructions crumbled before the argument that

American plenipotentiaries "in the manner most conformable to the dignity of the United States," and her rejection of a "plan of negotiation proposed by the mediating powers" which had "held up the idea" of the *status quo* for America. *Journals*, XXI. 1138-9. *Cf.* Doniol, V. 39-43. Doubtless, La Luzerne's report of June 13 had demonstrated to Vergennes the unfeasibility of accepting the *status quo* for the United States except as a very desperate measure.

[41] *Journals of the Continental Congress*, XXI. 1122 fn.

[42] See *ib.*, XXII. 44-5, 429, 458-60, XXIII. 870-5; Doniol, IV. 625-6 and 696-701; *Thomson Papers*, 63-5 and 93-108; and *Writings of James Madison*, I. 226 and 294-301.

such action, by the offense it would cause France, would do more harm than good, that while the instructions were doubtless a sacrifice of pride, they were a sacrifice of pride to more substantial interests.[43] Furthermore, Congress had before it the explicit assurance of Vergennes, who was now chief-minister, that the king "would use his influence and credit for the advantage of his allies whenever a negotiation should render their interests a subject of discussion."[44]

This assurance suggested to Congress a way out of its difficulty. By the resolutions of January 22nd, 1782, the Instructions of June 15th were still left standing, but the American commissioners were ordered to contend "with an earnestness becoming the importance of an object on which a great part of the United States absolutely depend" both for commerce and subsistence, "for an explicit acknowledgment of the common right of these United States to take fish in the North American seas and in particular on the banks of Newfoundland," and "with equal earnestness," "for the boundaries of the United States as described in the instructions" of August 14th, 1779, and further, "to represent to His

[43] Above references. See also notes 22, 24, 27, 29, 31, and 32, above.

[44] *Journals,* XX. 1138. Livingston makes the quite positive statement that this assurance was what decided Congress to continue the Instructions of June 15 in effect after Yorktown, Livingston to Jay, Jan. 4, 1783, Wharton, VI. 178-9 fn.

Most Christian Majesty" "the most sanguine expectations" of Congress that "His Majesty's friendship and influence will obtain for his faithful allies" both these objects.[45]

In other words, Congress solved the dilemma created by Yorktown—the dilemma, to wit, of American expectations on the one hand and French sensibilities on the other—by shifting the responsibility to the shoulders of the American commissioners. Ten weeks later Grasse's fleet encountered Rodney's in the Bahama Channel and was utterly defeated, Grasse himself being taken prisoner. Yet,—and it is a striking comment on the complex diplomatic situation in which the United States and France were mutually involved—the former derived distinct ad-

[45] *Ib.,* XXII. 44-5. Livingston communicated the resolutions to La Luzerne, Jan. 24, Wharton V. 126-7. The resolutions were preceded by Livingston's elaborate letter to Franklin of Jan. 7, 1782, in support of the claims of the United States to a boundary at the Mississippi, to the navigation of that river, and to a share in the Newfoundland fisheries, Wharton, V. 87-94. They were followed by the resolution of Apr. 30, in which Congress expressed approval of Jay's course as detailed in his report of the preceding Oct. 3 (see next chapter); and by a second resolution, adopted Aug. 6, 1782, ordering him to decline any propositions from Spain before transmitting them to Congress, unless his accession thereto "was necessary to the fulfilment of the stipulation on the part of the United States contained in the separate and secret article" of the treaty with France. *Journals of the Continental Congress,* XXII. 219-20 and 449-51. Whether these resolutions reached Jay in time to influence his conduct at the peace negotiations, I do not know, but conceivably they did.

vantage from this defeat of their ally, perhaps indeed, greater advantage than they would have from her victory. For it was Rodney's triumph, the news of which reached London on the evening of May 18th, that encouraged the British government in the idea of attempting to separate America from her allies in the peace negotiations that were just to begin, the theory being that if the wastage of the American war could be brought to an end, England could afford to continue the war on the sea with the Bourbon powers.[46] That this assault upon their loyalty contributed materially to the success with which the American envoys met in the negotiations is altogether unquestionable. In short, America at this period was the lucky banker at the wheel of fortune: she ventured little, leaving that to others but whoever won, she won.

[46] See Fitzmaurice's *Life of Shelburne*, III. 194-5 and 203. For the consolatory memoir which Vergennes presented the king on Grasse's defeat, see Doniol, V. 118-20. The moral he draws is that France must give the lie to Lord North's statement at the beginning of the war, "que la France débute toujours avec supériorité, mais qu'elle se relache dans ses efforts, autant que l'Angleterre multiplie et acroit les siens."

CHAPTER XIV

JAY'S MISSION TO SPAIN

The story of Jay's part in the negotiations of
1782 is one that has never ceased to interest
American students. In relating this well-known
episode, I have not sought to avoid the problems
of casuistry that, thanks to the opposed labors of
the pious and the critical it has come to involve.
At the same time, I have endeavored to organize
my treatment of these problems in conformity
with my main theme, wherefore I treat Jay's
action primarily as a foil to French policy touching the negotiations. But as French policy at
this point leaned heavily on Spanish policy, and
as Jay imbibed at Madrid the point of view
from which his course at the negotiations took its
departure, I feel that a brief review of his mission to the latter country will not be inap-
posite.[1]

[1] The following account of Jay's Spanish mission is drawn from
his long reports to the President of Congress, of May 26 and Nov.
6, 1780, Oct. 3, 1781, and Apr. 28, 1782, which are to be found in
Wharton, III. 707-34, IV. 112-50 and 738-65, and V. 336-77. The
constituent documents of these reports will also be found in the
Correspondence and Public Papers of John Jay (H. P. Johnston,
ed., New York, 1890, 4 vols.), vols. I and II, *passim.*

Jay set out for his post October 20th, 1779, and arrived at Cadiz January 22nd, 1780. Never received officially in the entire course of thirty month's sojourn at the court of His Catholic Majesty, snubbed personally by nobility and officials, often without funds from the failure of his salary to reach him, put constantly to great expense in following the migratory court from pillar to post, embarrassed by the remarkable course of Congress in drawing on him when he had not a *sou* in prospect, put off again and again with the most transparent excuses, his correspondence subjected to official espionage and molestation—he underwent, without doubt, one of the most trying experiences that has ever fallen to the lot of an envoy clothed with the dignity of his government's commission.

Yet at the outset, Jay's mission was not without signs of promise. He was received by Florida Blanca with great promptitude and given strong hopes of considerable financial aid before the end of the year, as well as of a treaty which, at no remote date, would establish the long sought *via media* between the legitimate interests of both Spain and America respecting the Mississippi question.[2]   But early in July, 1780, came the news of the loss of Charleston. "The effect of it," wrote Jay, "was as visible the next day as that of a hard night's frost on young leaves."[3]

[2] Wharton, III. 709-11, 722-5.
[3] *Op. cit.,* IV. 123.

Meantime, Congress was constantly drawing on its envoy, and bills of exchange were constantly accumulating against him in the hands of the brokers, with the result that his financial difficulties were soon appalling.[4] On July 5th, he had a long conference with the minister as to ways and means of meeting these bills, but, in his own expressive phrase, "not a single nail would drive."[5] Nor was he more successful in his efforts at correspondence. Four successive notes remained unanswered, and an attempt to see the minister proved equally unavailing.[6] Finally, on September 3rd, Don Diego Gardoqui, one of the friendly house of Bilboa merchants that since the beginning of the war had been carrying on a considerable trade in contraband with the United States, presented himself to Jay with Florida Blanca's compliments, and proceeded to propose point-blank that, in return for financial assistance, the United States should surrender their claims to the navigation of the Mississippi. Jay rejected the offer indignantly and was shortly after informed that even the limited credit which His Majesty had thus far extended was, for "reasons of state," withdrawn.[7]

[4] *Ib.*, III. 722; IV. 122 ff.

[5] *Ib.*, 125.

[6] *Ib.*, 127-8.

[7] *Ib.*, 133-5. There was much talk at this time and for some months later of sending Gardoqui to America to take the place filled by Rendon, as Miralles' successor, *ib.*, 741-2, 764. As a

At this moment, fortunately, "some glorious reports from America arrived," and the Spanish government reconsidered its harsh decision. On September 15th Gardoqui informed Jay that if he could find credit for that sum, His Majesty would be answerable for as much as one hundred and fifty thousand dollars,[8] and eight days later the minister himself conferred with Jay a second time on the subject of a treaty. The conference revealed, however, that a treaty was probably far distant. Actually, as Florida Blanca inadvertently admitted, the Spanish monarch was determined not to recognize the United States before England did.[9] Primarily this was because

matter of fact Gardoqui did not arrive in the United States till May, 1785. For the negotiations then undertaken between him and Jay, who was now secretary of Foreign Affairs, see Bancroft, VI. 421-2.

[8] Wharton, IV. 139.

[9] "After a variety of other remarks of little importance he made a very interesting observation, which will help us to account for the delays of the court, *viz.:* That all these affairs could with more facility be adjusted at a general peace than now, for that such a particular and even secret treaty with us might then be made as would be very convenient to both. . . . Throughout the whole conversation [May 23, 1781] the count appeared much less cordial than in the preceding one; he seemed to want self-possession, and to that cause I ascribe his incautiously mentioning the general peace as the most proper season for completing our political connections. I had, nevertheless, no reason to suspect that this change in his behavior arose from any cause more important than those variations in temper and feelings which they who are unaccustomed to govern themselves often experience from changes in the weather, in their health, from fatigue of business, or other such like accidental causes." *Ib.,* 746.

he feared the example and effect of American independence on his own dominions; but connected with this fear was Spain's desire, which Florida Blanca constantly stressed, to maintain her monopoly of commerce in the Gulf of Mexico. The Count, wrote Jay,

made several observations tending to show the importance of this object to Spain and its determination to adhere to it, saying with some degree of warmth that, unless Spain could exclude all nations from the Gulf of Mexico, they might as well admit all; that the king would never relinquish it; that the minister regarded it as the principal object to be obtained by the war, and *that obtained*, he should be perfectly easy whether or no Spain procured any other cession; that he considered it far more important than the acquisition of Gibraltar, and that if they did not get it, it was a matter of indifference to him whether the English possessed Mobile or not.[10]

Late in October Jay received word that Gates had been defeated at Camden and that the elder Laurens was in the Tower. "Our sky in this quarter," he wrote, "is again darkened with clouds not in my power to dispel."[11] Furthermore, this was the period of the Spanish government's negotiations with the Englishman Cumberland, which, as we have seen, menaced the United States with the *status quo*. Not until March, 1781, did Cumberland leave Madrid, that

[10] *Ib.*, 145-6.
[11] *Ib.*, 149.

is, several weeks after Spain had ostensibly agreed to a fresh campaign.[12]

Meantime, by the resolution of February 15th, Congress had instructed Jay to recede from his previous instructions so far as they insisted on the free navigation of the Mississippi below the 31st degree, "provided such cession shall be unalterably insisted on by Spain"; and on May 18th Jay received advices to this effect from the secretary of Congress.[13] He greatly regretted the step, arguing that, inasmuch as Spain was herself now "at war with Great Britain to gain her own objects," she would be apt to "prosecute it full as vigorously as if she fought for" ours.[14] Also, as certain papers that should have accompanied Lovell's letter did not arrive and the letter itself had passed through the post-office, he suspected that Florida Blanca knew as much about Congress' change of front as he did; and he

[12] "If they have rejected all the overtures of Britain," wrote Jay in Nov., 1780, "why is Mr. Cumberland still here? And why are expresses passing between Madrid and London through Portugal?" *Ib.*, 148. Jay records Cumberland's departure in his report of Apr. 25, 1781: "Mr. Cumberland is on the road home. I much suspect that he was sent and received from mutual views in the two courts of deceiving each other. Which of them has been most successful is hard to determine. . . . As to the assurances of the minister on this subject, they are all of little consequence, because on such occasions courts only say what may be convenient, and therefore may or may not merit confidence. Time and circumstances will cast more light on this subject." *Ib.*, 388.

[13] *Ib.*, 738-40.

[14] *Ib.*, 743.

wrote: "The moment they saw that the cession of this navigation was made to depend upon their persevering to insist upon it, it became absurd to suppose that they would cease to persevere."[15]

Finally on July 2, taking the bull by the horns, Jay informed Florida Blanca outright that the great obstacle to a treaty between the United States and Spain had been removed by the action of Congress itself, and expressed the hope that His Majesty would "now be pleased to become the ally of the United States."[16] Ten days went by and the communication still remained unnoticed by the Spanish minister. Jay then called at the Pardo and was informed that the reason for the seeming neglect was the press of business consequent upon the court's intention to remove shortly to San Ildefonso. On August 4th Jay himself repaired to the new capital and something over a month later was able to secure an interview with the minister, who had filled up the interval with alternating pleas of illness and business.[17] The conference was resultless, but a second one a fortnight later produced a request on Florida Blanca's part that "Mr. Jay . . . would offer him such a set of propositions as might become the basis of future conferences between him and the person whom he expected

[15] *Ib.*, 744.
[16] *Ib.*, 747.
[17] *Ib.*, 750-4.

His Majesty would appoint."[18]   The request was complied with four days later.   By the sixth article of the proposed agreement, the United States *relinquished* to His Catholic Majesty "the navigation of the river Mississippi from the 31st degree of north latitude . . . down to the ocean."   Accompanying the article, however, was the explanation that "the offer of this proposition, being dictated" by the circumstances of the war, "must necessarily be limited by the duration of them and consequently that if the acceptance of it should, together with the proposed alliance, be postponed to a general peace, the United States will cease to consider themselves bound by any propositions" now made in their behalf.[19]

Of course the offer came to nothing, and on November 21st we find Jay writing Franklin that "this court continues to observe the most profound silence respecting our propositions."[20] Three weeks later Jay secured another interview with the minister, who informed him that a certain M. del Campo "had been appointed nearly three months ago to treat and confer" with him, but that "shortly after the court removed from San Ildefonso that gentleman's health began to decline" and that it had only insufficiently checked its deplorable tendency very recently.[21]

[18] *Ib.*, 758.
[19] *Ib.*, 760-2.
[20] *Ib.*, V., 346.
[21] *Ib.*, 348.

However, Jay now began to pay court to M. del Campo, with whom he finally obtained an interview some six weeks later.

I found M. del Campo [he writes] surrounded by suitors. He received me with great and unusual civility and carried me into his private apartment. I told him that, as he was evidently very busy, I could not think of sitting down and wished only to detain him a few moments. He said that he was indeed much engaged but that we might, nevertheless, take a cup of chocolate together.[22]

A few weeks later Franklin wrote Jay from Paris requesting that he "render himself" there for the approaching peace negotiations as soon as possible. "You would," said the venerable doctor, "be of infinite service. Spain has taken four years to consider whether she should treat with us or not. Give her forty, and let us in the meantime mind our own business."[23] The middle of June Jay left for Paris, expectant of renewing negotiations there with Aranda. But these expectations proved as footless as preceding ones had been. Aranda refused to show Jay his powers to treat—for the good reason that he had

[22] *Ib.*, 356-7. For a good summary of the delays Jay had met with in Spain, see La Fayette to Vergennes, Mar. 20, 1782, *ib.*, 266. For the episode of the invitation that was sent to Jay by mistake, to dine with the Spanish minister, and was declined when renewed to him in his quality as "a private gentleman of distinction," see *ib.*, 373-7.

[23] Letter of Apr. 22, 1782, *ib.*, 321.

none—and Jay refused to proceed without this preliminary.[24]

Writers have implied that Jay went up to Paris in 1782 in a rather suspicious frame of mind, and it is certain that if he had ever been inclined to regard diplomatic questions in a sentimental light he had been pretty well cured of the tendency by the time he left Madrid. "In politics," he wrote Franklin at the close of this period, "I depend upon nothing but facts, and therefore never risk deceiving myself or others by a reliance on professions, which may or may not be sincere."[25] He, accordingly, warned Congress of the futility of attempting to form alliances "on principles of equality *in formâ pauperis*";[26] that the United States, to be "respectable anywhere," must be "formidable at home";[27] that we but deceived ourselves if we believed "that any nation in the world has or will have a disinterested regard for us."[28] France, he acknowledged ungrudgingly, was doing a vast deal for America and often in a handsome and generous spirit that added greatly to the value of the favors she rendered; and he held, that, "so long as" she was faithful to us, we were in honor bound to continue

[24] Jay to Livingston, Nov. 17, 1782, *ib.*, VI. 21-5, 28; same to same, Dec. 12, *ib.*, 130.

[25] *Correspondence and Public Papers*, II. 63.

[26] *Ib.*, 20.

[27] Wharton, IV. 147.

[28] *Ib.*, 148.

in the war for her objects as well as our own.[29]
At the same time, he was under no illusions as to
the obligations of France to Spain. The latter
power, he perceived, had been brought into the existing war only by special inducements, and he
did not hesitate to inform Montmorin of his belief that one of these was "the exclusive navigation of the Mississippi and the Gulf of Mexico."[30]
It is not remarkable, then, that he remonstrated
strongly against the Instructions of June 15th.
They had, he conceded, "an appearance of policy," but, he protested, they forced the American
envoys to

receive and obey (under the name of *opinions*) the *directions* of those on whom . . . no American minister
ought to be dependent and to whom, in love for our
country and zeal for her service, I am sure that my
colleagues and myself are at least their equal.

Indeed, he preferred to resign his commission as
peace negotiator rather than submit to such a
control. But he did not resign; and as events
were to prove, he had underestimated his own
hardihood of purpose.[31]

[29] *Correspondence and Public Papers,* II. 283.

[30] Wharton, IV. 137. This belief Montmorin challenged, but
he later admitted that Spain was desirous of modifying American
independence, Jay to Livingston, Apr. 28, 1782, *ib.,* V. 368.

[31] *Correspondence and Public Papers,* II. 71-2.

CHAPTER XV

JAY AND THE NEGOTIATIONS OF 1782

The story of the American negotiations for peace, which it was understood from the outset were to be carried on separately between the American envoys and such representatives as Great Britain should accredit for the purpose,[1]

[1] Vergennes to La Luzerne, Apr. 9, 1782: "Au reste, M., quoique nous désirons que le Congrès n'entame aucune négociation directe et qu'il ne fasse point une paix séparée, . . . nous sommes et serons toujours disposés à consentir que les plénipotentiaires Américains en Europe traitent conformement à leurs instructions, directement et sans notre intervention, avec ceux de la cour de Londres, tandis que nous traiterons de même de notre côté, à condition que les deux négociations chemineront d'un pas égal, et que les deux traités seront signés en même tems et ne vaudront point l'un sans l'autre," Doniol V. 78-9. See also Oswald to Shelburne, June 9, 1782: "Dr. Franklin then said he thought the best way to come at a general peace was to treat separately with each party, and under distinct commissions to one and the same, or different persons. By this method many difficulties . . . would be in a great measure avoided. And then at last there would only remain to consolidate these several settlements into one genuine and conclusive treaty of pacification . . . . He explained as to the commissions, that there might be one to treat with France, one for the Colonies, one for Spain, and, he added, one for Holland, if it should be thought proper." At the same time Franklin put in a bid for Oswald as the American negotiator. Lord Edmond Fitzmaurice, *Life of*

begins to all practical intents with Franklin's communication of July 9th to the British agent Oswald, wherein was laid down the basis for a treaty of peace between the two countries. The first four items of this basis, labelled "necessary," were as follows:

1. Independence full and complete in every sense, and all troops to be withdrawn; 2. A settlement of the boundaries of the Thirteen States; 3. A confinement of the boundaries of Canada to at least what they were before the Quebec Act, if not to still narrower limits; 4. A freedom of fishing on the Banks of Newfoundland and elsewhere, as well for fish as whales.[33]

William, Earl of Shelburne (London, 1876, 3 vols.), III. 207-8. The only effort made by the British government for a separate negotiation in the United States was through Sir Guy Carleton who arrived in New York on May 5, with a commission to make "peace or war in North America." Later Carleton was authorized to make peace either with Congress or "through General Washington" on the basis of "unconditional independence." See Wharton, V. 405-6, 413, 417, and 652, and VI. 15-6. The arrival of Carleton evoked the Congressional resolutions of May 31, 1782, assuring His Most Christian Majesty of Congress' determination "to hearken to no propositions for peace which are not perfectly conformable" to the Alliance, and in case such propositions were made by the court of London, not to depart from the measures which they have heretofore taken for preventing delay, and for conducting the discussions of them [such propositions] in confidence and in concert with His Most Christian Majesty," *Journals of the Continental Congress,* XXII. 312-3. See also to same effect, the Resolutions of Oct. 4, 1782, *ib.,* XXIII. 637-9.

[2] Fitzmaurice, *Life of Shelburne,* III. 243-4. Early in the year a correspondence had arisen between Hartley and Franklin touching peace. The former had hinted at a separate peace between England and America, which suggestion the American had spurned. Wharton, V. 80-4 and 112-4. See also Franklin to

Jay's participation in the negotiations began
on August 10th, when he and Franklin conferred
with Vergennes as to the sufficiency of Oswald's

Rayneval, Mar. 22, transmitting this correspondence, B. F. Stevens,
Peace Transcripts (Library of Congress). Meanwhile the
crumbling North cabinet had sent Forth to Paris to make some
bungling efforts to draw France off from her alliance with the
United States. Forth offered France her conquests in the West
Indies, the suppression of the commissionership at Dunkirk, and
certain advantages in the East Indies. Of course, he failed,
Revue d'Histoire diplomatique, XIV. 161 ff.; Wharton, V. 298,
303-5; *Journals of the Continental Congress*, XXII. 302-3. Over-
lapping this episode, and so antedating the formation of the Rockingham cabinet, a correspondence had also sprung up between
Franklin and Shelburne regarding peace. In consequence of this,
as early as April 12, Oswald was sent to Paris by Shelburne, who
was now secretary for Home and Colonial Affairs under Rockingham, to sound him on the question of peace. Franklin informed
Oswald "that America was ready to treat, but only in concert with
France, and that as Mr. Jay, Mr. Adams, and Mr. Laurens were
all absent from Paris, nothing of importance could be done in the
affair." At the same time Franklin urged the cession of Canada in
the interest of a durable peace and gave Oswald a minute of his
views on the subject. This proposal Franklin afterward renewed
in his communication of July 9, cited above, but without result.
On Apr. 23, the Rockingham cabinet agreed to a minute requesting
that His Majesty have Oswald return to Paris in order to set on
foot a negotiation with Franklin looking to a general peace and
"the allowance of independence to America," and that Fox, the
secretary of Foreign Affairs, suggest a proper person to the king
to begin a like negotiation with France. In consequence of this
minute Oswald was sent again to Paris to treat with Franklin,
while Thomas Grenville was sent by Fox to treat with the French
minister. On May 18, the cabinet asked the king to direct Fox to
empower Grenville "to treat and conclude at Paris" "on the basis
of independence to the Thirteen Colonies in North America"; and
five days late instructed the latter in negotiating *with France*, to
propose the acknowledgment by England of the independence of

commission, which empowered that amiable gentleman to treat, not with the United States of
America, but with "the said colonies and plantations."[3] Jay urged that "it would be descending
from the ground of independence" to treat under
such a description. Vergennes, however, urged
that names signified little; that the king of Great Britain's styling himself the king of France was no obstacle
to . . . France's treating with him; that an acknowledgment of our independence, instead of preceding, must
in the natural course of things be the effect of the treaty.

America "in the first instance." Fox, interpreting these minutes
as establishing a single negotiation, that with France, who, accordingly, was to be assured at the outset of England's intention
to recognize American independence, now authorized Grenville to
take over the whole business of peace-making. At first his plan
was checked by the refusal of Vergennes to treat with regard to
American interests, both because His Majesty had no power to do
so and also because "the dignity of the king of England and of
the United States required the establishment of a direct negotiation between the two," Vergennes to La Luzerne, June 28, 1782,
Doniol, V. 88. In order to meet this objection Fox now empowered Grenville to treat with the king of France "and any
other Prince or State," Fitzmaurice, *op. cit.*, III. 214-7. Meantime, however, Shelburne had protested against the American
negotiation being removed from his department and the king had
sided with him. From the confusion thus resulting the situation
was relieved by the death of Rockingham on July 1st, and the
accession of Shelburne the day following to the Prime Minister-
ship. Fox now left the cabinet and Grenville threw up his commission as envoy. Meantime, the Parliamentary Enabling Act
had been passed, and on July 25 Oswald received his first commission, while, a fortnight earlier, Fitzherbert, the British minister
at Brussels, had been appointed to take the Grenville's place. Fitzmaurice, *op. cit.*, III. chs. IV and V; Doniol, V. ch. III.

[3] *Wharton*, V. 613-4.

Upon leaving Vergennes' presence Franklin imputed the minister's attitude to a desire to remove
"every obstacle to a speedy negotiation." But
Jay, who had been led to believe by the mystifying conduct and language of another British
agent, Grenville, that there was still some doubt
about the British government's according independence, drew the conclusion that Vergennes
was prepared to profit by this uncertainty by
getting Spain out of the war before England and
America could come to terms. They wish, said
he to Franklin, "to make their uses of us": the
Count foresaw "difficulties in bringing Spain into
peace on moderate terms, and that if we once
found ourselves standing on our own legs . . .
we might not think it our duty to continue in the
war for the attainment of Spanish objects."[4]

[4] Jay to Livingston, Wharton, VI. 12-9. This letter, *ib.*, 11-51, is
Jay's apology for the course described in the text. It is also to
be found in the *Correspondence and Public Papers*, II. 366-452.
The statement by Grenville that is referred to is his assertion,
upon leaving Paris, that Shelburne had no intention of granting
America her independence, Fitzmaurice, *op. cit.*, III. 246. This entirely unwarranted assertion was the source of the whole misunderstanding between Jay and Vergennes on the matter of
independence. As is clear from his course with both Grenville
and Fitzherbert, Vergennes was determined not to begin negotiations till he was definitely assured that the British government was
ready to recognize American independence, Doniol, V. ch. III,
passim; Fitzmaurice *op. cit.*, III. 251-2. *Journals of the Continental Congress*, Sept. 24, 1782, XXIII. 596-604. Jay, on the other
hand, felt that Grenville's declaration was sufficient to call into
question any mere statement by the British government henceforth

Jay was, of course, quite right in suspecting that the great difficulty in the way of peace was the necessity France was under of satisfying Spain, and from this it was a reasonable deduction that the French Foreign Office might be tempted to resort to underhand expedients to prolong the negotiations between the United States and England.[5]   On the other hand, it does

of its intentions as to independence, and that nothing could now remove uncertainty save the act of recognition itself, or what would be equivalent to an act of recognition if peace succeeded. To his view, therefore, Vergennes' willingness to forego *the actual recognition of independence* by England till the treaty of peace was tantamount to willingness to postpone, till the end of the negotiations perhaps, *the question whether there should be such a recognition* at all. Herein, he was wrong. "We may judge of the intentions of the court of London," Vergennes wrote La Luzerne, Aug. 14, "by their first propositions. If they have independence for their basis we may proceed; if not, we must break off," Doniol, V. 110.

[5] "When once independence has been *definitely offered* to the United States, if it is not followed immediately by peace it will not be difficult to persuade them that the continuation of the war has an entirely different object from their interests," Montmorin to Vergennes, Aug. 12, 1782, Stevens, *Peace Transcripts*. It should be noted in passing that, in an effort to reassure the Americans of his good faith, Shelburne had furnished Franklin with a copy of his letter to Sir Guy Carleton of June 25. This letter mentions that Grenville had been instructed to propose American independence "in the first instance, instead of making it the condition of a general peace." At the same time, however, this letter also brought forward the point, "that if the negotiation is broken off it will undoubtedly be for the sake of" France and Spain and not America, and that any delay in obtaining peace would be attributable to the same cause, Wharton, VI. 15-6. While, therefore, this document was reassuring in one way, in another it confirmed Jay's suspicions. These suspicions were in formation be-

not appear how the postponement, to the conclusion of peace, of British recognition of American
independence—a matter which, Vergennes had
informed himself was a foregone result—would
have delayed proceedings. The truth is that, owing
to his misapprehension of Shelburne's good-
faith, Jay was playing the very game that, by his
assumption, Vergennes wished to have played,
that is, he was creating delay. Nevertheless, in so
doing he forwarded American interests. For in
an effort to meet his demands and to bring to an
end the delay they were causing, Townshend, acting for Shelburne, authorized Oswald on September 1st "to agree to the plan of pacification"
that had been proposed by Franklin, "to the full
extent" of the "necessary" articles and, further,
"to waive any stipulation" in behalf either of
British creditors or of the American loyalists.[6]

But even this concession did not abate Jay's
determination to treat on no other footing than
as the representative of independent states; and
there now followed a succession of events which
galvanized his obstinacy to swift and positive

fore he left Spain. "France," he wrote Livingston, in his report
of Apr. 28, "is ready for a peace, but not Spain. The king's eyes
are fixed on Gibraltar . . . . If England should offer us peace
on the terms of our treaty with France, the French court would
be very much embarrassed by their alliance with Spain, and as yet
*we are under no obligations to persist in the war to gratify this
court"* (the emphasis is mine), *ib.*, 373.

[6] Fitzmaurice, *op. cit.*, III. 254-6; Bancroft, History, V. 563-4.

action. It should be mentioned that, on the same
occasion when Oswald's commission had been first
discussed with Vergennes, the conflicting claims
of Spain and the United States in the region west
of the Mountains had also been brought into the
conversation. The minister himself, Jay records,
"was very reserved and cautious; but M. Rayneval, his principal secretary, who was present,
thought that we claimed more than we had a right
to."[7] This tone on Rayneval's part, it is probable, was somewhat material in forming Jay's
unfavorable opinion of the minister's argument
on the question of Oswald's commission. Be that
as it may, Rayneval next proceeded to develop
his views to Jay more at length, and on September 7th sent him an elaborate memorandum in
support of them and proposing that the lands
south of the Ohio be divided into two Indian pro-
tectorates, the one toward the Mississippi to be
under Spain, the one toward the Mountains to be
under the United States, and that the lands north
of the Ohio be left to England.[8] Then on September 9th Jay "received certain information that
on September 7th M. Rayneval had left Versailles
and was gone to England, that it was pretended
he was gone into the country, and that several
precautions had been taken to keep his real destination a secret."[9] Finally, on September 10th

[7] Wharton, VI. 23.
[8] Cf. p. 309 supra.
[9] Wharton, VI., 28.

"a copy of a translation of a letter from M. Marbois to the Count de Vergennes against our sharing in the fishery" was put into the American's hands.[10]

[10] *Ib.*, V. 740 and VI. 29. Jay states that he is "not at liberty to mention the manner in which this paper came" to his hands, but Fitzmaurice says that it was communicated "by means of one of the secret agents in the employment of the English government," *op. cit.*, III. 257. Writers have attempted to cast doubts on the authenticity of this document, but these doubts are adequately met by the following passage from Vergennes' despatch of Aug. 12, 1782, to La Luzerne: "Le Sr. de Marbois propose un expédient pour arrêter les espérances des Américains et les menées de M. Samuel Adams; mais le Conseil du Roi juge que comme nous ne sommes liés par aucun engagement, nous n'avons aucune mesure à prendre pour prévenir les clameurs et les reproches, et toute démarche de notre part tendante à ce but seroit au moins prématurée; d'ailleurs, nous avons du tems de reste pour nous expliquer lorsque la matière des pêcheries sera sérieusement discutée entre les plénip'res Américains et le commissaire de la cour de Londres." Doniol, V. 157. In his despatch of Jan. 4, 1783, to Jay, Livingston, Congress' secretary for Foreign Affairs, belittles the significance of Marbois' communication. He is not, he says, surprised by it, "since he [Marbois] always endeavored to persuade us that our claim to the fisheries was not well founded." Then he continues: "Yet one thing is very remarkable, and I hope evinces the determination of France to serve us on this point: The advice given to discourage the hope is certainly judicious, and yet we find no steps taken in consequence of it. On the contrary, we have been repeatedly told in formal communications since that period, 'that the king would do everything for us that circumstances will admit.' . . . This communication was made on the 21st of last November from letters of the 7th of September . . . . Congress, relying upon it, have made no alteration in their instructions since the change in their affairs by the blow the enemy received at Yorktown. This letter of Marbois, and the conduct of the court of France, evince the difference between a

Jay was now thoroughly aroused and thoroughly alarmed, especially for American interests in the West. France stood ready, he now felt

great politician and a little one . . . . Our exclusion from the fishery would only be beneficial to England." Wharton, VI. 177-80 fn. This argument would be more persuasive if the letters of September 7th, relied upon by Livingston, had not been followed by such expressions as that quoted above, from the despatch of August 12, 1782, where Vergennes clearly contemplates the possibility of intervening in the discussion of the fisheries question between the British and American negotiations, against the American pretensions. And to the same effect is the following passage from the French minister's despatch of June 28: "Je prévois, M., qu'il y aura encore de grands débats au Congrès au sujet des limites de quelques états. Si le Congrès ne se laisse pas entraîner par l'intérêt personnel et les clameurs des provinces du Nord, il envisagera la paix comme le plus grand des bienfaits qu'il puisse désirer; il se gardera bien d'exiger la moindre faveur, à titre de droit, d'un puissance à laquelle une portion énorme de son domaine va échapper; il se bornera à demander ce que le droit commun assûre aux Américains, et il se réservera de demander une plus grande extension lorsque l'Angleterre lui proposera des arrangements de commerce. Je me flatte surtout, M., que les Américains ne prétendront pas que le Roi se fasse fort de leur procurer l'extension de pêche qu'ils convoitent, et encore moins qu'il fasse le sacrifice de ses propres pêcheries pour les dédommager du refus de la Grande-Bretagne. Sa M'té ne consentira ni à l'un ni à l'autre; tout ce qu'elle pourra faire sera d'accorder ses bons offices selon que les circonstances le lui permettront; mais elle est invariablement résolüe de ne point sacrifier le rétablissement de la paix à une pretention mal fondée." Doniol, V. 90-1. To like effect are Vergennes' despatches of Oct. 14 and Nov. 23 to La Luzerne, Stevens, *Peace Transcripts;* Doniol V. 176-9. Also, we should not ignore the testimony of Lord St. Helens (formerly Fitzherbert, the British negotiator with France), in his letter to Judge William Jay, in 1838, that Vergennes had argued strongly, in 1782, against the Americans being admitted to the fisheries, convinced, in case the United States would not give Spain the territory she wanted in that region, to aid the latter in negotiating with England for it; and Rayneval, he believed, had gone to England to sound Shelburne on the American claims, to impress upon him France's disapproval of them, and "to hint the propriety of such a line as would on the one hand satisfy Spain and on the other leave to Britain all the country north of the Ohio."[11] He at once determined on aggressive measures. Without consulting Franklin, he sent Benjamin Vaughan, a friend of both Franklin and Shelburne, to London to combat Rayneval's reasoning and to urge a new commission for Oswald authorizing him to treat with "the United States of America."[12] Vaughan's mission proved successful, and upon the new basis the negotiations proceeded till November 30th, when "provisional articles" were signed, embodying the conditions of a treaty to be concluded when terms of peace should "be agreed upon between Great

on the ground that it would be dangerous to accord them so great a nursery of sea-power. Henry Flanders, *Lives and Times of the Chief Justices* (Phila., 1858), I. 343. Then, there is the point made by Adams, "that, aiming at excluding us from fishing upon the north side of Newfoundland, it was natural for them [the French] to wish that the English would exclude us from the south side," Wharton, VI. 93. For an estimate of the fisheries as a nursery of seamen, see *ib.*, III. 789.

[11] Wharton, VI. 29.

[12] *Ib.*, 29-32, 45-7.

Britain and France," which did not occur till some six weeks later.[13]

Was Jay's conduct, which by their ratification of it became that of his fellow commissioners also, justifiable? The severest criticism meted out to the commissioners was that of Vergennes in his heated letter to Franklin of December 15th, which was called forth by the latter's announcement that he was about to forward the Provisional Articles to Congress by a vessel for which a passport had been secured from the king of England.[14]

I am at a loss, sir, [wrote the irate minister] to explain your conduct and that of your colleagues on this occasion. You have concluded your preliminary articles

---

[13] The Provisional Articles are given in Appendix V. A question raised in Parliament with reference to them was whether "American independence was to take effect absolutely at any period, near or remote, whenever a treaty of peace was concluded with the court of France, or was contingent merely, so that if the particular treaty now negotiating with France should not terminate in a peace, the offer was to be considered revoked and the independence left to be determined by events," *Parliamentary History,* XXIII. col. 306. Shelburne denounced the question as "unwise" and "unprecedented" and refused to answer it: "he was bound to keep the secrets of the king . . . the thing was done, the treaty signed and sealed, and whether good or bad, its production could not vary it," *ib.* What was the character of the contract in the provisional articles? This question was discussed in Congress, and the opinion arrived at by Wilson of Pennsylvania was that it was "contingently definitive," *Writings of Madison,* I. 448-50. See also a question raised as to the interpretation of the preamble, *ib.,* 410.

[14] Wharton, VI. 137-8.

without any communication between us, although the instructions from Congress prescribe that nothing shall be done without the participation of the king. You are about to hold out a certain hope of peace to America without even informing yourself on the state of the negotiation on our part. You are wise and discreet, sir; you perfectly understand what is due to propriety; you have all your life performed your duties. I pray you to consider how you propose to fulfill those which are due to the king?[15]

Technically, of course, the violation by the commissioners of their instructions was a matter exclusively between them and Congress, besides which these instructions had been voted with the mediation of the Imperial courts in view, while the negotiations of 1782 proceeded along quite different lines. Nor again, did the action of the commissioners technically violate the pledge given in the Treaty of Alliance, that the United States would conclude neither truce nor peace with Great Britain without first obtaining the formal consent of France. The

[15] *Ib.*, 140. Franklin's soothing answer is given *ib.*, 143-4. Franklin admitted that the Americans had "been guilty of neglecting a point of *bienséance*." But he urged that "this little misunderstanding . . . be kept a secret," as *"the English, I just now learn, flatter themselves they have already divided us"* (the emphasis is Franklin's). At the same time, Franklin insisted that the articles ought to be sent to America, arguing that it would be better for Congress to have the commissioners' account of them than the British account. On the 24th, the articles were sent off, *ib.*, 153 fn. For a further expression of the attitude of the Foreign Office toward the conduct of the commissioners, see Vergennes to La Luzerne, Dec. 19, *ib.*, 150-2.

Provisional Articles were not a separate peace nor did they "hold out a certain hope of peace." It may be admitted, however, that they were intended to convey a warning that the United States reserved the right to make a separate peace, if a final peace should be obstructed by France for reasons not covered by the Treaty of Alliance. In other words, the articles reclaimed for the United States that right to construe their treaty obligations which, when exercised in good faith, belongs to all sovereignties, and which Congress had surrendered by its instructions.[16]

[10] There is, therefore, no necessary contradiction between Jay's language to Oswald and to La Fayette. "Upon my saying," Oswald wrote Townshend, Oct. 2, "how hard it was that France should pretend to saddle us with all their private engagements with Spain, he [Jay] replied: 'We will allow no such thing. For we shall say to France: The agreement we made with you we shall faithfully perform; but if you have entered into any separate measures with other people not included in that agreement, and will load the negotiation with their demands, we shall give ourselves no concern about them.'" Stevens, *Peace Transcripts*. On Jan. 19, 1783, Jay wrote La Fayette, with reference to the Provisional Articles, thus: "It appears to me singular that any doubts should be entertained of American good faith. . . . America has so often repeated and reiterated her professions and assurances of regard to the treaty alluded to [the Treaty of Alliance], that I hope she will not impair her dignity by making any more of them." *Correspondence and Public Papers*, III. 25. But see also Edward Channing, *History of the United States*, III. 384-5, for proof of the fact that Jay urged Oswald to press his government to undertake the reconquest of West Florida from the Spaniards, and even suggested to that end that some of the British troops at New York and Charleston be used for the purpose. In this way the British forces in the United States would have been weakened; the Brit-

The question that at once prompts itself is
whether the United States, having regard to the
kinds and scope of the assistance they had had
from France, were altogether free to claim the
prerogatives of sovereignty in relation to their
engagements with that country. No doubt, in
theory the United States were "sovereign and independent" allies of France; but more imposing
than any theory is the fact that, at the very moment of communicating the Provisional Articles
to Vergennes, Franklin was obliged by instructions from Congress to solicit a fresh loan from
His Most Christian Majesty.[17] And the circumstance is indicative of what had been the actual
situation from the very outset of the alliance.
But such being the case, was not the Foreign
Office at liberty, within reasonable limits, to make

ish concession to the United States of the right to navigate the
Mississippi would have been rendered effective; and Spain would
have been humiliated.

[17] Congress wanted a loan of twenty millions, and on Dec. 21 a
loan of six millions was extended, Wharton, VI. 152 fn. Some
writers have attributed this concession to the pleasing effects of
Franklin's note of Dec. 17, quoted above. It is much more probable that the concession was instigated by the consideration
suggested in the text, that so long as Congress was the recipient
of such favors from France it was not likely to cut loose from
the French leading-strings. In justice to the commissioners, however, one should recall the principle invoked by Jay in Spain, that
the United States, being a sovereign nation, were free to borrow
money "on the same consideration that other nations did," namely,
"the repayment of the principal with interest," and accordingly,
without putting their more permanent interests in pawn. See
Wharton, IV. 134-6.

the best arrangements it could in the interest of a cause which was certainly not less that of America than of France; and granting the measures so taken to have been taken in good faith, were not the United States in honor bound to shoulder their legitimate consequences? Jay himself had owned that it was farcical to seek an equal alliance *in formâ pauperis*. It was, perhaps, a little less than honest to pretend to maintain one on that footing.

"The separate and secret manner in which our ministers had proceeded with respect to France and the confidential manner with respect to the British ministers," Madison records, "affected different members of Congress very differently."[18] Madison himself thought the conduct of the commissioners censurable, taking substantially the point of view just expounded. He admitted that France had mingled too much artifice in her dealings with America, and that her truest policy would have been a more straightforward course. He also conceded that the ties of France with Spain, "whom she had drawn into the war, required her to favor Spain, at least to a certain degree, at the expense of America."[19] None the less, he contended that, "instead of coöperating with Great Britain" to take advantage of "the embarrassment in which France was placed by

[18] *Writings*, I. 404.
[19] *Ib.*, 296.

the interfering claims of Spain and the United States," the envoys "ought to have made every allowance and given every facility to it consistent with a regard to the rights of their constituents." The facts alleged by the envoys, he continued, showed no "hostile or ambitious designs" against our claims on France's part, nor any other design "than that of reconciling them with those of Spain"; wherefore, an impartial world must regard the action of the commissioners as striking "a dishonorable alliance with our enemies as against our friends." Indeed, a measure of consideration had been due Spain herself, for notwithstanding the disappointments and indignities which the United States had received from her, "it could neither be denied nor concealed that the former had derived many substantial advantages from her taking part in the war, and had even obtained some pecuniary aids."[20]

Rightly or wrongly, the commissioners modelled their course upon more robust principles. Jay, a quick and sensitive temperament, who had in Congress shown himself not a little compliant with French views, had been cast by his experiences in Spain into an attitude of patriotic self-assertiveness, an attitude to which the Congressional instructions added fresh fuel. Adams' hardy provincialism needed no special incentive to patriotic self-assertion, though it had this in his

[20] *Ib.,* 418.

intense interest in seeing Massachusetts restored to her fishing privileges off the Grand Banks. Franklin, burdened with years, was perhaps overborne to some extent by his more vigorous colleagues but he also felt, and had from the first, a keen desire to see the United States reach to the Mississippi.[21] All these men, moreover, had been of the pioneers of American independence, among the first to conceive a national destiny for the American Provinces.

But the immediately provoking cause, of course, of the independent policy adopted by the commissioners was Jay's suspicions, and these, it has been frequently urged by writers, were not altogether well-placed. Nevertheless, I think it has to be conceded that most of Jay's errors were rather as to the motives represented by certain facts than as to the facts themselves or their natural tendency; and even such mistakes as he made were compensated for to a singular degree by facts that he did not know. Today, however, the essential elements of the situation that confronted the commissioners are plain; they may be summarized thus: First, the necessity France was under to obtain peace as speedily as possible; second, the positive obligation she was under not

[21] See Jay's testimony on this point, *Correspondence and Public Papers,* II. 390. See also the commissioners' letter to Livingston, Dec. 14, in which Franklin assents to the statement, "We knew this court and Spain to be against our claims to the Western country," Wharton, VI. 132.

to accept peace until Spain was satisfied;[22] third, British resistance, ever becoming stiffer, to Spain's principal demand, the surrender of Gibraltar;[23] fourth, Spain's scarcely secondary interest in thrusting the Americans back from the Mississippi; fifth, Vergennes' denial that the reciprocal guaranty of the Treaty of Alliance was yet operative except as to American independence; sixth, his entire disbelief that there was any likelihood of England's conceding the American claims, either as to the fisheries or the Western lands, and his repeatedly announced intention of bringing the Americans to reason if they persisted in untenable claims;[24] seventh and

[22] Peace, Vergennes had written in August, 1779, could be concluded only on two conditions: "la satisfaction plénière du roi d'Espagne et la reconnaissance des Etats-Unis dans leur état de liberté et d'independance," Donïol, IV. 339-40.

[23] Even on his first mission to London Rayneval had reported the British reluctance to the cession of Gibraltar as almost insuperable. "My lord Shelburne s'est apesanti sur Gibraltar; il s'est apliqué avec chaleur à me prouver que la cession en est impossible, il m'a parlé de la résistance que cet article éprouveroit au Conseil; que le lord Keppel, lorsqu'il lui en a parlé, lui dit nettement qui si on parloit de céder Gibraltar, il prendroit son chapeau et s'en iroit," ib., V. 616. See also Fitzmaurice, op. cit., III. 262, 275, 289, 305, 312.

[24] See note 10 supra. See also Vergennes to La Luzerne under dates of Oct. 14 and Nov. 23, 1782, Stevens, Peace Transcripts; Doniol, V. 176-8. Note the following expressions from the latter document: "Le Roi ne sera moins exact à les tenir de son côté [certain conditions], mais il n'en existe aucune [condition] dans nos traités qui l'oblige à prolongér la guerre pour soutenir les prétentions ambitieuses que les Etats-Unis peuvent formér soit par rapport

last, the procedure governing the negotiations, whereby the Americans were left to shift for themselves, while the Foreign Office took the Spanish interest under its wing from the beginning. No one of these facts was necessarily of fatal import for American interests, but the *ensemble* is somewhat impressive. To it, moreover, may be quite legitimately lent the coloration of one or two other circumstances. The first of these is Rayneval's early mission to England. True, the primary purpose of this had to do with Gibraltar, but the young secretary took what opportunity the occasion offered, none the less, to disparage the American claims with the British ministers, if quietly yet not ineffectively.[25]

à la pêche, soit par rapport à l'etendue des limites . . . . Malgré toutes les cajolleries que les ministres anglois prodiguent aux Américains, je ne me promets qu'ils se montrent facils ni sur les pêches ni sur les limits . . . ," *ib.,* 177. The earlier document is even more positive in tone. It is interesting to compare this tone with that taken by Rayneval with reference to Gibraltar: "le Roi, s'il en étoit besoin, se feroit un devoir d'exhorter le roi d'Espagne à être modéré dans ses pretensions, mais Sa Majesté ne pourroit aucunement parler de l'abandon de Gibraltar," *ib.,* 618.

[25] The following extracts from Rayneval's report of his conferences with Shelburne are the significant ones: "Mais mylord craint les Américains et les Hollandois; j'ai encore dit qu'il y auroit moien de les dérouter, principalement en leur laissant ignorer l'état de la négociation entre la France, l'Espagne, et l'Angleterre. Cet article tient infiniment à coeur à mylord Shelburne," Doniol, V. 614. (It is interesting to compare this suggestion with Vergennes' later complaint to Franklin, that the Americans had not tried to inform themselves as to the state of

Again, one should, perhaps, not altogether ignore this further consideration: "The French are interested in separating us from Great Bri-

the Anglo-French negotiation, note 15, *supra*). "Est venu le tour de l'Amérique; mylord Shelburne a prévu qu'ils auroient beaucoup de difficultés avec les Américains, tant par rapport aux limites que par rapport à la pêche de Terre-Neuve, mais il espère que le Roi ne les soutiendra pas dans leurs demandes. J'ai répondu que je ne doutois pas de l'empressement du Roi à faire ce qui dépendra de lui pour contenir les Américains dans les bornes de la justice et de la raison; et mylord ayant désiré savoir ce que je pensois de leurs prétentions, j'ai répondu que j'ignorois celles relatives à la pêche, mais que telles qu'elles puissent être il me sembloit qu'il y avoit un principe sûr à suivre sur cette matière, savoir, que le pêche en haute-mer est *res nullius* et que la pêche sur les côtes apartenoit de droit au propriétaire des côtes, à moins de dérogations fondées sur des conventions. Quant à l'étendue des limites j'ai suposé que les Américains la puiseroient dans leur chartres, c'est à dire qu'ils voudront aller de l'Ocean à la mer du Sud. Mylord Shelburne a traité les chartres de sottises, et la discution n'a pas été poussée plus loin parceque je n'ai voulu, ni soutenir la prétention Américaine, ne l'anéantir. J'ai seulement dit que le ministre Anglois devoit trouver dans les négociations de 1754 relatives à l'Ohio les limites que l'Angleterre, alors souveraine des 13 Etats-unis croyoit devoir leur assigner," *ib.*, 618-9. The reference to the negotiations of 1754 is explained by the following passage from the memoir which Rayneval had only a few days before this presented to Jay on the Mississippi question: "It is known that, before the Treaty of Paris, France possessed Louisiana and Canada, and that she considered the savage people situated to the east of the Mississippi as either independent or as under her protection. This pretension caused no dispute; England never thought of making any [pretension?] except as to the lands situated towards the source of the Ohio, in that part where she had given the name Allegheny to that river." Wharton, VI. 25. The reaction of the English ministers to what Rayneval had to say about the American claims is recorded

tain . . . but it is not their interest that we should become a great and formidable people."[26] The words are Jay's, but Vergennes himself had said as much time and again.

In short, the commissioners were confronted with an appreciable danger, in meeting which they displayed sagacity and spirit. However, it may still be a question whether their policy really netted the United States a profit or a loss; and in fact, it has been argued that it did the latter. The pivotal fact upon which this contention hinges is the rejection by Shelburne on October 20th of a draft treaty which had been agreed to by Oswald, and which, in addition to granting the Americans everything they had asked for with reference to the fisheries and the West, accorded the United States a northern boundary that included much that is today Canada and maintained complete silence as to the claims of British creditors and of the loyalists, whereas the

by Shelburne's biographer, thus: "They then proceeded to speak about America. Here Rayneval played into the hands of English ministers by expressing a strong opinion against the American claims to the Newfoundland fishery and to the Valley of the Mississippi and the Ohio. These opinions were carefully noted by Shelburne and Grantham," *op. cit.*, III. 263. When the Provisional Articles arrived in London, Rayneval was there on a second mission. Being shown them he remarked upon the embarrassment that the article according the United States the navigation of the Mississippi would cause Spain, but elicited a very unfeeling response from Shelburne, Doniol, V. 229.

    [26] Wharton, VI. 48.

Provisional Articles of November 30th made certain concessions on the two latter points and drew a much more restrictive northern boundary. Now, it is urged that the rejected draft treaty was in entire accord with Townshend's letter of September 1st to Oswald, that the motive of the British minister in authorizing such extensive concessions to the Americans was the hope of separating them from the French, that Vaughan's mission, by revealing to Shelburne that this end had already been accomplished, instigated him to retract in a measure his policy of concession, and that, therefore, the unfavorable differential between the draft treaty and the later Provisional Articles must be charged against Jay's headiness and precipitancy.[27]

The argument is ingenious but not convincing. To begin with, it will be recalled that, whatever the ulterior motive of Townshend's letter, it was called out immediately by Jay's demand that the British government should recognize American independence preliminary to treating. Again, while this letter empowered Oswald to agree to "a settlement of the boundaries," there is plainly some difference between an adjustment of boundaries and such a cession of territory as that made by the draft treaty of lands to the west of the

[27] Phillips, *The West in the Diplomacy of the American Revolution*, pp. 220-1. See also to same effect *Works of Benjamin Franklin* (ed. Bigelow), VIII, 164 fn.

Mountains and later repeated by the Provisional Articles. But again, it was not Vaughan's mission that first informed Shelburne and his associates that there was a rift in the French-American lute, it was Rayneval's mission and his attack on American pretensions. Finally, the assertion that Vaughan's mission persuaded Shelburne that the objective of his policy had been realized and that, consequently, he might abandon the policy, is mere conjecture, and not very plausible conjecture at that. Unquestionably, it was Shelburne's purpose to divide France and America but it was also his purpose to *keep* them divided till peace was obtained, and peace had not yet been obtained when, on October 20th, he rejected the draft treaty "as in no way adapted to our present circumstances."[28] Indeed, it seems to me that a more plausible conjecture would be, that it was not so much the *success* of his policy as its comparative *failure* that may have influenced Shelburne to some extent at this moment. For the draft treaty, like the later Provisional Articles, was to go into effect only when France had also arrived at terms with England. However, the circumstance that really determined the fate of the draft treaty is no mystery. It was the arrival at this moment of the news that Howe had lifted the siege of Gibraltar; and the day following his letter to Oswald, Shelburne also wrote Rayneval

[28] Shelburne to Oswald, Oct. 20, Fitzmaurice, *op. cit.*, III. 283.

that England would not yield Gibraltar to Spain nor St. Lucia and Dominica to France.[29]

Naturally, it would be impossible to determine with minute exactitude the extent to which the United States profited by the action of the commissioners in ignoring their instructions; and yet it is a matter that admits, I think, of rather confident speculation when the two controlling factors of the situation are clearly set forth. The first and more important of these is the hope that was held out to the British cabinet by the independent attitude of the Americans that if the United States were satisfied with the terms they received from England, they would refuse to continue in the war in the interest of Spain. It was because of this hope that the cabinet yielded the Americans their demands as to the boundaries and the fisheries, and it is almost inconceivable that they would otherwise have done so. But in the second place, once this concession was ratified, the hands of the British government were tied, and it could neither offer nor demand equivalents within the field of American pretensions.[30] At one point, however, this statement demands qualification, but only with the result of reinforc-

[29] Ib., 280.

[30] It must be recognized in this connection that it was not only the possibility that England would deny Gibraltar to Spain that was dangerous to American interests. For if England had given up Gibraltar, she would have demanded equivalents, and these might very well have lain within the field of the American pretensions. See Phillips, op. cit., 210 and Doniol, V. 617.

ing the principal argument. By the separate and
secret article of the Provisional Articles, England retained the right for herself to a northern
boundary to West Florida at the line running due
eastward from the mouth of the Yazoo river, but
not the right to accord Spain a boundary to the
same province north of the thirty-first degree.

The contemporary estimate of the achievement
of the commissioners confirms this analysis most
strikingly. The commissioners themselves in
communicating the articles to Congress, though
somewhat apologetic for the concessions that had
finally been made in the interest of the loyalists
and the British creditors, used the quiet terms of
profound satisfaction: "We can not but flatter
ourselves that they [the articles] will appear to
Congress as they do to all of us, to be consistent
with the honor and interest of the United
States."[31]   Congress' estimate of the terms was
governed in part by the jealousies of sections and
factions, but it is to be noted that those who had
expected most were most gratified. "Mr. Wolcott," Madison records, "conceived it unnecessary
to waste time on the subject"— a proposition to
communicate the separate article to the French
envoy—"as he presumed Congress would never
so far censure the ministers who had obtained
such terms for this country as to disavow their

[31] See their letter to Livingston, Dec. 14, Wharton, VI. 131-3.

conduct."[32] The event proved that Wolcott had judged rightly, for the proposition referred to never came to a vote. The directest testimony, however, is that afforded by the comments of the Foreign Office on the articles:

You will notice [Vergennes wrote Rayneval] that the English buy peace rather than make it. Their concessions indeed, as well in the matter of the boundaries as in that of the fisheries and the loyalists, exceed all that I could have thought possible.[33]

Rayneval agreed: 'the treaty with America appeared to him a dream, and the English ministers in according it had had in view ultimately the defection of the Americans.'[34]

However, it must be remembered that the Provisional Articles were *provisional*. Indeed, their immediate effect was to diminish the likelihood of peace, by encouraging the British cabinet to set an impossible price upon Gibraltar.[35] And, of course, had the war been renewed, the Americans

[32] *Writings*, I. 411. Note also his statement: "The terms granted to America appeared to Congress on the whole extremely liberal," *ib.*, 403.

[33] Dec. 3, Wharton, V. 293-4; Doniol, V. 188. See also his letter of July 21, 1783, to La Luzerne where he says: "The boundaries in the Mississippi region must have astounded the Americans. Surely they did not flatter themselves that the English ministry would go beyond the mountains that hem in the United States from the Ohio to Georgia," *ib.*, 293-4.

[34] *Ib.*, 270.

[35] *Ib.*, 228-30 and 251-6. The equivalent first demanded by England for Gibraltar was the French islands, Guadaloupe and Dominica, *ib.*, 220. After the arrival of the news of the American signature St. Lucia was added to the list; or in its place, Trinity;

would have had either to part with their winnings or with the French alliance. Aid came from an unexpected quarter. Early in December the Spanish ambassador received a despatch from Madrid, dated November 23rd, in which inquiry was made as to "what considerable advantage Spain could expect from the treaty, if, for any reason," His Catholic Majesty "made the sacrifice of withdrawing from" the engagement created by the Treaty of Aranjuez. On December 5th Aranda placed this despatch before Vergennes, who at once wrote Rayneval, now in London a second time, to offer the abandonment of Gibraltar if Spain were given Minorca and the two Floridas. Ten days later came an affirmative response from Rayneval, and Aranda, though without instructions from Madrid, gave his approval. Florida Blanca's wrath when he learned the bold course of his envoy was tremendous, and even Charless III's chagrin is badly concealed in his letter of January 2nd to Louis sanctioning peace. Vergennes' delight, on the other hand, was boundless. "I bow before the Sovereign Being," he exclaimed to Aranda, "and return him my heartfelt thanks for His infinite

or for all three, Porto Rico, *ib.*, 256. It seems to me unlikely, however, that Parliament would have accepted peace if Gibraltar had been included among the concessions made to England's enemies. As it was, though the peace was accepted, a vote of censure was passed against it in the House of Commons, *Parliamentary History*, XXIII. cc. 514 and 571.

wisdom, which has disposed the heart and mind of the Catholic king to give up the cession of Gibraltar." To Montmorin he expressed himself to like effect: While he would not like to see such diplomatic usage established as that followed on this occasion by the Spanish ambassador, "it is none the less true that we owe peace to his courageous resolution."[36]

On January 20th preliminary articles were signed by the representatives of France and Spain on the one hand and of Great Britain on the other.[37] The same day Adams and Franklin—Jay being absent from Paris—signed a declaration asserting that the Provisional Articles were not designed to "alter the relation of the United States toward England so long as peace should not be concluded between His Most

[36] François Rousseau, "Participation de l'Espagne à la Guerre d'Amérique," *Revue des Questions historiques,* LXXII. 484-9. See also Doniol, V. 237-41, and ch. VIII *passim.* Even after the Gibraltar question was settled, the negotiations were nearly wrecked by England's demand that Dominica be given her. At the same time there was a strong war party at the French court as well as the British, among the opponents of Vergennes' policy being his own minister of the Marine, Castries, *ib.,* 270. According to Florida Blanca, at the moment peace was signed a joint French-Spanish expedition consisting of seventy ships of the line and 40,000 men was ready to sail for the West Indies, Coxe's *Memoirs of the Kings of Spain,* III. 344-6. The negotiations were finally saved by England's proffer of Tobago and certain concessions in Pondicherry to France in return for Dominica, Doniol, V. ch. VIII.

[37] They will be found in the *Parliamentary History,* XXIII. 346-54.

FRENCH POLICY AND

Christian Majesty and His Britannic Majesty"
and "repudiating any interpretation of them contrary to this assertion." Thus, says M. Doniol,
was "the alliance in some sort renewed."[38]

In reality, the one entangling alliance of our
history, the indispensable instrument of our
deliverance as a nation, was now at an end. Ten
years and one day from the promulgation of this
declaration Louis XVI mounted the guillotine.
One month after that war began between France
and England. Two months later Washington
proclaimed American neutrality. His action
represented the deliberate decision that the most
vital interests of the United States would not
admit of its adhering to the pledges given in
1778. But indeed, France had long since become reconciled to the idea that America was
not an available ally. Some six years before
Washington and his cabinet determined to cast
aside the Treaty of Alliance, the French representative at Philadelphia was urging his government to seize New York and Newport to prevent
their falling into the hands of Great Britain in
the event of war. The Foreign Office replied
that it had anticipated just such developments,
but that it consoled itself that France had
"never pretended to make America a useful
ally," that she had had "no other end in view than
to deprive Great Britain of that vast continent."[39]

[38] Doniol, V. 277 and fn.
[39] The Cabinet of Versailles to Otto, the French chargé at Phila-

delphia, Aug. 30, 1787, Bancroft, *History of the Formation of the Constitution of the United States* (N. Y., 1882, 2 vols), II. 438. The attitude of France toward her American alliance after the War of Independence looked primarily toward preventing the restoration of English influence. In this connection the following passages from the Instructions of Montmorin, Vergennes' successor, to the Count de Moustier, who became the French envoy at Philadelphia in the fall of 1787, are interesting: Le Comte de Moustier jugera par là qu'il devra s'attacher à fortifier les Américains dans les principes qui les ont engagé à s'unir à la France: il leur fera sentir pour cet effet, qu'ils ne sauroient avoir d'Allié plus naturel que le Roi, tandis qu'ils peuvent être certains que l'Angleterre jalouse leur prospérité, et qu'elle y nuira autant qu'elle en trouvera l' occasion. . . . Ce seroit se tromper volontairement que de supposer que cette puissance [England] ne cherche pas à diminuer les sentiments qui doivent attacher les Etats-Unis à la France, et à opérer insensiblement leur raprochement de leur ancienne Mère-patrie. Il sera utile que le Ministre du Roi suive la marche des agens anglais, et qu'il fasse ce qui dépendra de lui, mais sans affectation, pour rendre nulles leurs insinuations." "Mémoire pour servir d'Instructions au Sieur Comte de Moustier," Oct. 10, 1787, *American Historical Review*, VIII. 710-1. Montmorin expected that if war broke out between France and Great Britain "the Americans would wish to remain neutral," and indicated the probability that France would favor this disposition. However, he continued, "circumstances may counteract our principles," Bancroft, *op. cit.*, II. 444. A few months later Moustier reported an argument by Jay to the effect that the Treaty of Alliance no longer subsisted, to which proposition Montmorin demurred strongly: "Le Roi et son conseil, M., ont été singulièrement étonnés de l'opinion òu est M. Jay que l'Alliance entre le Roi et les Etats-Unis ne subsiste plus. Ce ministre a donc oublié les termes dans lesquels cette Alliance a été conçue: s'il veut bien relire le traité du 6. février 1778 et se convaincre qu'elle est perpétuelle. . . . Il convient, M, que vous rectifiez les idées de M. Jay sur ces différents objets: vous l'assurerez que le Roi regarde son alliance avec les Etats-Unis comme inaltérable; que Sa. M'té. a toujours pris et qu'elle ne cessera de prendre un intérêt véritable à leur prospérité, et que Sa. M'té. continue a à y contribuer autant qu'elle le pourra sans préjudice à ses propres intérêts. Violà, M., la doctrine que vous devez faire germer et que le Conseil du Roi a été surpris de voir si mal établie." Montmorin to Moustier, June 23, 1788, *American Historical Review, loc. cit.*, 728. Four years later the monarchy gave place to the republic and Genêt came to the United States. His "Instructions d'Arrivée" contained an interesting attack on the "Machiavellism" of Vergennes' policy toward America, the basis of the charge being the former minister's opposition to American acquisition of Canada; and the implication was that the new government would be controlled by much more liberal principles. *Annual Report of the American Historical Association for 1903*, II. 202-3. At the same time Genêt was instructed to get a new treaty with the United States extending the articles with reference to commerce and navigation, "as the just price of the independence which France won for the United States," and renewing the guaranty of the Treaty of Alliance of French possessions in the West Indies. *Ib.*, 207-11. Both the Treaty of Amity and Commerce and the Treaty of Alliance were declared "void" by the Senate on June 25, 1798, and by the House of Representatives on July 7. This action of the Houses was posited on the right of Congress to judge of infractions of the Law of Nations, *Annals of Congress*, 5th Congress, I. 586-8, II. 2116-28.

CHAPTER XVI

PROFIT AND LOSS

In the ensuing chapter I shall discuss the outcome of French intervention in the War of Independence from the point of view of the objective of that enterprise. The treaty of peace between France and England throws little light on the subject, albeit France obtained some minor advantages by it, an island in the West Indies which she had lost in 1763, a strip of land on the West African coast, an enlargement of her fishing rights in Newfoundland, the suppression of the articles relative to Dunkirk. The treaty is significant rather as a symbol. England, exhausted by the war, "had not blushed to be the first to petition for peace," and the treaty itself had "erased the stain" of 1763. Thus Vergennes writes in his *Mémoire* to the King, of March 29th, 1784, where, moreover, he presents the treaty as the consummation of a period of conspicuous triumph for his entire system.[1]

Louis, the minister records, had ruled but a decade, yet within that brief period he had re-

[1] Ségur, *Politique de Tous les Cabinets,* III. 196-219.

stored peace to Europe no fewer than four times. In Germany by the Treaties of Teschen he had vindicated afresh France's prerogative as guarantor of the Treaty of Westphalia. Twice in the Southeast he had rescued Turkey, at the cost to that power of some small subtractions of territory, from the clutch of its enemies. Meanwhile, the transparent disinterestedness of His Majesty's principles had won the confidence of Europe, so that all nations had been content to see him "lower the pride of England and labor for her enfeeblement."[2] In brief, France was once more what she had been, "the moderator and arbiter" of Europe, the power that "gave the tone" to the European concert. "Placed in the center of Europe, strong by virtue of the contiguity and unity of her provinces, and by the wealth and population of her soil," girt round by protecting fortresses and by neighbors mutually isolated, she was free to forego aggrandizement and to devote all her influence "to the preservation of the established order and to preventing the different states which compose the European balance from being destroyed."[3]

Over against this chant of victory and accentuating its triumphal note, stand the contemporary lamentations of Englishmen at the downfall of Britain through the loss of her American empire.

[2] *Ib.*, 201.
[3] *Loc. cit.* See also p. 218.

"The greatest statesmen whom England had produced," writes Wraxall of this period, "though
they concurred in scarcely any other political
opinion, yet agreed on the point that, with the
defalcation of the Thirteen Colonies from the
crown, the glory and greatness of Britain were
permanently extinguished."[4]   The Parliamentary debates support his assertion.   "Are we,"
Burke caustically inquired in his speech on the
address from the throne following the receipt of
the news of Yorktown,

are we to be told of the rights for which we went to war?
Oh, excellent rights!   Oh, valuable rights . . . that
have cost England thirteen provinces, four islands,
100,000 men, and seventy millions of money!   Oh, won-
derful rights, that have lost to Great Britain her empire on the ocean, her boasted, grand, and substantial
superiority which made the world bend before her!   Oh,
inestimable rights, that have taken from us our rank
among nations, our importance abroad, and our happiness at home; and that have taken from us our trade,
our manufactures, and our commerce; that have reduced
us from the most flourishing empire in the world to
one of the most unenviable powers on the face of the
globe![5]

The same sentiment was voiced on one occasion or other by men of all parties, by Lord
George Germaine, North's minister of War,
who maintained that "from the instant when

[4] *Historical Memoirs* (Phila., 1845), 366.
[5] *Parliamentary History,* XXII. col. 721.

American independence should be acknowledged the British empire was ruined";[6] by Sir John Cavendish of the Whig opposition, who declared that "the great and splendid empire of Britain was nearly overturned";[7] by Shelburne, who asserted that "whenever the British Parliament should recognize the sovereignty of the Thirteen Colonies, the sun of England's glory was forever set."[8] A writer in the *Gentleman's Magazine,* commenting on Great Britain's "astonishing decline" "from being the first maritime power in the world," accounted for it in the following strain of philosophic resignation:

In these vicissitudes the hand of Providence, by which the government of the world is directed, is most manifest. Nations and peoples are permitted to arrive at a certain pitch of greatness, and when at the height are doomed to fall to decay. None of the great monarchies of ancient time, so celebrated in history, nor even the Republic of Rome itself, were ever in possession of half the territory which Great Britain could boast at the commencement of the reign of George III. By its so suddenly crumbling to pieces, part after part, does it not seem that this is a devoted Empire?[9]

[6] Wraxall, *op. cit.,* 367.

[7] *Parliamentary History,* XXII. col. 1114.

[8] Same as note 6. And see generally the debates on the treaties, *Parliamentary History,* XXIII. cols. 373-571.

[9] Vol. LII. 123. See also John Adams to Vergennes, July 13, 1780: "Breaking off such a nation as this [America] from the English so suddenly and uniting it so closely with France is one of the most extraordinary events that ever happened among mankind," Wharton, III. 855.

And not only had Britain declined: by the same token France had become predominant once more. The dominion of America, a Tory writer had urged shortly before Cornwallis' surrender, gave dominion of the seas, and France's calculations had proceeded from this postulate: "The balance of power which has from the beginning of the reign of Charles V been so diligently studied in every part of Europe as a science, and which is now brought to a degree of improvement unknown to the rusticity of former ages, could not but obtrude itself in her councils."[10] "What," inquired the learned Dr. Fothergill, in an "Address" to his countrymen, some months later, "can France gain by all these expenses if she seeks not for territorial possessions in America?" and answered his own question thus:

Why, the uncontrolled superiority in Europe. For, where is the power, when America is divided from us, that can withstand her? Whilst we had America France knew, and all Europe felt, that every distant possession they had were so many obligations for her peaceable behaviour. They saw America growing so populous and so powerful, her commerce increasing and increasing the power of Great Britain, that nothing was secure from us.[11]

[10] *Rivington's Royal Gazette* (New York), Sept. 29 and Oct. 3, 1781.

[11] Quoted in the Boston *Evening Post and General Advertiser* of Feb. 23, 1782. The learned doctor continued that, "by the people of New England only New Spain would have been added to the British Empire in a few years with the succour of the

"Happy would it be for us," exclaimed another writer,

if the loss of America was the only evil we have this day to deplore. The independence of that country is so great an object with the different nations of Europe that we have armed nearly one-half of them in its favor. . . . The influence of France in the course of this war has risen to such a pitch that renders it almost a degree of vanity in us to call her any longer the rival of this country. She has occupied its place in foreign courts and has become in a few years the arbiter of Europe.[12]

Even as late as the end of 1782, we find a writer declaring in the London *Chronicle,* that the people of Great Britain were

ready to part with an eighth or a quarter of all they are worth rather than accede to the independence of America and suffer so disgraceful and ruinous a dismemberment of the empire, which must in its consequences give to France the dominion and commerce of the European seas and render Great Britain the least significant among nations.[13]

British fleet, and France knew that her West Indian islands were held by them at our courtesy should a war break out."

[12] Quoted *ib.,* in issue of Mar. 9, 1782. See also the London *General Advertiser* of Mar. 6, 1782, where the following sentiments appear: "To how infamous and degraded a situation are we reduced! . . . What a contrast is the king of France! He is without doubt, not only the first monarch of his time, but the wisest, greatest, and best of monarchs that ever sat upon any throne!"

[13] London *Morning Chronicle,* Nov. 30 and Dec. 5 and 11, 1782.

The common sense of mankind has pilloried in numerous disdainful maxims that odious species of wisdom which parades itself after the event. And yet if the historian is to be wise, *quâ* historian, it must be after the event. The testimony we have just reviewed goes far to stamp Vergennes' policy with the sanction of the statesmanship of that generation. Indeed, the very stubbornness with which England had resisted American independence implies the same thing. We of today, however, easily see that the French program, precisely as it was deduced from certain premises, rested upon too restricted a foundation of fact, that its results were neither solid nor durable, and that, trifling as they were, they were obtained at suicidal cost. Nor is this altogether the wisdom of the autopsy. Vergennes himself betrayed no little disappointment in the outcome of his labors.

The first respect in which the course of events cheated the calculations underlying French intervention in the War of Independence was the swift recuperation of England from her losses. For this phenomenon, which, he asserts, had "no parallel in the history of the world," Wraxall adduces three causes: "the preservation of the British Constitution"; the institution of the sinking fund by Pitt; and the extension of British acquisitions in India, whence an annual revenue of fifteen millions sterling, payable in specie, was soon drawn.[14] The last two causes were no doubt potent, but they coöperated with still more powerful ones, the rise of the factory system at this same period and the opening up of England's mineral resources. In these circumstances, the fact upon which perhaps more than any other England's enemies had counted to produce her downfall, became a blessing in disguise, the public debt. Stabilized by Pitt's measures, the famous "consols" rendered British resources fluid and turned them into the channels of trade and industry as nothing else could have done.

Still it may be urged that these developments would have occurred anyway and that the loss of America contributed to offset them. Is this so? Vergennes' purpose was to break down both the political and the commercial connection between England and America, and so far as the former was concerned his success was unquestionable. Not only was the aid which France lent America the efficient cause of the outcome of the war, but the sentiment of gratitude which this aid engendered among the American people at large was a factor of no little importance in weaning the country from its natural predilection for the former mother-land.[15] As we have seen, the al-

[14] *Op. cit.,* 367-71.

[15] For a very pessimistic account, from the French point of view, of the American propension for things English and the English themselves, despite the war, see a letter from Kalb to Broglie, quoted in Doniol, IV. 19 fn. This letter was probably

liance with France was soon discarded, but the motive back of the act was not sympathy for England but a real vision of national destiny which would be foiled and frustrated were the nation to be drawn into "the European vortex."[16]

But the more important objective with the Foreign Office had been the termination of America's commercial dependence on England, to which, indeed, the severance of the political bond stood somewhat in the relation of means to end.   Yet

known to Vergennes, as it is among the archives of the Department of Foreign Affairs. The chief reason for Vergennes' dismay at Jay's behavior was the idea that it sprang from a pro-English inclination. "If," he wrote La Luzerne, "we may judge of the future from what has passed here under our eyes, we shall be but poorly repaid for all we have done for the United States and for securing to them a national existence," Wharton, VI. 152. On this score, however, he was reassured by La Luzerne: "I do not credit him [Jay]," the envoy wrote, "with gratitude to us, but he is incapable of preferring England to us; he glories in being independent," etc., La Luzerne to Vergennes, Sept. 26, 1783, Steven, *Peace Transcripts*. On American gratitude to France, see the opening paragraph of Pickering's despatch of July 15, 1797, to Pickney, Marshall, and Gerry, *American State Papers*, "Foreign Relations," II. 153. *Cf.* Hamilton's estimate of the motive of French aid and of French policy following the War of Independence, *Works of Alexander Hamilton* (Constitutional ed.), VI. 206-14.

[16] Hence, of course, the American policy of isolation, the first and main pillar of the Monroe Doctrine. In the same connection see the lengthy letter (probably by Samuel Adams) addressed "To the Public," in the Boston *Continental Journal and Weekly Advertiser* of May, 1783, warning against suffering "ourselves, either from gratitude or any other principle, to engage in any future controversies or quarrels on the other side of the Atlantic, if we mean to keep our independence, independent of all the world." See also letter of John Adams in Wharton, III. 621 ff.

it is at this point exactly that Vergennes' reckoning, which, like that of his alarmed English
contemporaries, was based on the teachings of
Mercantilism, went most awry. The peace negotiations had not yet begun when his auxiliary,
Dupont, wrote Hutton, early in 1782, that "if
the war is not too long continued, the Americans
will be more to England than to us, since the
language they speak and their former relations
will naturally lead them to carry on trade with the
English rather than with France."[17] To be sure,
it does not appear whether Dupont, who was a

[17] Doniol, V. 36-7 fn. It would seem that there was considerable
trade between England and America even while the war was still
in progress. "This," writes Adams to the President of Congress,
June 26, 1781, "is a subject which deserves the serious consideration of every American. British manufactures are going in vast
quantities to America from Holland, the Austrian Flanders,
France, and Sweden, as well as by the way of New York and
Charleston, etc.," Wharton, IV. 521. For a Congressional ordinance designed to check this trade, see *Journals of Congress*, Dec.
4, 1781, XXI. 1152. For some evidence of England's rapid recovery of her American trade after the Revolution, see Moustier
to Montmorin, Feb. 8, 1788, *American Historical Review*, VIII. 716,
where the writer complains that the Americans use the monetary
proceeds of their trade with the French islands to pay for the merchandise which they import from England; also Baring's
*Inquiry into the Causes and Consequences of the Orders in
Council* (London, 1808), pp. 19 ff. As to French commerce with
the United States, see a pamphlet in the Pennsylvania Historical
Society's library entitled *Causes qui se sont opposées au Progrès du
Commerce entre la France et les Etats-Unis* (Paris, 1790).
Franklin's hope was to see the United States become commercially
independent of Europe, Lee's *Lee*, I. 354.

disciple of Quesnay, expressed in the passage just quoted the views of his superior. But the commercial treaty which he negotiated with England early in 1786 affords unmistakable evidence that Vergennes' own economic creed had undergone considerable change since the date of the *Exposé Succinct.*[18] Even earlier, moreover, he had recorded his recognition of the fact that American independence had not touched the vital sources of British sea-power. In the memoir of March 29th, 1784, while asserting that France had recovered her influence on the Continent, he warned the king that the English fleet would soon be "more numerous and more powerful than it was at the moment of peace," and that the only guaranty of continued good relations with that country was the maintenance of the French marine on a respectable footing.[19]

At this point, however, it behooves us to remember that in Vergennes' thinking the crippling of English sea-power was to be contributory to a far more important end, the restoration of French leadership on the Continent and the establishment

---

[18] This treaty abolished or lowered many protective duties between the two countries, French wines thus obtaining entry to the English market in competition with Portuguese, and English manufactures being admitted to the French market. The treaty was a distinct triumph for the views of Adam Smith and the French Physiocrats. For contemporary discussion of its provisions, see *Annual Register,* XXIX. 65 ff.

[19] Ségur, III. 217-8.

there of a reign of peace. Unhappily, this dream
—for it was little more—was based on the tradition of a Europe that no longer existed, of a
Europe in which Poland, Sweden, and Turkey
were still effective units of the balance of power;
in which Prussia was still dependent on France;
in which the House of Austria was definitely secondary to the House of Bourbon; in which Russia
had no voice. Once again, in other words, had
the minister premitted the conventional creed of
his office to blind him to the actual facts; and
once again, in consequence, is he forced to record
his own disillusionment. "What had rendered
peace so necessary" the year before, he informs us
in the document just cited, was "the swift *rapprochement*" of "the courts of Vienna and St.
Petersburg, which for twenty years had dwelt in
open enmity." It was, he continues, a development "calculated to arouse disquiet and alarm";
and indeed, his whole tone reveals his own most
serious concern.[20] Yet it is difficult to see how,
even if the outcome of the war had been the total
annihilation of British sea-power, France would
have been in any better position to deal with this
formidable and unprecedented combination in the
Southeast.[21]

[20] *Ib.,* 203 ff.

[21] In this connection it should be recalled that in 1774 Vergennes had considered the feasibility of an Anglo-French *rapprochement* directed against Russia, See chapter III, *supra.*
After the war Shelburne propounded the same idea to Rayneval.

In a word, the restoration of French prestige
had altered the actual balance of forces on the
Continent very little, if at all; and by the same
sign, it had gone but little way toward guaranteeing the *status quo* or a lasting peace. Vergennes'
own recognition of this unpleasant truth was as
frank as possible: 'It was difficult to flatter
one's self of a long peace or even to regard the
existing one as more than precarious, unless the
power to which alone it belonged to give the tone
found itself in position to make itself respected.'
This was France's "superb prerogative"; but
'good example would not of itself suffice, were
it not backed up by imposing means.' 'Of all
human passions, ambition was the most active,
the one held in leash with greatest difficulty.
Defect of power alone could render it passive;
and this could exist only if His Majesty was
ready and willing to repell all designs on the

Not only, said the former, were France and England not natural
enemies but they had many interests in common which ought to
cause them to come to an understanding. There had been a time
when no one dared set off a cannon in Europe without the consent
of England and France, while today the powers of the North
assumed to stand by themselves. "Let us unite and we shall give
the law to Europe." Certainly, they were too clear-sighted in
France not to be convinced that the system of the German empire was an unnatural one, and that Russia wished to enjoy a
rôle and had views which were not harmonious with the interests
of France and England. "If we are in accord we shall take our
old place once more and shall be able to arrest all revolutions in
Europe," etc. Rayneval's Report of his Second Mission to England, Doniol, V. 619-20.

public security and tranquility.' "Force is the surest measure of respect, particularly when it is exercised with wisdom and employed with justice."[22]

In 1785 Vergennes scored his last great diplomatic triumph, a settlement of difficulties between the emperor and Holland and a close offensive and defensive alliance between the latter power and France. "The Count de Vergennes," commented the writer in the *Annual Register*, this year

acquired the honor to his country and the glorious distinction to himself of being the pacificator general of the universe. It could not but be a grevious consideration to Englishmen that, while France, through the happiness of great ministers at home and their choice of able negotiators abroad, was spreading her consequence and extending her influence through the nations of the earth, Great Britain through some unaccountable fatality seemed to be fallen from that high seat in which she had so long and so gloriously presided and to be no longer considered . . . in the general politics and system of Europe.[23]

In fact, the triumph, resting as it did on the unstable basis of the temporary preponderance of the Dutch Republican party, was for France an empty one. Within a few months the House of Orange, actively backed by Pitt, was again in control, and France was signing a declaration

[22] Ségur, III. 216-8.
[23] *Ib.*, XXVII. 137.

"agreeing to a general disarmament and asserting that the king of France had never any intention of interfering in the affairs of the Dutch Republic." "France," said the emperor maliciously, "has just fallen. I doubt if she will ever recover."[24]

The words were prophetic, more prophetic than their author could willingly have intended them to be. There were others, however, who had already begun to perceive how unreal France's triumph over England had been and, on the other hand, how terribly real its cost was like to prove. One of these was Burke, who in the *Annual Register* for 1787 wrote as follows:

It seemed a grand stroke of policy to reduce the power and humble the pride of a great and haughty rival. . . . Nor was this all; for as it was universally supposed that the loss of America would prove an incurable, if not a mortal wound to England, so it was equally expected that the power of the Gallic throne would thereby be fixed on such a permanent foundations as never again to be shaken by any stroke of fortune. . . . This speculation, like many others, when tried by the test of dear-bought experience, came to nothing, and their fond hopes have already vanished in smoke. . . . But though the American war failed in producing its wished for effects in respect to France, it left behind it other relics of a less pleasing nature. An immense new debt, being laid upon the back of the old,

[24] Hassall, *The Balance of Power*, p. 379, citing Marquis de Barral-Montferrat, *Dix Ans de Paix armée entre la France et l'Angleterre, 1783-93*, I. 54.

already too great, the accumulation became so vast . . .
as to exceed all inquiry." "And as the minds of men grow
attached to those principles which they are embarked in
require them to maintain . . . , the French nation, re-
sorting more to provision and principle by which the
abuses of power are corrected than those by which its
energy is maintained, have imbibed a love of freedom
nearly incompatible with royalty.[25]

Seldom indeed has the course of events displayed a more ironical, yet juster logic, than that
whereby the last considerable achievement of the
Classical diplomacy—an achievement that had
been planned to secure Europe peace and repose
for many years—had within a decade become the
funeral pyre of the Old Régimé and the starting-
point of a conflagration more than Continental.

Early this same year Vergennes died, just as
the Assembly of Notables was convening to make
a last effort to rescue the monarchy from bankruptcy without at the same time invading prescriptive rights. So his passing was synchronous
with the passing of the order on whose outworn
ideals and outlook he had reared his whole ambitious and mistaken structure. Yet the temper of
his purpose was something more permanent; for
the cold sophistry of the diplomat enwrapped the
ardor of the patriot, as witness the words in which
he shaped, for the last time as it seems, an apology for his American venture:

[25] *Annual Register,* XXIX. 174-8.

A nation [he wrote] can experience reverses, and it ought to yield to the imperious law of necessity and its own preservation; but when such reverses and the humiliation they entail are unjust, when they have for their end the gratification of the pride of a powerful rival, then the nation owes it to its own honor, dignity, and self respect, to retrieve itself when occasion offers. If it neglects to do so, if fear holds it back from duty, it adds abasement to humiliation and becomes the object of contempt of its own age and of ages to come. These important truths, Sire, have never been absent from my thoughts. They were already deeply graven on my heart when Your Majesty called me to His Council, and I awaited with lively impatience the opportunity of following their lead. These are the thoughts that fixed my attention on the Americans, that made me watch for and seize the moment when Your Majesty could assist that oppressed people with a well-founded hope of effectuating their deliverance. If I had had other sentiments, other principles, other views, I should have betrayed your confidence and the interests of the State; I should regard myself as unworthy of serving Your Majesty, I should regard myself as unworthy the name of Frenchman.[26]

[26] Doniol, I. 3-4.

BIBLIOGRAPHICAL NOTE

My principal source has been the material from the Archives of the French Department of Foreign Affairs to be found in Henri Doniol's *Histoire de la Participation de la France à l'Etablissement des Etats-Unis d'Amérique, Correspondance Diplomatique et Documents,* a work in five large quarto volumes, containing some four thousand pages, and in process of publication for fifteen years (1884-99). The work embodies four sorts of text: first, the author's narrative, which is in large type and is frequently a running paraphrase of documentary material; secondly, documentary material in small type set in the narrative; thirdly, footnotes in fine type containing further documentary material and the references to the Archives; fourthly, documentary appendices to the individual chapters in small type. The proportion of purely documentary material to the author's narrative may be illustrated from volume II, which is fairly illustrative of the set. This volume contains 864 pages, of which the extracts from documents fill better than 580 pages, printed in small and fine type. Making the proper allowance for the different sizes of type, I calculate that nearly, if not quite, four-fifths of the material in these volumes is source material. Nor can there be any doubt as to the thoroughly representative character of this material; indeed, its essential completeness. Primarily, of course, I base this conclusion upon my perusal of the work, but I am confirmed in it by the examination of such works as the Stevens *Facsimiles,* Circourt's *Histoire de l'Action Commune,* and Mr. Phillips' scholarly essay on *The West in the Diplomacy of the American Revolution.* It may be confidently asserted that conclusions which are securely based on the material in Doniol can only be confirmed by further research in the Archives. Conversely, for an American student, with limited time at his disposal, to attempt an investigation of the Archives without a thorough acquaintance with Doniol to begin with, would be deliberately to incur the risk of one-sided and ill-considered, however surprising, results.

But, of course, there are certain phases of the subject of French intervention in the War of Independence with which Doniol does not pretend to deal, while on the phases with which he does deal he throws, for the most part, only the light shed by the French correspondence. Thus he ignores altogether the background afforded the subject by the history of eighteenth century French diplomacy, and by Choiseul's attitude toward the initial phases of the British-American dispute. To sketch in this background is, accordingly, the purpose of the first two chapters of the present volume, with which should also be grouped the last chapter. The material there used, of which the most important items are the voluminous *Recueil des Instructions,* the elder Ségur's *Politique de Tous les Cabinets,* De Witt's *Thomas Jefferson,* Soulange-Bodin's *Pacte de Famille,* Bourguet's *Duc de Choiseul et l'Alliance Espagnole,* Flassan's *Histoire Générale et Raisonnée de la Diplomatie Française,* and various memoirs, is cited in the footnotes with full bibliographical data, which need not be repeated here.

It is also valuable, particularly in connection with the dealings of the French envoys with the Continental Congress and with the final Peace Negotiations, to supplement the French material from the American sources. These are to be found principally in Wharton's great work and the *Journals of the Continental Congress,* both of which have been thoroughly utilized in the present volume. In the same connection, I had also previously gone through a large mass of newspaper material, but my gleanings from this have turned out to be of use only to illustrate public opinion at times. Finally, of the writings of American public men of the period, those of Jay, Madison, Charles Thomson, the secretary of Congress, and Deane have proved to be of most value.

Hardly less important, however, than the American aspect of French intervention is the Spanish phase, and for that I have had to rely again principally on Doniol; but for a reason stated in the text, this is hardly matter for regret, for as I point out, the Spanish ambassador at Paris throughout the Revolution, the Count d'Aranda, did not enjoy the confidence of his government, with the result that the French-Spanish negotiations were conducted almost exclusively through the French ambassador at Madrid, the despatches to whom and the reports from whom are given by Doniol with his usual thoroughness. Only at two points, and those bearing only remotely on the subject of this volume, is it possible that the Spanish archives might prove of material value. Thus, in connection with the Spanish mediation of 1778 it would be interesting to have the correspondence between Florida Blanca and Almodovar, the Spanish ambassador at London; while in connection with Cumberland's secret mission to Spain in 1780, there may be Spanish material that would clarify Florida Blanca's rather ambiguous attitude at this period. But for the most part, it is clear, that the Spanish material touching the subject of French intervention is of negligible worth, a conclusion which is well borne out by such portions of this material as are to be found in the Sparks Mss. in the Harvard University Library.

Lastly, there are points at which the English point of view is of importance in connection with the theme of this volume. In such cases, for the Parliamentary debates I have used the *Parliamentary History;* as a record of English public opinion and a repository of public documents, the *Annual Register;* for the correspondence of the British government with its ambassador at Paris and the reports of British spies, the Stevens *Facsimiles;* and for material bearing on the final Peace negotiations, the *Peace Transcripts,* also compiled by Stevens and now in the Library of Congress.

For further data bearing on the works just mentioned, as well as on the numerous lesser works, pamphlets, articles in periodicals, etc., that were also used in the preparation of the present volume, the reader is referred to the footnotes.

APPENDICES

I

(a)

TREATY OF ALLIANCE,[1]

concluded at Paris, February 6, 1778; ratified by Congress May 4, 1778.

ARTICLES

   I. Alliance against Great Britain.
  II. Independence of the United States.
 III. Efforts to be made against Great Britain.
 IV. Concurrent operations.
   V. Conquests to belong to United States.
 VI. Relinquishment of territory by France.
VII. Conquests to belong to France.
VIII. Islands in Gulf of Mexico.
 IX. Renunciation of Claims.
  X. Powers invited to accede to alliance.
 XI. Proprietary rights.
XII. Duration.
XIII. Ratification.

The Most Christian King and the United States of North America, to wit: New Hampshire, Massachusetts Bay, Rhode Island, Connecticut, New York, New Jersey, Pennsylvania, Delaware, Maryland, Virginia, North Carolina, South Carolina, and Georgia, having this day concluded a treaty of amity and commerce, for the reciprocal advantage of their subjects and citizens,

[1] Text from Wm. Malloy, *Treaties, Conventions,* etc. (Washington, 1910).

have thought it necessary to take into consideration the means of strengthening those engagements, and of rendering them useful to the safety and tranquility of the two parties; particularly in case Great Britain, in resentment of that connection and of the good correspondence which is the object of the said treaty, should break the peace with France, either by direct hostilities or by hindering her commerce and navigation in a manner contrary to the rights of nations, and the peace subsisting between the two Crowns. And His Majesty and the said United States, having resolved in that case to join their councils and efforts against the enterprises of their common enemy, the respective Plenipotentiaries impowered to concert the clauses and conditions proper to fulfil the said intentions, have, after the most mature deliberation, concluded and determined on the following articles:

ARTICLE I

If war should break out between France and Great Britain during the continuance of the present war between the United States and England, His Majesty and the said United States shall make it a common cause and aid each other mutually with their good offices, their counsels and their forces, according to the exigence of conjunctures, as becomes good and faithful allies.

ARTICLE II

The essential and direct end of the present defensive alliance is to maintain effectually the liberty, sovereignty, and independence absolute and unlimited, of the said United States, as well in matters of government as of commerce.

ARTICLE III

The two contracting parties shall each on its own part, and in the manner it may judge most proper, make all the efforts in its power against their common enemy, in order to attain the end proposed.

ARTICLE IV

The contracting parties agree that in case either of them should form any particular enterprise in which the concurrence of the other may be desired, the party whose concurrence is desired, shall readily, and with good faith, join to act in concert for that purpose, as far as circumstances and its own particular situation will permit; and in that case, they shall regulate, by a particular convention, the quantity and kind of succor to be furnished, and the time and manner of its being brought into action, as well as the advantages which are to be its compensation.

ARTICLE V

If the United States should think fit to attempt the reduction of the British power, remaining in the northern parts of America, or the islands of Bermudas, those countries or islands, in case of success, shall be confederated with or dependant upon the said United States.

ARTICLE VI

The Most Christian King renounces forever the possession of the islands of Bermudas, as well as of any part of the continent of North America, which before the treaty of Paris in 1763, or in virtue of that treaty, were acknowledged to belong to the Crown of Great Britain, or to the United States, heretofore called British Colonies, or which are at this time, or have lately been under the power of the King and Crown of Great Britain.

ARTICLE VII

If His Most Christian Majesty shall think proper to

attack any of the islands situated in the Gulph of Mexico, or near that Gulph, which are at present under the power of Great Britain, all the said isles, in case of success, shall appertain to the Crown of France.

Article VIII

Neither of the two parties shall conclude either truce or peace with Great Britain without the formal consent of the other first obtained; and they mutually engage not to lay down their arms until the independence of the United States shall have been formally or tacitly assured by the treaty or treaties that shall terminate the war.

Article IX

The contracting parties declare, that being resolved to fulfil each on its own part the clauses and conditions of the present treaty of alliance, according to its own power and circumstances, there shall be no after claim of compensation on one side or the other, whatever may be the event of the war.

Article X

The Most Christian King and the United States agree to invite or admit other powers who may have received injuries from England, to make common cause with them, and to accede to the present alliance, under such conditions as shall be freely agreed to and settled between all the parties.

Article XI

The two parties guarantee mutually from the present time and forever against all other powers, to wit: The United States to His Most Christian Majesty, the present possessions of the Crown of France in America, as well as those which it may acquire by the future treaty of peace: And His Most Christian Majesty guarantees on his part to the United States their liberty, sovereignty and independence, absolute and unlimited, as well in matters of government as commerce, and also their possessions, and the additions or conquests that their confederation may obtain during the war, from any of the dominions now, or heretofore possessed by Great Britain in North America, conformable to the 5th and 6th articles above written, the whole as their possessions shall be fixed and assured to the said States, at the moment of the cessation of their present war with England.

Article XII

In order to fix more precisely the sense and application of the preceding article, the contracting parties declare, that in case of a rupture between France and England the reciprocal guarantee declared in the said article shall have its full force and effect the moment such war shall break out; and if such rupture shall not take place, the mutual obligations of the said guarantee shall not commence until the moment of the cessation of the present war between the United States and England shall have ascertained their possessions.

Article XIII

The present treaty shall be ratified on both sides, and the ratifications shall be exchanged in the space of six months, or sooner if possible.

In faith whereof the respective Plenipotentiaries, to wit: On the part of the Most Christian King, Conrad Alexander Gérard, Royal Syndic of the city of Strasbourgh, and Secretary of His Majesty's Council of State; and on the part of the United States, Benjamin Franklin, Deputy to the General Congress from the State of Pennsylvania, and President of the Convention

of the same State, Silas Deane, heretofore Deputy from
the State of Connecticut, and Arthur Lee, Councellor
at Law, have signed the above articles both in the
French and English languages, declaring, nevertheless,
that the present treaty was originally composed and
concluded in the French language, and they have here-
unto affixed their seals.

Done at Paris, this sixth day of February, one thousand seven hundred and seventy-eight.

(Seal.)	C. A. GERARD.
(Seal.)	B. FRANKLIN.
(Seal.)	SILAS DEANE.
(Seal.)	ARTHUR LEE.

(b)

Act Separate and Secret Reserving Right of King of
Spain to Agree to the Foregoing Treaties,
concluded February 6, 1778; ratified by the Continental
Congress May 4, 1778, ratifications exchanges at
Paris July 17, 1778.

The most Christian King declared in consequence of
the intimate union which subsists between him and the
King of Spain, that in concluding with the United
States of America this treaty of amity and commerce,
and that of eventual and defensive alliance, his Majesty
hath intended, and intends, to reserve expressly, as he
reserves by this present separate and secret act, to his
said Catholick Majesty the power of acceding to the
said treatys, and to participate in their stipulations at
such time as he shall judge proper. It being well understood, nevertheless, that if any of the stipulations
of the said treatys are not agreeable to the King of
Spain, His Catholick Majesty may propose other conditions analogous to the principal aim of the alliance

and conformable to the rules of equality, reciprocity and friendship.

The Deputies of the United States, in the name of their constituents, accept the present declaration in its full extent, and the Deputy of the said States who is fully impowered to treat with Spain promises to sign, on the first requisition of His Catholic Majesty, the act or acts necessary to communicate to him the stipulations of the treaties above written; and the said Deputy shall endeavor, in good faith, the adjustment of the points in which the King of Spain may propose any alteration conformable to the principles of equality, reciprocity, and the most sincere and perfect amity, he, the said Deputy, not doubting but that the person or persons impower'd by His Catholic Majesty to treat with the United States will do the same with regard to any alterations of the same kind that may be thought necessary by the said Plenipotentiary of the United States.

In faith whereof the respective Plenipotentiaries have signed the present separate and secret article, and affixed to the same their seals.

Done at Paris this sixth day of February, one thousand seven hundred and seventy-eight.

(Seal.)	C. A. GERARD.
(Seal.)	B. FRANKLIN.
(Seal.)	SILAS DEANE.
(Seal.)	ARTHUR LEE.

Deputy, Plenipotentiary for France and Spain.

II

Reflexions which may perhaps present some New Ideas upon the great and important Affairs of America.[1]

7 January 1777.

The arrival of Mr. Franklin in France has given rise to reflections which may perhaps, present some new ideas upon the great and important affairs of America.

The present state of those affairs and the rôle which Mr. Franklin plays therein does not allow an observant person to doubt that this American is deputed to come with certain propositions to France in the critical position in which his country finds herself of having to achieve absolute independence or of falling again under the rule of England, and even of seeing her position aggravated, if the fortune of war is against her.

If we turn our attention more closely to the true interests of America, of France and of England with regard to this important object, we easily recognize that, in the actual position of things, America has propositions so absolute, so urgent, to make to France, that it is as difficult for her not to come to a decision, as it is essential and pressing for her to determine wisely.

It is not for us, (the writer) supposing that such propositions existed, to go so far as to pronounce upon what it is expedient to do. That point exceeds our province. But one may be justified, as a good subject of the King, and without overstepping the zeal with which one is animated for his service in considering what may be the consequences of the course for or against, to be taken in the circumstances.

One may suppose then that America has at the present time a twofold plan of action demanding equal

[1] Smss. no. 619. Though the work of a "private citizen," this memoir was probably prepared for the Council, Doniol II. 118.

urgency: either to obtain with the aid of France and Spain, her complete independence or to extort an acknowledgment of it from England itself.

The argument which the United Colonies of North America may use to France is to say to her: "Assist us to win our complete liberty and you will derive therefrom honour and advantage by the Treaty Offensive and Defensive and that of Commerce which we offer you, or leave us to treat with England at your peril and risk if it is achieved."

On the other hand the proposition which America, to arrive equally at the goal of her independence, may make to England is the following:

"We have been fighting," she may say, "for two years past for a rightful liberty. The probabilities for and against, so to speak, are at the present time equal; the issue will become a certainty if we join with France and Spain. Grant us generously what we are in a position to wrest from you, and here is the price we put upon the just independence which we desire. A treaty, as glorious for the mother country as for her colony, being signed, take twenty, thirty thousand men of our troops which are all ready, you have your vessels on our coasts, go possess yourselves therewith of St. Domingo, Martinique, Guadaloupe, drive the French entirely out of America and you will have in the new possessions which you acquire an ample equivalent for what you cede to us; an equivalent more productive, better suited to the nature of your territories, and one henceforward impregnable in your hands because we will be its guardians, its defenders, as well as the nurses of its prosperity, and, being already your brothers by blood and becoming bound to you by a memorable treaty we shall thus be doubly your allies and much more sure allies than if we remained subordinate and discontented subjects."

. . . .

If it were permitted to a private citizen to extend his reflections further upon the question of the justice of a war with England in the present conjuncture it might be observed that the war which we may have with that crown, as things stand, would not exactly possess the characteristics of which we have been speaking. It would indeed be rather a war of self-defense, if the propositions of which we have spoken above existed. Indeed, France having the safety of her own possessions compromised has thenceforth only to choose between the course of furnishing America with the aid she asks for or of seeing an oppressed colony or (and) an ambitious mother country treating on their own account and of taking upon herself the consequence of their agreement. If that danger has any foundation in fact, then it is a league prejudicial to her own repose, prejudicial to her possessions, which she breaks. It is a peril which she provides against and averts, and that peril well defined, which politically speaking is most certain, is perhaps a sufficient reason, of justice as much as of state, to warrant a determination of that kind.

. . . .

Basing our conclusion upon all these reflections as well as upon justice, it remains for us to give our idea of the extent and consequences of the revolution which is preparing, the main object of this writing.

If it is accomplished by our means, it ought while lowering England to raise France in a corresponding degree and restore her to her rank. It may even offer the most fortunate opportunities for making a sure work, seeing that England, with her resources already wasted, is almost unguarded at home, and that she presents there and elsewhere opportunities to strike a nearly certain and absolutely decisive blow. Lastly the present conjuncture, a conjuncture which the revolutions of time so rarely offer, is such that it may have an influence upon the state of France and upon that of Europe, always to the advantage of this kingdom, which the longest ages will not be able to disturb.

If America is severed from England with our aid, thenceforward all the possessions of that country in that part of the world fall, and ours establish themselves there upon the firmest foundations. Since the two great sources of England's commerce, the sole basis of her fortune, are in America and in Asia, one of the great sinews of that power is thenceforth cut; and if we hasten promptly and effectually to provide for the safety of the Isle of France (a post which can alone preserve India entire and give security to our future projects there) we shall at leisure and at opportunity provide suitably against the excessive power which England is tending to usurp there: in which we shall be the more assisted as the finances of England must needs be thrown completely out of gear by the ill-success of this war; and her public wealth being nothing but an exaggerated and almost artificial credit, she ought to be doubly overthrown both by the expenses of this war and by the loss of her possessions, the only pledge for the truly imaginary credit which has grown up in that nation, and which her constitution, aided by successes, has much favoured.

The consequences of this revolution ought, as we think, to be still more widespread. Such an event in our opinion, changes forthwith, to the advantage of France, the political state of Europe and even repairs the bad effects of the fatal war of Poland which has destroyed the balance of the Germanic body established with so much difficulty by a war of forty years and the celebrated treaty of Westphalia.

England, who weighed too heavily in the contrary balance which produced this change, reduced to her natural state, could no longer be of any assistance to Russia and to the King of Prussia, who as yet have only a forced extension of power the unconsolidated fortune of which depends much on the rare qualities of the rulers, who, in spite of their success, have only succeeded in disturbing the equilibrium of Germany without having given it another fixed constitution, since there are two rival monarchies seeking to establish themselves upon the ruin of that aristocracy and a third monarchy, Russia, strives to force a way into it, a state of things which substitutes a conflict or a new war for the old condition of things, the decaying condition of the Germanic body.

It is true that the new house of Austria, by this revolution regains the preponderance in Germany which we had taken away and that naturally she also ought to find in the weakening of England means of increasing her power. But in what respect may France find her interests injured thereby? In their common elevation the point is so strongly in her favour that she has nothing to wish for in that respect. If the maritime power of England falls, France naturally and invincibly takes her place whether by the advancement of her distant acquisitions or by the favourable position of her territories. Her pre-eminence in this respect, too, will be so constant, so certain; besides, the new kind of power which she will acquire is in itself so important, so decisive, considering the present customs of Europe, that it is much rather to be feared this excessive pre-eminence may be noticed and may excite resistance. Consequently, looking at this double increase, the desire of the houses of Bourbon and Austria for union would be better fulfilled by these circumstances than by any others which could ever arise, for, lastly, firm treaties are not formed nor maintained except by mutual advantages. In short nothing can happen more essential for France, in her real and in her relative power, than the absolute consummation of this revolution. By her position alone she inherits all that England loses; and without even going so far as to pluck them, she sees drop from the hands of her rival the chief branches of that rival's fortune; all this debris comes of itself to increase her own, and time alone assures her without any effort, a two-fold power, on sea and on land, which she has never been able to unite and which strengthening each other will put her above attack.

Taking now a collective view of this statement of facts all the importance of the resolution which France is called upon to make presents itself to the mind. The question is, according to the laws of nature, as to the liberty of one of the four quarters of the world held captive by one of the European powers: in two words, it is a question of giving America to the whole world; politically, it is a question of putting right the state of Europe and chiefly that of France. Finally, if it is permissible in a political memoir to consider the subject philosophically, one can see with some interest a people forming itself into a national body, creating itself a civil state embodying a mixture of the manners of a state of nature and of the wisdom of an age most fruitful of knowledge, a people which is about to give laws to itself, having before its eyes the laws of all civilized peoples. This is not a collection of savages gradually emerging from barbarism, and which rather receives than gives to itself the constitution which circumstances impose upon it. This is a people already civilized by its understanding and which, after having acquired its political independence, is about to choose for itself the legislation that is to establish its destiny for all time. The history of the world perhaps shows no spectacle more interesting, and the political stage has never perhaps presented an event the consequences of which are more important and more widespread in the general condition of this globe.

Summarizing what has been said in this memoir, the result is that finance must dictate the course to take in the present state of things always after justice shall have spoken. The impression with which one is filled in writing this is such that it cannot too often be repeated that it is a question of taking from England, our natural and actual enemy, more than half her power, and that for ever, and of giving it to France; or of seeing England make an agreement which will give her more strength and cover her with glory, will change into good fortune an occasion of disaster, and all that at our expense; and the course to be taken ought to be taken actively and without delay or it is very possible that the other part of the dilemma just spoken of may be accomplished before our eyes.

The writer here closes the reflections which the fulness of his zeal for the King's service may render acceptable.

III

CONSIDERATIONS UPON THE NECESSITY OF FRANCE DECLARING AT ONCE FOR THE AMERICAN COLONIES, EVEN WITHOUT THE CONCURRENCE OF SPAIN.[1]

13 January 1778.

The quarrel which exists between England and the Colonies of North America is as important to France as to Great Britain, and its issue will have equal in-

[1] Smss. no. 1835. Though unsigned this document contains expressions from earlier papers from Vergennes' pen. Cf. for example, Doniol, II. 144 and 733 ff. Besides the points for which it is cited in the text, the memoir is interesting as an omnium gatherum of all the arguments for French intervention.

fluence on the reputation and power of those two Crowns. It is, therefore, essential that France should decide upon and fix the policy it is advisable she should adopt in such a conjuncture.

The Americans have been struggling for the last three years against the efforts of Great Britain, and they have up to the present maintained a sort of superiority; but the war which they wage fatigues and exhausts them, and must necessarily weary the people and awaken in them a desire for repose.

England, for her part, crushed by the expenditure occasioned by this same war, and convinced of the impossibility of reducing the Colonies, is occupied with the means of re-establishing peace. With this view she is taking the most urgent and animated steps with the Deputies from Congress, and it is natural that the United States should at last decide to listen to their proposals.

In this state of affairs it is desirable to examine what course it is proper for France to take.

There exist two courses only,—that of abandoning the Colonies, and that of supporting them.

If we abandon them, England will take advantage of it by making a reconciliation, and in that case she will either preserve her supremacy wholly or partially, or she will gain an ally. Now it is known that she is disposed to sacrifice that supremacy and to propose simply a sort of family compact, that is to say, a league against the House of Bourbon.

The result of this will be that the Americans will become our perpetual enemies, and we must expect to see them turn all their efforts against our possessions, and against those of Spain. This is all the more probable as the Colonies, require a direct trade with the sugar islands. England will offer them that of our islands after having conquered them, which will be easy for her.

Thus the coalition of the English and the Americans will draw after it our expulsion, and probably that of the Spaniards, from the whole of America; it will limit our shipping and our commerce to the European seas only, and even this trade will be at the mercy of English insolence and greed.

It would be a mistake to suppose that the United States will not lend themselves to the proposals of the Court of St. James's. Those States took up arms only in order to establish and defend their independence and the freedom of their commerce; if, therefore, England offers them both, what reason will they have for refusing? Their treaty with that Power will give them more safety than the engagements which they might make with other Powers, or than all the guarantees which we might offer them. Indeed, what opinion can they have of our means, and even of our good-will, since we have not dared to co-operate in securing an independence of which we would afterwards propose the empty guarantee? Their surest guarantee will be in the community of interests and views which will be established between them and their former mother-country; we have nothing to offer which can counterbalance that.

Such will be the effects of the independence of the United States of America, if it is established without our concurrence.

It follows from this that the glory, the dignity and the essential interest of France demand that she should stretch out her hand to those States, and that their independence should be her work.

The advantages which will result are innumerable; we shall humiliate our natural enemy, a perfidious enemy who never knows how to respect either treaties or the right of nations; we shall divert to our profit one of the principal sources of her opulence; we shall shake her power, and reduce her to her real value; we shall extend our commerce, our shipping, our fisheries; we shall ensure the possession of our islands, and finally, we shall re-establish our reputation, and shall resume amongst the Powers of Europe the place which belongs to us. There would be no end if we wished to detail all these points; it is sufficient to indicate them in order to make their importance felt.

In presupposing that the independence of the Americans is to be the work of France, it is necessary to examine what line of conduct it is desirable for us to observe in order to attain that end; there is but one,— to assist the Colonies.

But in order to determine the sort of assistance to be given, it is essential not to deviate from the two following truths: 1st, that whatever sort of assistance we give the Americans, it will be equivalent to a declaration of war against Great Britain: 2nd that when war is inevitable, it is better to be beforehand with one's enemy than to be anticipated by him.

Starting with these two principles, it appears that France cannot be too quick in making with the Americans a treaty of which recognised independence will be the basis, and that she should take her measures for acting before England can anticipate her.

It is all the more urgent to hasten the arrangements to be made with the Americans, as the Deputies are hard pressed by emissaries of the English Ministry, and as, if we are not the first to bind them, they will give the Court of London a foundation for proposing a plan of reconciliation at the re-assembly of Parliament, which will take place on the 20th instant, and then all will be over with us, and it will only remain for us to prepare to undertake war against the English and against the insurgents, whereas we could and ought to have begun it in concert with the latter.

In all that has just been said, the co-operation of Spain has been presupposed.

But in the event of that Power not adopting the principles and plan of France, or of her judging the moment of putting it into execution not yet arrived, what course will France, thus isolated, have to follow?

The independence of the Colonies is so important a matter for France, that no other should weaken it, and France must do her utmost to establish it, even if it should cost her some sacrifices; I mean that France must undertake the war for the maintenance of American independence, even if that war should be in other respects disadvantageous. In order to be convinced of this truth, it is only necessary to picture to ourselves what England will be, when she no longer has America.

Thus France must espouse the American cause, and use for that purpose all her power, even if Spain should refuse to join her. From this one of two things will happen; either that Power will still remain neutral, or she will decide to join France. In the first case, although she will be passive, she will nevertheless favour our operations, because she will be armed, and England will see her constantly placed behind us, and ready, if need be, to assist us: but in order to maintain this opinion, we must also maintain that of a good understanding between the two Courts. The second case has no need of development.

But Spain is awaiting a rich fleet from Vera Cruz, and that fleet will not arrive until about next spring. Its arrival must unquestionably be ensured, and that may be done in two ways; 1st by prolonging the period of our operations, or else, 2nd, by sending a squadron to meet the fleet. Spain has vessels at Cadiz and Ferrol; they are armed and ready to put to sea. A cruise might be given as a pretext in order to mask their real destination.

If the King adopts the course of going forward without the participation of Spain, he will take away from that Power all just reason for complaint, by stipulating for her eventually all the advantages which she would have claimed, had she been a contracting party. These advantages will be the same as those which His Majesty will ask for himself.

IV

Extracts from the "Observations on the Justicative Memorial of the Court of London."[1]

While the ambassador of England put the King's patience to the strongest proofs . . . an event came to pass in America which essentially changed the face of things in that quarter of the world. This event was the defeat of the army under General Burgoyne. The news of this unexpected disaster . . . astonished the British ministers, and must have the more sensibly affected them, as it overthrew the plan they had laid for the reduction of the Colonies. We shall be convinced of this truth by reading the speeches occasioned by it in Parliament. The first result of the tumultuous debates of both Houses was the naming of commissioners of peace, to carry to America conciliatory bills; and

---

[1] The original (though quite different) form of this document is to be found in Beaumarchais' *Oeuvres complètes* (Paris, 1835), 530-42. The present document was published in Paris in 1779 over Beaumarchais' name, but the edition of 1780, which is unchanged, is anonymous, though it is attributed in the catalogue of the Bibliotèque Nationale to J. M. Gérard de Rayneval, Vergennes' Secretary. The English-American translation (Philadelphia and London, 1780), from which the above extracts are made, is also anonymous. There are four copies of this translation in the Pennsylvania Historical Society's library at Philadelphia, and one of the French edition of 1779.

that of the secret deliberations of the council at S^t.
James' was to make advances and to sound the American
commissioners residing at Paris, and to propose to them
peace and a coalition against the Crown of France.

This last proposition was the consequence of the im-
putations which the ministry of London had incessantly
made against that of Versailles: They have affected to
consider France as the cause, the support, in a word
as the author, of the revolution of which America presented them a view; and this opinion would naturally
inspire them with the desire of vengeance. . . . This
prospect was so much the more proper to console, and
even to dazzle the British ministers, as it perfectly cor-
responded with their most dear and most constant wish,
a wish which for a long time had been the very essence
of British policy, that of humbling France; and as the
presumptuous confidence of that nation must have still
grown greater, when they beheld the extraordinary
armaments they had got ready, with a despatch which
surprised all Europe [the armaments referred to are
stated to be those prepared in January, 1777].

The British ministry, led astray by this brilliant
phantom, delayed not putting in motion all the secret
springs by means of which they would be able to realize
it. Emissaries came one after another and watched the
American commissioners: Their discourse to every one
of them was, that *they should no longer continue the
dupes of France, but must unite with the court of London, and fall upon that power, etc.*

The court of London denies the facts and represents
them as *a supposition destitute of truth and even of
probability, and calls upon France to produce the
proof of it.* But can a subterfuge like this possibly
impose on any one? Who will suspect the British ministry to have carried their want of address or impru-
dence so far as to leave direct marks of a darksome

manouvre, and of not having on the other hand, taken the most effectual measures that, in case of discovery, it might not be imputed to them! . . . True it is, that according to the British ministry, *the King of Great Britain could not be suspected of not being offered peace to his subjects, after a long and hard contest, but with design of entering into a new war against a respectable power;* [this is a mistranslation of the French: the second *not* and the *but* should be omitted]. But some very plain reflections will make it clear how illusory this affected language is, and how little it deserves belief.

If the court of London . . . either sincerely, or in order to impose upon the English nation or even on its king . . . has experienced unpardonable injuries from France, if it has reason for reproaching her with the defection of the Colonies, they must consider her dignity and most essential interests as wounded, and from that time must feel the most ardent desire, not only of taking vengeance, but also of recovering from France what the crown of England lost in America. In consequence of this plan, it was natural for the British ministry, unable to subdue her Colonies, to seek to be reconciled to them and to engage them to espouse her resentment: They might so much the more flatter themselves that they should succeed herein as the proceedings of France with regard to American privateers . . . and especially the dislike the king had at all times manifested to any engagement with the Congress, must have given disgust and dissatisfaction to their deputies, and induce them, notwithstanding their well known aversion, to seek even in England the safety of their country when they failed to find it in France. . . .

In this situation ought it not to be supposed that, the moment the British ministry perceived the necessity of yielding to the efforts of the Colonies, they perceived the project and the hope of punishing France for the wrongs they had imputed to her? Such have, indeed, been the intention and conduct of the ministers of the king of Great Britain. We have already affirmed, in the *Exposé de Motifs* and we repeat it here, with that assurance which nothing but truth can give; and the King dares flatter himself that the opinion which all Europe has of his rectitude and probity will have more weight than a denial merely hazarded and which they have not even had the address to render probable.

Moreover, although the king had not had certain proof of the hostile views of the court of London, it would have been sufficient for him to have had probable grounds to suspect that they existed; now, what must His Majesty have thought of the sight of the immense and hasty warlike preparations of the court of London! her arbitrary proceedings, her denials of justice, her arrogant pretensions! What must he have allowed to the last words of the idol and oracle of the British nation, Lord Chatham, who dragged himself to Parliament, there to expire exclaiming, *Peace with America, and war with the House of Bourbon!* The court of London herself had justified the suspicion and foresight of the king, by the hostile orders sent to India before the declaration of the Marquis de Noailles, and even before the signing of the Treaty of February 6, 1778. . . .

The King well informed of the plan of the court of London and of the preparations which were the consequence of it, perceived that no more time was to be lost if he would prevent the designs of his enemies: His Majesty determined, therefore, to take into consideration, at length, the overtures of the Congress [pp. 60-6]. . . . .

Whilst the British ambassador renewed without intermission complaints unjust in their object . . . the British ministry, convinced that notwithstanding their formidable armaments any subjugation whatever of the Colonies was in future impossible, proposed to Parliament the means of conciliation; they endeavored at the same time to open a secret negotiation with the commissioners of Congress at Paris; they were disposed to yield everything, even independence in fact, provided they could retain a *nominal dependence*. But war against France was to be the price of so great a sacrifice. The king apprised on the one side of the offers and hostile views of the court of London, and on the other side of the unshaken resolution of Congress not to suffer the least trace of its former subjection to remain: The king, I say, did not hesitate to take a part. . . .

To deceive the other nations with regard to the real motives which have directed the conduct of the king, the British ministry maintain that he entered into treaty with the Americans, not because he feared the secret views of Great Britain, but because he foresaw that the Americans defeated, discouraged without support and without resources, were about to return to their mother-country. . . . It was without doubt for the sake of this assertion that the British ministry have thought it beneath the dignity of their sovereign to search for the period at which France formed connections with the United States. . . . The king is willing to spare the British ministry a task so disagreeable and so embarrassing, by observing for them that the conversations which led to the Treaties of the 6th of February, 1778, were considerably posterior to the capitulation of General Burgoyne. Now it is notorious that this event elevated the courage and the hopes of the Americans as much as it dejected the British nation, and principally the court of London. If then the king has listened to the propositions of Congress after this period so disastrous to the British, it has not been, and could not have been for any other reason, but because the thought with the United States that their independence was thenceforward irrevocable; England herself thought as the Americans did" [93-6].

V

PROVISIONAL ARTICLES[1]

agreed upon, by and between Richard Oswald, Esquire, The Commissioner of His Britannic Majesty, for Treating of Peace with the Commissioners of the United States of America, in behalf of His Said Majesty on the One Part, and John Adams, Benjamin Franklin, John Jay, and Henry Laurens, Four of the Commissioners of the Said United States for Treating of Peace with the Commissioners of His Said Majesty, on Their Behalf, on the Other Part. To be Inserted in, and to Constitute the Treaty of Peace Proposed to be Concluded Between the Crown of Great Britain and the Said United States; but which Treaty is not to be Concluded until Terms of a Peace Shall Be Agreed Upon Between Great Britain and France, and His Britannic Majesty Shall Be Ready to Conclude Such Treaty Accordingly.

Concluded November 30, 1782. Proclamation ordered by the Continental Congress April 11, 1783.

ARTICLES

    I. Independence acknowledged.

   II. Boundaries.

 III. Fishery rights.

 IV. Recovery of Debts.

  V. Restitution of estates.

 VI. Confiscations and prosecutions to cease.

VII. Withdrawal of British armies.

[1] Text from Malloy.

VIII. Navigation of the Mississippi River.

IX. Restoration of territory.

Separate Article. Boundary of West Florida.

Whereas reciprocal advantages and mutual convenience are found by experience to form the only permanent foundation of peace and friendship between States, it is agreed to form the articles of the proposed treaty on such principles of liberal equity and reciprocity, as that partial advantages (those seeds of discord) being excluded, such a beneficial and satisfactory intercourse between the two countries may be established as to promise and secure to both perpetual peace and harmony.

ARTICLE I

His Britannic Majesty acknowledges the said United States, viz., New Hampshire, Massachusett's Bay, Rhode Island and Providence Plantations, Connecticut, New York, New Jersey, Pennsylvania, Delaware, Maryland, Virginia, North Carolina, South Carolina, and Georgia, to be free, sovereign and independent States; that he treats with them as such, and for himself, his heirs and successors, relinquishes all claims to the Government, propriety and territorial rights of the same, and every part thereof; and that all disputes which might arise in future on the subject of the boundaries of the said United States may be prevented, it is hereby agreed and declared that the following are and shall be their boundaries, viz.:

ARTICLE II

From the northwest angle of Nova Scotia, viz., that angle which is formed by a line drawn due north from the source of St. Croix River to the Highlands; along the Highlands which divide those rivers that empty themselves into the river St. Lawrence, from those which fall into the Atlantic Ocean, to the northwesternmost head of Connecticut River; thence down along the middle of that river to the 45th degree of north latitude; from thence, by a line due west on said latitude until it strikes the river Iroquois or Cataraquy; thence along the middle of said river into Lake Ontario, through the middle of said lake until it strikes the communication by water between the lake and Lake Erie; thence along the middle of said communication into Lake Erie, through the middle of said lake untill it arrives at the water communication between that lake and Lake Huron; thence along the middle of said water communication into the Lake Huron; thence through the middle of said lake to the water communication between that lake and Lake Superior; thence through Lake Superior northward to the isles Royal and Phelippeaux, to the Long Lake; thence through the middle of said Long Lake, and the water communication between it and the Lake of the Woods, to the said Lake of the Woods; thence through the said lake to the most northwestern point thereof, and from thence on a due west course to the river Mississippi; thence by a line to be drawn along the middle of the said river Mississippi untill it shall intersect the northermost part of the 31st degree of north latitude. South, by a line to be drawn due east from the determination of the line last mentioned, in the latitude of 31 degrees north of the equator, to the middle of the river Apalachicola or Catahouche; thence along the middle thereof to its junction with the Flint River; then strait to the head of St. Mary's River; and thence down along the middle of St. Mary's River to the Atlantic Ocean. East, by a line to be drawn along the middle of the river St. Croix, from its mouth in the bay of Fundy to its source, and from its source directly north to the aforesaid highlands which divide the rivers that fall into the Atlantic Ocean, from those which fall into the river St. Laurence; comprehending all islands within twenty leagues of any part of the shores of the United States, and lying between lines to be drawn due east from the points where the aforesaid boundaries between Nova Scotia on the one part, and East Florida on the other, shall respectively touch the bay of Fundy and the Atlantic Ocean; excepting such islands as now are, or heretofore have been, within the limits of the said province of Nova Scotia.

ARTICLE III

It is agreed that the people of the United States shall continue to enjoy unmolested the right to take fish of every kind on the Grand Bank, and on all the other banks of Newfoundland; also in the Gulph of St. Lawrence, and at all other places in the sea, where the inhabitants of both countries used at any time heretofore to fish; and also that the inhabitants of the United States shall have liberty to take fish of every kind on such part of the coast of Newfoundland as British fishermen shall use, (but not to dry or cure the same on that island;) and also on the coasts, bays and creeks of all other of his Britannic Majesty's dominions in America; and that the American fishermen shall have liberty to dry and cure fish in any of the unsettled bays, harbours and creeks of Nova Scotia, Magdalen Islands, and Labrador, so long as the same shall remain unsettled; but as soon as the same or either of them shall be settled, it shall not be lawful for the said fishermen to dry or cure fish at such settlement, without a previous agreement for that purpose with the inhabitants, proprietors or possessors of the ground.

ARTICLE IV

It is agreed that creditors on either side shall meet with no lawful impediment to the recovery of the full value in sterling money of all bona fide debts heretofore contracted.

Article V

It is agreed that the Congress shall earnestly recommend it to the legislatures of the respective States to provide for the restitution of all estates, rights and properties which have been confiscated, belonging to real British subjects, and also of the estates, rights and properties of persons resident in districts in the possession of His Majesty's arms, and who have not borne arms against the said United States: And that persons of any other description shall have free liberty to go to any part or parts of any of the thirteen United States, and therein to remain twelve months unmolested in their endeavours to obtain the restitution of such of their estates, rights and properties as may have been confiscated: And that Congress shall also earnestly recommend to the several States a reconsideration and revision of all acts or laws regarding the premises, so as to render the said laws or acts perfectly consistent, not only with justice and equity, but with the spirit of conciliation which, on the return of the blessings of peace, should universally prevail: And that Congress shall also earnestly recommend to the several States that the estates, rights and properties of such last-mentioned persons shall be restored to them, they refunding to any persons who may be now in possession the bona fide price (where any has been given) which such persons may have paid on purchasing any of the said lands, rights and properties since the confiscation. And it is agreed that all persons who have any interest in confiscated lands, either by debts, marriage settlements or otherwise, shall meet with no lawful impediments in the prosecution of their just rights.

Article VI

That there shall be no future confiscations made, nor any prosecutions commenced against any persons for or by reason of the part which he or they may have taken in the present war, and that no person shall, on that account, suffer any future loss or damage, either in his person, liberty or property; and that those who may be in confinement on such charges, at the time of the ratification of the treaty in America, shall be immediately set at liberty, and the prosecutions so commenced be discontinued.

Article VII

There shall be a firm and perpetual peace between His Britannic Majesty and the said States, and between the subjects of the one and the citizens of the other, wherefore all hostilities, both by sea and land, shall then immediately cease: All prisoners, on both sides, shall be set at liberty; and His Britannic Majesty shall, with all convenient speed, and without causing any destruction, or carrying away any negroes or other property of the American inhabitants, withdraw all his armies, garrisons and fleets from the said United States, and from every port, place and harbour within the same, leaving in all fortifications the American artillery that may be therein; and shall also order and cause all archives, records, deeds and papers belonging to any of the said States or their citizens, which in the course of the war may have fallen into the hands of his officers to whom they belong.

Article VIII

The navigation of the river Mississippi, from its source to the ocean, shall forever remain free and open to the subjects of Great Britain and the citizens of the United States.

Article IX

In case it should so happen that any place or territory belonging to Great Britain or to the United States should be conquered by the arms of either from the other, before the arrival of these articles in America, it is agreed that the same shall be restored without difficulty and without requiring any compensation.

Done at Paris the thirtieth day of November, in the year one thousand seven hundred and eighty-two.

(Seal.)	Richard Oswald.
(Seal.)	John Adams.
(Seal.)	B. Franklin.
(Seal.)	John Jay.
(Seal.)	Henry Laurens.

Witness: Caleb Whitefoord,
Sec'y to the British Commission.
W. T. Franklin,
Sec'y to the American Commission.

Separate Article

It is hereby understood and agreed that in case Great Britain, at the conclusion of the present war, shall recover, or be put in possession of West Florida, the line of north boundary between the said province and the United States shall be a line drawn from the mouth of the river Yassous, where it unites with the Mississippi, due east, to the river Apalachicola.

Done at Paris the thirtieth day of November, in the year one thousand seven hundred and eighty-two.

(Seal.)	Richard Oswald.
(Seal.)	John Adams.
(Seal.)	B. Franklin.
(Seal.)	John Jay.
(Seal.)	Henry Laurens.

Witness: Caleb Whitefoord,
Sec'y to the British Commission.
W. T. Franklin,
Sec'y to the American Commission.

INDEX

Adams, John: Suggests French intervention, 52-3 fn.; opposed to a military connection with France, *ib.;* prophesies American greatness, 218; appointed envoy to negotiate peace, (Oct. 4, 1779), 261; wishes to communicate his powers to treat to the English government, 273-5; defends the "40 to 1" act, 275-6; endeavors to demonstrate France's indebtedness to the United States, *ib.;* thinks France should aid America more positively, 276-7; is snubbed by Vergennes and goes to Holland, 278; Congress asked to curb, 295, 299; superseded by a commission, 301; participation of, in the peace negotiations, 340, 345-6; signs a declaration (Jan. 20, 1783) explaining the Provisional Articles, 357.

Almodovar: Spanish ambassador at London, 182.

Aranda, Count d': Spanish ambassador at Paris and bitter enemy of England, 82; enthusiastic for an American alliance, 97, 107-8, 179-80 fn.; not a real ambassador, 108; recognizes the extension of the United States to the Mississippi, 241 fn.; action of, in facilitating peace, 356-7.

Argenson, Marquis d': Diplomatic policy of, 26-7.

Austria: Value of alliance with, to France, 39, 51, 59.

Balance of Power, Doctrine of: Connected with the balance of trade idea, 15-6, 33-4; logic of connected with French policy in the Revolution, 17-22; stated by Vergennes as an argument for French intervention in America, 86-9, 101, 137 ff.; to be applied to North America, 21-2, 176, 184.

Bancroft: An agent of the American commissioners, 127 and fn.

Bancroft the Historian: Explanation of French intervention in the Revolution, 2.

Bavarian Succession, War of: Cause and settlement of, 169-70.

Beaumarchais: Alarmist report on situation in England (1775), 65; proselytes the king in behalf of secret aid, 72-3; his *La Paix ou la Guerre,* 79; activities as Hortalez et cie, *ib.;* alarmism after Saratoga, 121 fn., 129-30; memoir of, urging immediate American recognition (Jan., 1778), 155 footnote; author of the original form of the *Observations sur le Mémoire,* etc., 145 and appendix IV; charges Arthur Lee with treachery to France, 166 fn.; controversy over claims of, 207-8; witty comment of, on Spain's entry into the war, 216 fn.

415

Belligerency: A status unknown to the Law of Nations
in 1776, 81 and fn.

Berkeley, Bishop: Predicts
greatness of America, 217 fn.

Bernis, Cardinal: Minister of
Foreign Affairs (1756), 32.

Bonvouloir: Mission of, to
America (1775), 73-4; re-
ports favorably on American
prospects (Mar., 1776), *ib.*

Boston: Siege of, impresses
French opinion, 68.

Broglie, Count de: His *Conjectures raisonnées,* 46 ff.;
plan for invasion of England
preserved at request of Vergennes, 61-2; plans to become
temporary "Statholder" of
the United States, 90-2; memoir on England's enfeeblement (Jan., 1778), 154-5 fn.

Burgoyne: British general
captures Ticonderoga, 117;
surrenders at Saratoga, 120.

Burke: Predicts French intervention in America, 52 fn.;
assesses the cost to France of
her intervention in America,
375-6.

Canada: Lost to France by
the Treaty of Paris (1763),
37; significance of English re-
tention of, in preference to
Guadaloupe and Martinique,
19-20; not a French objective
in the Revolution, 9-11, 70,
74, 200-1 and fn.; French
withdrawal from, assists
French intervention, 51, 65,
74; wish of France and Spain
to leave, in the hands of England, 12 fn., 111, 176, 201-4
and fns.; Vergennes' idea of
making a free state of, under
French protection, 201-2 and
fn.; Washington opposes a
French expedition into, 204.

Carleton, Sir Guy: Authorized

to negotiate peace in America, 330 fn.

Carmichael: Memoir of, to
Vergennes cited, 118 and fn.

Cartography: Evidence of, on
the Western Land question,
222 fn.

Castejon, Marquis de: Member
of the Spanish royal council,
and opposed to American
recognition, 109.

Castries: Becomes secretary
of state for the Marine, 285;
opposes peace (1782), 357 fn.

Catherine II: Assists in partition of Poland, 45; forms the
First League of Neutrals
(1780), 172; joins with Joseph II in offering to mediate
between Great Britain and
her foes (1781), 286.

Charles III, of Spain: A loyal
Bourbon, 34; concern at
French - American alliance,
161-2; deep resentment at independent course of France,
176-8; character of, sketched
by Florida Blanca, 176-7 fn.;
pleased with the idea of mediating between France and
England, 184; urges upon
Louis the acceptance of a
qualified recognition by England of American independence, 185-6; will not recognize
American independence be-
fore England, 195; disap-
pointment of, at not obtaining
Gibraltar, 356.

Chatelêt: Correspondence with
Choiseul regarding American
affairs, 42; joins Choiseul in
opposing Vergennes' policy,
287.

Chatham: Attitude toward
France and French view of,
3, 35 fn.; lament on Saratoga,
18-9; rumors of prospective
return to power, 64-5; in

eclipse, 66; no likelihood of his being called to power after Saratoga, 124 fn.; rumors respecting, 130, 155; opposed to recognizing American independence after Saratoga, 133 fn.; also, after the announcement of the French-American treaty, 168 fn.

Chaumont: A secret agent of the French Foreign Office, 126, 129.

Choiseul, Duke de: Succeeds Bernis (1758), 33; his Mercantilism, 33-4; obtains the second Family Compact, 35-6; cedes Louisiana to Spain, 36; *Mémoire* of (1765), 39-40; considers intervening in England's dispute with her Colonies (1766-8), 40 ff.; sends Kalb to America, 43; disliked by Louis XVI, 54; attacks of, on Vergennes' foreign policy, 78, 287.

Clark, George Rogers: Expedition of, against British posts in the Northwest, 269.

Commissioners, The American: Agree to transcend their original instructions, 96-7; would like to involve France with England, 114; endeavor to force the French government's hand, 118; abandon these tactics after Ticonderoga, 118-9 and fn.; prefer a coalition with France, 125 fn.; not citable in support of Vergennes' alarmism after Saratoga, 143-4; negotiations with the Foreign Office, ch. VII; propose a treaty of amity and commerce, 149; state their terms, 152-4; fail in their effort to procure immediately effective guaranties from France, *ib.;* presented at court, 168. See "Deane," "Lee," and "Franklin."

Congress, The Continental: Sends an agent to France, 84; authorizes a treaty of amity and commerce with France, 96; enlarges its instructions to the American commissioners, 97; effect of British gold on, feared by Vergennes, 163-4; declares against the idea of a separate peace, 209; debates in, of the Western Land question, 220 fn., 231-2 fn.; parties in, 247-8 and fns.; relations of, with the French envoys, chs. XI-XIII; developes aggressive views respecting American claims in the West and to the Newfoundland fisheries (1779), 256 ff.; adopts instructions of Aug. 14, 1779, 260; instructions of, to Jay, respecting the navigation of the Mississippi, see "Jay." See further "Instructions of June 15, 1781" and "Provisional Articles."

"Corsairs": The question of, 99-101.

Courier de l'Europe: Sensationalism of, 132 and fn.

Deane, Silas: First American agent to France, arrives in Paris, 84; approves Broglie's scheme to become "Stat-holder" of the United States, 90; presents Vergennes a plan of alliance between France, Spain, and the United States (Mar. 1777), 97; negotiations of, with the English spy, Wentworth, 127; famous controversy of, with Arthur Lee, 207-9; holds lands west of the Mountains to be at Congress' disposal, 219; endeavors to raise money in France on the Western lands as security, 238-9 and **fn.**

Deslandes: Urges importance of naval power to France, 29-30.

Diplomatic Revolution, The: motive for, 23; consummation of, 31-2.

Dunkirk: Treaty provisions regarding, 38; stipulation of Convention of Aranjuez with reference to, 193-4; articles concerning, s u p p r e s s e d (1783), 361.

Durand: Correspondence of, as ambassador at St. James' with Choiseul regarding American affairs, 41.

England: Begins Seven Years' War without warning, 3, 73; offers France and Spain a guaranty of their American possessions (1776-7) 6-7, 115-6; re-assesses colonial empire in consequence of Seven Years' War, 19-20; colonies, commerce, and marine the basis of the power of, 18-21, 29, 31, 41, 44, 48, 50, 87, 154-5; hereditary rival of France and enfeeblement of, sought by France, 18 ff., 40, 47-50, 69-70, 86, 89, 101, 137, 139-40; overbearing naval policy of, 47, 51, 73, 102-3; plays a waiting game with Spain (1778), 181-2; rejects proffer of Spanish mediation (Mar., 1779), 214-5; supposed to be enfeebled by the loss of America, 362-4; subordination of, to France resented, 365-6; causes of swift recuperation of, 367-8; recovery by, of American trade, 369-71 and fn.; rapid restoration of fleet of, 371; regains the predominance in Holland, 374-5.

Estaing, Count d': Sent with a fleet to North America, 169; address of, to French-Canadians (Oct., 1778), 202 fn.

Family Compact (1761): Formation and provisions of, 35-6; maintenance of, urged by Choiseul, 40; called by Vergennes "the corner-stone" of French policy, 59; loyalty to, pledged by Florida Blanca, 106; put in jeopardy by Vergennes' American policy, 135; appeal to, by France feared by Florida Blanca (1778), 175; supplemented by the Convention of Aranjuez, ch. VIII.

Favier: Associated with Broglie in the preparation of the *Conjectures raisonnées*, 46; influence of his work, 48-9.

Fitzherbert: British peace negotiator, 332 fn.

Fleury, Cardinal: His *Système de Conservation* and its great success, 23-5; defect of the *Système*, 28.

Florida Blanca, Don José Moniño Count de: Succeeds Grimaldi as prime-minister of Spain (1777), 105; characteristics of policy of, toward America, ch. V, *passim;* his idea of intervention, 112 ff.; opposes a pledge of financial aid to the Americans, 119; favors financial aid after Saratoga, but opposes an alliance with the colonies, 157; extreme anger at intelligence of French-American negotiations, 158-60; calculates on leisurely negotiations between France and Spain, 160-1; declines French offer of naval protection for Mexican treasure fleet, 164; fears an appeal by France to the Family Compact, 175; compared with Aranda, 175 fn.; crystallization of views of, respecting the American peril, 176-78;

angry correspondence with Aranda, 179-80 fn.; efforts of, to make Spain mediator rebuffed by England, 181; better success of, 182; wishes to see American independence neutralized, 184-5; discloses his intention to make Spanish objectives the *sine quâ non* of peace, 185, 189; definite objectives sought by, for Spain, 190; shapes the Convention of Aranjuez, 191-2; offers England Spanish mediation on the basis of the *status quo* in America, 214-5; recognizes the extension of the United States to the Mississippi, 240, 242; urges the *status quo* for the United States (1780), 271-2; eccentric conduct of, with Jay, 319 ff.; admits that Spain will not recognize American independence before England, 321-2; lack of self-possession of, *ib.* fn.; emphasizes Spain's interest in her monopoly of commerce in the Gulf of Mexico, 322; solicits terms of a treaty from Jay, 324-5; anger of, with Aranda in consequence of Spain's failure to obtain Gibraltar by the peace, 356.

Floridas, The: Holker's instructions with reference to (Nov. 25, 1777), 12 fn.; exchanged by Spain for Havana, 36; recovery of, sought by Spain, 112, 161, 190-1, 197-8. See also Appendix V.

Forth: British emissary to France (1777), presents informally English demands with reference to American privateers, 115; offers France a guaranty of her West Indian possessions, *ib.;* representations of, go unsupported, 116-7; offers France a separate peace, 331 fn.

Fox, Charles: Quarrel of, with Shelburne over the control of the peace negotiations, 331-2 fn.

France: Motives for entering the Revolution, chs. I and II, especially pp. 49-53, ch. VI, and appendices II and III; diplomatic object of, in the 18th century, 23 ff., 50; guarantor of the Treaty of Westphalia, 28, 59, 169-70; neglects her navy, 28-30; losses by the Seven Years' War, 37-8; humiliated by the Treaty of Paris, 38; also, by the partition of Poland, 45-6; intervention of, in the Revolution foretold, ch. II, note 52; weak navy of (1776), 87 fn.; hazardous position of, early in 1777, 99; apology of, to Europe for entering the Revolution, 144-5 fn.; breaks with England, 168-9; champion of neutral rights, 170-2; attitude of, on the Western Land question, 232 ff.; benefits received by, from the Treaty of Peace, ch. XVI; prestige of, restored on the Continent, 361-2; position of, arouses English jealousy, 365-6; failure of, to secure American trade, 369-71 and fn.; influence of, threatened by an Austro-Russian *rapprochement,* 372; temporary triumph of, in Holland, 374; terrible cost to, of her intervention in America, 375-6; see also "Spain" and "Vergennes."

Franklin: Foresees French intervention in the British-American dispute, 44 fn. 38, 52 fn.; arrives in France

(Dec., 1776), 93; immense reputation of, and its effect on the American cause, 93-4; first audience with Vergennes and demands of, 95; joins with Deane and Lee in transcending the Congressional instructions, 96-7; proposes a plan of alliance to Aranda, 97; intervenes in behalf of American privateers, 100; prepares memoir to the French government with Deane and Abbé Niccoli, 118 fn.; acquiesces in the idea of a truce, 186; holds lands west of the Mountains to be at Congress' disposal, 219 and fn.; personal interests of, in an English grant west of the Mountains, 226, 302 fn.; treats the Mississippi as the western boundary of the United States (Dec., 1775), 241 fn.; appointed peace negotiator, 301; views of, on method of negotiating peace, 329 fn.; articles proposed by, to Oswald as "necessary," 330; confidence of, in good faith of Vergennes, 333; joins with Jay and Adams in negotiating without regarding the Instructions of June 15, 1781, 340; returns a soothing answer to Vergennes' reproaches, 341 fn.; signs a declaration (Jan. 20, 1783) explanatory of the Provisional Articles, 357-8.

Frederick II: Makes treaty of Westminster with England (1756), 31; participates in partition of Poland, 45.

Gardoqui, Don Diego: Interest of, in American trade, 320; negotiations of, with Jay concerning the naviga-

tion of the Mississippi, *ib.* and fn.

Garnier: *Chargé d'affaires* at London, 64; reports of, on the English situation, 64-6; communicates news of the Declaration of Independence, 84; sends news of the American defeat at Long Island, 85.

George III: Control of Parliament, 4; calls the Americans "rebels" (Aug., 1775); dislike of, for Chatham, 64-5, 124 fn.; obstinacy in matter of American independence, 121-2; slow to recognize that France intends war, 163 fn.

Gérard (Conrad Gérard de Rayneval): Secretary to Vergennes, 69; *Réflexions* of (Nov., 1775), 69-72; denies that the Americans will become a conquering nation, 110; interview of, with the three American Commissioners (Dec. 17, 1777), 150-1; communicates to the commissioners the king's decision to make an alliance with the United States (Jan. 8, 1778), 152-3; sent as first French envoy to America, 169; instructed to prepare Congress for a truce and indirect recognition, 187; fails to obtain a favorable declaration from Congress on this subject, 195; fails to obtain concessions from Congress for Spain respecting the Floridas, 197-8; participation of, in Deane-Lee controversy, 208; obtains declaration from Congress against a separate peace; (Jan., 1779), 209; negotiations of, with Congress respecting the Western Land and Fisheries questions, ch.

XI; characterization of, 247 fn.; leaves America in broken health, 261-2; influence of, seen in La Luzerne's instructions, 265-7.

Gibbon the Historian: Author of the *Mémoire justicatif*, etc., 144.

Gibraltar: Vergennes' willingness to exchange French possessions to secure, for Spain (1782), 6; recovery of, desired by Spain, 178, 190, 347; pledge of Convention of Aranjuez, with reference to, 193-4; struggle for (1781-2), 287, 293, 313, 352; question of, delays peace, 347 fn., 348, 353, 356-7 and fn.

Grand: A secret agent of the French Foreign Office, 129.

Grasse, Count de: Commander of French fleet in American waters, 293; correspondence of, with Rochambeau, 310-2; credit due, for Yorktown, 313.

Grenville, Thomas: British peace envoy, 331-2 fn.; mystifying assertions of, 333 and fn.

Grimaldi, Marquis de: Prime minister of Spain, 86, 98; is succeeded by Florida Blanca, 105; cautions Aranda against the dangers of the American example, 108; meets Lee at the Spanish frontier and turns him back, *ib*.

Guines, Count de: Ambassador to England, sends Bonvouloir to America, 73-4; favors an understanding with England and is superseded by Noailles, 78.

Hartford Conference: Proceedings of, 291-2.

Hartley: An English friend of Franklin, 186, 330 fn.

Holker: First emissary sent to America after Saratoga and first French consul at Philadelphia, 120 and fn.

Holland: Relations of, to France under Treaty of Vervins, 184, 186-7; the Republican party of, and France, 83; breaks with England (1781), 285; enters into close alliance with France (1785), 374; French influence in, overthrown by England, 375.

Howes, The: British commanders in America, and rumored to be in negotiation with the Americans, 129-30 and fn.; victory of Lord Howe before Gibraltar, 352.

Hutton: An English friend of Franklin, 126.

Independence: Scope of the French guaranty of, 176, 183 fn., 193. See also "Treaty of Alliance," "Truce," *"Status Quo."*

Instructions of June 15, 1781: Terms of, 300-1; Congressional debates on, 301 ff. *passim;* explanation of Congress' action in voting, *ib.;* instructions supplementing, 315-7; criticized by Jay, 328; broken by Jay and his associates, 338 ff.

Jamaica: Vacillating attitude of Spain toward proposition to conquer, 178, 190, 287.

Jay, John: President of Congress, 249-50; confers with Gérard on the Western Land and Fisheries questions, 250-2, 259; appointed envoy to Madrid, 261; instructions of Congress to, respecting the navigation of the Mississippi, 261, 270 fn., 280 and fn., 323; appointed peace negotiator, 301; mission of, to Spain, ch.

XIV; submits scheme of treaty with Spain, 325; requested by Franklin to come to Paris, 326; fruitless attempts at negotiation with Aranda, *ib.;* effect upon, of his Spanish experiences, 327-8; part of, in the negotiations of 1782, ch. XV; is opposed to Oswald's first commission, 331-3; suspicions of, and their validity, 333-9, 346-9 and notes; sends Vaughan to England, 339; insists on America's fidelity to France, 342 fn.; willing to see Great Britain reconquer West Florida, *ib.;* beneficial results of conduct of, 350-5.

Jefferson, Thomas: Governor of Virginia, appointed peace negotiator, 301-2 and fn.

Jenifer: Member of Congress from Maryland, a leader of the "landless" state party, 280 fn., 304.

Kalb, John (later Baron de): Sent to America by Choiseul (1767), 42-3; report of, unfavorable to French intervention, *ib.;* acts as agent of Broglie, 90.

La Fayette, Marquis de: Comes to America (1777), 90; plans joint French-American campaign in Canada, 203; visits France and secures the despatch to America of forces under Rochambeau and Ternay, 287-8.

La Luzerne, Chevalier de: Second plenipotentiary to the United States, characterization of, 263-4 and fn.; Vergennes' first instructions to, 256-6; negotiations of, with Congress respecting Spain's interests, 267 ff.; Vergennes' later instructions to, touch-

ing this matter, 278-9, 281; negotiations of, with Congress leading to the Instructions of June 15, 1781, 297 ff.; assents to an American invasion of Canada (1781) 305; details American expectations from the treaty of peace, 308-9 and fn.

Laurens, Henry: Appointed peace negotiator, 301; is captured by the British and lodged in the Tower of London, 302 fn.

Laurens, Col. John: Is sent to France by Congress to obtain a loan (Feb., 1781), 292 and fn.

Lee, Arthur: In London (1775), 66; goes to Spain and is turned back (Mar., 1777), 98; accused of communicating the French-American Treaty to the British government, 166-7 fn.; controversy with Deane, 207-8; is prevented by La Luzerne from becoming secretary of Foreign Affairs, 265; criticism of, on the Instructions of June 15, 1781, 305 fn.

Lee, Richard Henry: Attitude of, on question of a separate peace, 208 and fn.

Livingston, Robert R.: Election of, to secretaryship of Foreign Affairs is promoted by La Luzerne, 265; letter of, to Franklin (Jan., 1782) in support of American claims in the West, 316 fn. See "Marbois."

Long Island, Battle of: Bad effect of, on American prospects in France, 85-8.

Louis XV: His *Secret du Roi,* 45; unpopular at death on account of France's humiliations abroad, 51 fn.

Louis XVI: Pledges reforms, 7, 60 and fn.; dislikes idea of aiding rebels, 8 fn. and appendix IV; chooses cabinet, 54; ratifies the policy of secret aid, 79; extends financial aid to the Colonies, 95-6, 120; agrees to war with England and an alliance with the United States if Spain is favorable, 103-4; decides to make new gift to America, 120; convinced of "the moral certainty of peril," 129 and fn., 142-3; point of view of, to be distinguished from that of the Foreign Office, 148; authorizes the declaration of the Treaty of Amity and Commerce (Mar. 7, 1778), 166-7; sends letters to Congress, 168-9; on the point of stopping the war for financial reasons (1780), 284-5; goes to the guillotine, 358.

Louisiana: Not a French objective in the Revolution, 9-11; transferred by France to Spain (1762), 36. See "Mississippi and Western Land Question."

Madison, James: Argument of (Oct., 1780), against Spain's claim of a right to conquer British possessions along the Mississippi, 270-1 fn.; criticizes the conduct of the American peace negotiators, 344-5.

"Manifest Destiny": Origins of the idea, 217-19 fn.

Marbois: Secretary to La Luzerne, urges Spain's claims upon Congress, 280-1; letter of, opposing the American claims to the fisheries, 337-8 and fn.

Maria Theresa: Assists in the partition of Poland (1772),

45; desires peace (1778), 170.

Maryland: Opposes the claims of the "landed" states, 220 fn., 232.

Maurepas, Count de: Urges restoration of French Marine (1730-40), 28-9; urges a belligerent policy toward England, 78-9 and fn.

Mercantile System: Leading ideas of, 15-7 and fn., 28-9, 33-4; connection with French intervention, 18-9, 41-2, 44.

Miralles, Juan de: Spanish agent, arrives in America, 243-4; views of, on the conflicting interests of Spain and the United States, 244-5 and fn.; determines views of Gérard, 245 ff.; proposes purchase of American claims in the West, 251-2; spreads false reports respecting Spain's attitude, 255; admits lack of powers or instructions from Madrid, 269; dies, 280.

Mississippi and Western Land Question, The: See chs. X-XII; also chs. XIV-XV passim.

Monroe Doctrine, The: Some antecedents of, 201 fn., 369 fn.

Montmorin, Count de: Friend of Louis and Vergennes, becomes ambassador at Madrid, 156; urged by Vergennes to arouse the Spanish government to an appreciation of the opportunity presented by the Revolution, 156-7; encounters Florida Blanca's wrath at the action of France in negotiating with the Americans, 158-60; says that Spain wants "shining objects," 161; is sceptical of value of Spanish aid, 180; signs the Convention of Aranjuez (Apr. 12, 1779), 192; warns Vergennes of Spain's hostility toward America, 216.

Morris, Gouverneur: Views of, on the Western Land question, 248-9.

Nentrals, Rights of: French government champions, against English sea-power, 21, 80-1 and fn., 170-2. See "Catherine II."

Newfoundland Fisheries, The: An enlargement of rights in connection with, offered France by England (1778), 7 fn.; a share in, desired by Spain, 161, 178; French pledge with reference to, to Spain, 191, 197-9 and fn.; Congressional views respecting American rights in, 257 ff.; final instructions of Congress concerning, 314-6. See appendix V.

Noailles, Duke de: Opposes France's entrance into the War of the Austrian Succession, 29; succeeds the Count de Guines as ambassador to England (1776), 78; reliability of reports of, from London, 131; points of disagreement of, with Vergennes, 131-2; communicates the Treaty of Amity and Commerce to the British government, 168; leaves England, ib. and fn.

North, Lord: Sentiments attributed to, by Vergennes, 131, 133; introduces plan of conciliation into Parliament, 165 and fn.; fall of, from power, 331 fn.

Ossun, Marquis d': Ambassador at Madrid, 103; supplanted by the Count de Montmorin, 156.

Oswald, Richard: British peace negotiator, 330 ff. passim.

Parliament: Debates in, after Saratoga, 133 fn.

Peace Negotiations of 1782: Early stages of, 329-32 fns. See "Jay."

Phillips, Dr. P. C.: Views of, respecting the results of Jay's conduct of the peace negotiations considered, 350 ff.

Poland, First Partition of: in relation to French diplomacy, 45; denounced by Vergennes, 57.

Pontleroy: Early French agent to America, 40-1.

Price, Dr. Richard: Predicts American greatness, 218 fn.

Proclamation of 1763, The: considered in connection with the Western Land question, 224-7 and notes.

Provisional Articles, The: Provisions of, see appendix V; the signing of, 339-40; questions respecting the interpretation of, 340 fn.; real import of, 342; reception of, by Congress, 344-5, 354-5; estimate of, by the French Foreign Office, 355 and fn.

Quebec Act, The: Bearing of, on the Western Land question, 226-7 and fn.

Raynal, Abbé: His Histoire des Indes on the importance of naval power, 48-9; influence of his work, ib.

Rayneval, J. M. Gérard de: Secretary to Vergennes, on the status quo, 296-7 fn.; representations of, to Jay on the Mississippi question, 336; mystery surrounding journey of, to England, ib.; Jay's suspicions regarding, 339; finds Shelburne stiff on the question of Gibraltar, 347 fn.; conversations of, with Shelburne respecting American interests, 348 ff. and fn.; marvels at the success of the Americans, 355.

Rendon: Successor to Miralles, 280.

Richmond, Lord: Advocates American independence, 133.

Rochambeau, Count de: Brings a military force to the United States (1780), 276-7, 288-9; deep concern of, on account of American conditions, 292, 310-1; credit due, for Yorktown, 311, 313.

Rochford, Lord: Scheme for joint guaranty of French, Spanish and English possessions in America, 6-7; friend of Beaumarchais, 65.

Rockingham, Lord: Rumored hostile intentions of, toward France, 65; advocates unqualified independence for the Americans, 133 fn., 168 fn.; succeeds North, 331 fn.; dies, 332 fn.

Rodney: British admiral, defeats Grasse in the West Indies (Apr., 1782), 316-7.

Rouillé: Minister of the Marine, (1749), 31.

Saint-Contest: Secretary of state (1751), 30.

St. Germain: Secretary of state for War, and favorable to an aggressive diplomatic policy, 78; sends Steuben to America, 90; is supplanted by Ségur, 285.

Sandwich, Lord: Member of the British ministry, not author of sentiment attributed to him, 132; estimates British naval strength, 134.

Santo Domingo: Question of defense of, 6 fn., 89-90 fn.

Saratoga, Battle of: Brings about the French-American alliance, 120, 121 and fn., 141.

Sartines: Secretary of state for the Marine, favorable to an aggressive diplomatic policy, 78; is displaced by Castries, 285.

Ségur, The Elder: Becomes secretary of state for War (1781), 285.

"Sea-to-Sea" Charters, The: As basis of the claims of the United States in the West, 220 ff.

Secret Aid, Policy of: See "Vergennes" and "Beaumarchais"; kept a secret even from the Americans at first, 80; raises diplomatic questions, 80-1; the secret of, known to the British government, 93 and fn.

"Secret Article": Of the Treaty of Alliance, see appendix I; of the Provisional Articles, see appendix V.

"Secret du Roi," The: See "Louis XV".

Separate Peace: Origin of the idea of, between England and America, 206; notion combatted by Vergennes, ib.; disavowed by Congress, 209 and fn.

Seven Years War: Begun by England without warning, 3; auspicious opening of, for France, 31; calamities of later stages of, 32 ff.

Shelburne, Lord: Part of, in instituting the peace negotiations of 1782, 331-2 fn.; good faith of, doubted by Jay, 333-5 and notes; authorizes Oswald's second commission, 339; conferences of, with Rayneval, 339, 347 fn., 348-50 fn.; refuses to take Parliament into his confidence respecting the Provisional Arti-

cles, 340 fn.; effect on, of
Howe's victory before Gibraltar, 352-3; urges a French-
E n g l i s h *rapprochement*
against the northern powers,
372-3 fn.

Spain: Dispute of, with
Portugal over interests in
South America (1774-7), 61,
81-3, 104; is alarmed at the
prospect of American independence, chs. V and VIII
passim; temporizing attitude
of, 178-9 and fn.; question of
the value of aid of, to France,
180, 211-2 and fn.; seeks rôle
of mediator 180 ff.; self-
seeking policy of, 106, 161,
178, 180, 192; desires a monopoly of trade in the Caribbean, 178, 190, 322; desires to
recover the Floridas and a
share in the Newfoundland
fisheries, see under those
headings; final terms of
mediation of, 214-5; enters
the war (June, 1779), 216;
grant by, of navigation of the
Mississippi to British subjects (1763), 227-8 fn.; opposes American extension to
the Mississippi, 227-30; attempts of, to make conquests
along the Mississippi arouse
American opposition, 268-9
and fn.; secret negotiations
of, with England (1780), 271-
2; re-enters the war (1781),
287; interests of, preferred
by France to those of the
United States, 293-4; ambitions of, a bar to peace, 333-
4, 346-7, 353, 355-7; American
gratitude claimed for, 345.
See "Florida Blanca," "Rayneval," "Vergennes."

Spies: Numerous in Paris in
1777, 98.

Status Quo, The: Opposition

of Vergennes to, for the
United States, 215, 271-2; acceptance of, by France for
the United States admitted
by Vergennes to be possible
(1781), 296-8 and notes; rejected by Vergennes for the
United States, 314 fn.

Steuben, Baron von: Sent to
America by St. Germain, to
train the American army
(1777), 90.

Stormont, Lord: British ambassador at Paris (1774 ff.),
67; discusses, the American
situation with Vergennes
(Sept., 1775), *ib.;* remonstrates against secret aid, 93
and fn.; remonstrates against
the admission of American
privateers to French harbors,
100; charges Vergennes with
negotiating with the Americans, 163-5; avoids a categorical answer from the
French government, *ib.;*
leaves France, 168 and fn.

Sullivan, General: "Hero of
Newport," sells out to the
French envoy, 303.

Sweden: *Coup d'état* in, effected by Vergennes (1771), 55.

Ternay: French naval com-
mander, see "Rochambeau."

Ticonderoga: British capture
of, injures American prospects in France, 117.

Treaty of Alliance (Feb. 6,
1778): Principal features of,
authorized by the royal council (Jan. 7, 1778); final draft
of, signed, 154; text of, appendix I; existence of, suspected in England from an
early date, 163 fn., 165-6 and
fn.; meaning of the word
"continent" in article VI of,
199 and fn.; interpretation
of articles XI and XII of,

233 ff.; after the Revolution, 358-60 and fn.

Treaty of Amity and Commerce (Feb. 6, 1778): Difficulty respecting articles XI and XII of, 155 fn.; articles XXIII-XXVIII summarized, 171; declaration of, urged by Vergennes (Jan. 22, 1778), and authorized by Louis (Mar. 7), 166-8.

Treaty of Aranjuez (Apr. 12, 1779): Signed, 192; provisions of, 193-4; compared with the French-American treaty, ch. IX.

Treaty of Kutchuk-Kainardji: Turkey menaced by, 60-1.

Treaty of Paris (1763): Provisions of, 36-7.

Treaty of Teschen: A triumph for Vergennes' policy, 170.

Truce: Suggestion of, in lieu of a final peace, 183-4, 186-7, 195-6.

Turgot: As Louis XVI's controller-General contends for economy and domestic reform as against an aggressive diplomatic policy, 1, 72; answers Vergennes' *Mémoire de Considérations*, 76-7; fights a losing fight and retires, 77-9.

Turner, Professor F. J.: Theory that France sought American territory in the Revolution, 9-11 and fn.

United States: Commerce with, as an inducement to French intervention, 12-4 and fn.; naval capacity of, predicted by Vergennes, 67-8; not likely to become a conquering state, 111; permanent separation of, from England Vergennes' principal objective, 137 ff. and notes; a disappointing ally, 177 footnote, 188; basis of claims of, to

the West, ch. X; argued to be a sovereign entity, 230-2 and notes; struggle of, for independence near collapse (1780-81), 288-9; French views of, 290 fn.; significance for, of the Provisional Articles, see under that title. See also "Commissioners," "Congress," "Manifest Destiny," "Monroe Doctrine."

Van Tyne, Prof. C. H.: Views of, respecting French motives considered, 146-8 note.

Vaughan, Benjamin: Friend of Franklin and Shelburne, sent by Jay to London, 339, 352.

Vergennes: Argument to show that French intervention in the Revolution was a defensive measure, 3-9, and ch. VI; little interested in French colonies, 6 fn. 4; alleged *Mémoire* of, published in 1802, 10-3 and fn.; on commerce with the United States, 13-4; becomes secretary of state for Foreign Affairs (1774), 54; early career of, 54-5; characteristics and diplomatic creed of, 56-60; initial attitude toward England and the American Revolution, 60-2; denunciation of England, 62-3; alarmed at prospect of return of Chatham to power, 64-5; takes a more positive interest in the American situation, 66 ff.; *Mémoire de Considérations* of (Mar., 1776), 74-6; claims right for France to trade with the American rebels and receive their merchantmen in her harbors, 80-1; opposes Spanish conquest of Portugal, 82, 85, 104; urges war with England (July-August, 1776), 83-5; receives Deane and learns of Declaration of Independence, 84 and fn.; draws back after the news of Long Island, 85-6; congratulates Stormont on British successes, 86; pursues a policy of "watchful waiting" (Jan.-July, 1777), 87 ff.; urges the preëminent interest of France and Spain in procuring the separation of England and North America, 86-9; delivers a homily on peace, 88, opposes a general disarmament and an understanding with England, 89 and fn.; question of attitude of, toward Broglie's Statholderate idea, 91-2; receives Franklin but evades a formal audience, 95; promises financial aid to the Colonies (Jan. 1777), 95-6; precautions in behalf of secrecy, ib. fn.; is sceptical of the substance of the American revolt (Mar., 1777), 97; is sceptical of rumors of an hostile English-American coalition (early 1777), 99; policy of toward American privateers, 99 ff.; again urges war with England (July, 1777), 101-4; endeavors to allay Spanish apprehensions regarding American independence, 111, 177 fn.; consents to follow Madrid's lead (Aug., 1777), 113-4; urges that Forth's demand that American privateers be excluded from French ports be rejected, 115-6; anticipates the early outbreak of war with England (Sept., 1777), 116; again retreats after the arrival of the news of Ticonderoga, 117; proposes a pledge of financial aid to the

Americans, 119-20; renews in a new form after Saratoga the idea that French possessions in the West Indies are in danger of being attacked by an English-American coalition, 121-5; evidence brought forward by, to support this notion, 126-34; instances of disingenuousness of, in this connection, 132-4; contradictions and inconsistencies of, 135-8; declares enfeeblement of England to be France's principal objective, 139-40 and fns.; urges defensive aspect of his program, 140, 167, fns.; real concern of, after Saratoga, 141; reason for alarmism of, 142 ff.; initial advances to the American commissioners after Saratoga, 149-50; offers a defensive alliance, 151-3; resists American demand for an offensive alliance, 154; urges his policy on the Spanish government, 155-7; finesse of, in delaying transmission to Spain of news of the French-American negotiations, 159; significant interview with Stormont (Jan. 22, 1778), 161; presses for an open breach with England, 161 ff.; distrust of Arthur Lee, 166-7 fn., 187; policy of, in War of Bavarian Succession, 169-70; adopts liberal policy toward neutral rights, 170-2; impatience of, to bring Spain into the war, 173, 178, 180, 188; willing to support Spanish mediation, 182; careful of American rights, 183 fn.; attitude of, toward idea of a truce instead of a peace for America, 186-7; gives Montmorin carte-blanche in negotiating with Spain, 189; sends Montmorin a draft of treaty with Spain, 190; aims to safeguard France's honor with respect to American interests, 192-3; instructions of, to Gérard with reference to a truce, 196; same, with reference to the Floridas and Canada, 197 ff., 254; plans a free state in Canada under French protection, 201-2; combats the idea that America may make a separate peace with England, 206; bitterly criticizes Florida Blanca's terms of mediation (Apr., 1779), 215; recognizes the extension of the United States to the Mississippi, 240-2 and notes; favors American navigation of the Mississippi, 254-5; adopts the Spanish point of view in his *Instructions d'Arrivée* to La Luzerne, 265-6; fears that Spain seeks to impose the *status quo* on the United States (1780), 271-2 and fn.; altercations of, with John Adams, 273-8; instructs La Luzerne not to take sides in matters at issue between Spain and America, 278-81; review of attitude of, on the Mississippi question, 281-3; intercedes with the king to continue the war (Sept., 1780), 284-5; reorganizes the Departments of War and Marine, *ib.*; favors the offer of mediation by the imperial powers and a vigorous campaign, 286-7; disappointed in the Americans as allies, 289; response of, to the demands of the Hartford Conference, 292-3; considerations governing, at this time, 293-4; demands of, upon

Congress in respect to peace-making, 295-6; admission of, that France may accept the *status quo* for the United States, 295-8 and notes; broad scope of the program of, in intervening in the Revolution, 307; not directly responsible for the Yorktown campaign, 313; recognizes the unfeasibility of the *status quo* for America, 313-4 fn.; views of, as to the method to be pursued in peace-making, 329 fn.; refuses to treat with Grenville respecting American interests, 332 fn.; urges the American commissioners, to accept Oswald's first commission, 332-3; announces that France will not proceed with England unless she is ready to recognize American independence, 334 fn.; is noncommittal as to the conflicting claims of Spain and the United States, 336; comment of, on Marbois' letter respecting the fisheries, 337 fn.; announces that France will not continue the war to secure American demands respecting the fisheries and Western territory, 337-9 fn., 347-8 fn.; letter of (Dec. 15, 1782), to Franklin protesting against the course taken by the American commissioners, 340-2; states the two essential conditions of peace, 347 fn.; expresses surprise at the favorable terms secured by the Americans, 355 and fn. presses the negotiations in Spain's behalf, 355-6; delight of, at the conclusion of peace, 356-7; opposed by a war party at court, 357 fn.; reviews the success of his policy

(Mar., 1784), 361-2. desires the gratitude of the American people for France, 368-9 and fn.; negotiates a commercial treaty with England (1786), 371; urges a strong fleet for France, *ib.;* is dismayed by the *rapprochement* of Austria and Russia, 372; admits that Continental peace is precarious, 373; wins his last diplomatic triumph, 374; death of, 376; final apology of, for his American venture, 376-7.

Virginia: Claims of, in the West, 221, 222-4 fn.

Washington, General: Opposes French participation in a campaign in Canada, 204; views of, on the Western Land question, 251 fn.; growth of French regard for, 291 and fn.; attends Hartford Conference (Sept., 1780), *ib.*

Wentworth, Paul: Activities as British spy, 118 fn. 127 and fn., 130 fn., 163. fn.

West Indies, The French: and the Treaty of Paris, 19-20,

37; value of, after 1763, 5-6 and fn., 44, 63, 75-6, 136-7; independence of, proposed by Choiseul's secretary-general of Commerce, 44; asserted to be in danger from a joint English-American attack, 3, 75, 98-9, 121 ff.; English offers to guarantee, 6-7 and fn., 115-16; American offers to guarantee, 21, 95, 97; chosen for the scene of French-Spanish naval efforts (1781), 287, 293; Grasse's defeat in, by Rodney, 313, 316; equivalents demanded in, by England in return for Gibraltar, 355-6 fn., 357 fn.; great French-Spanish expedition prepared for (1783), *ib.;* French gains in, by the Peace of 1783 insignificant, 361.

Witherspoon: Member of Congress from New Jersey, a leader of the "landless" state party, 304.

Wolfe, General James: Prophecy by, of America's destiny, 218 fn.